THE LAST WILL & TESTAMENT FOR YOUR BUSINESS

BUY-SELL
AGREEMENTS

L. PAUL HOOD, JR.

Published by Paul Hood Services
Design & Distribution by Bublish, Inc.

ISBN: 978-1-647043-43-8 (eBook)
ISBN: 978-1-647043-44-5 (Paperback)
ISBN: 978-1-647043-45-2 (Hardback)

To Carol,
my favorite person

CONTENTS

INTRODUCTION

Welcome to this book! All nonfiction book authors have different reasons for writing books. Sometimes, it's purely to make money; other times, it's the recognition that the world would be well served by a good book on the subject. In part, I fall into the latter category, because there is no really good book on buy-sell agreements for the lay audience. But that's not the principal reason why I was driven to write this book.

For me, the principal motivator for writing this book was personal. My family was forced out of our two-generation family business due, in large part, to deficient buy-sell language. It changed the lives of my uncle and my maternal grandfather forever.

This happened when I was still quite young, but I recall hearing snippets about it around the dinner table. Unfortunately, by the time I became a lawyer, my grandfather was deceased, and I never had a chance to discuss the ordeal with my uncle—who was fired from the company by the son of my grandfather's partner in this ordeal, and he had died too. It wasn't until after I became a lawyer that I was able to investigate the corporate records on file with the Louisiana Secretary of State to determine what really happened.

My grandfather was bought out for book value (the value of the assets of the business as per the accounting books and records), which was far less than what his stock was worth—as is usually the case. The corporate documents provided for book value redemptions, which I counsel *strongly* against. The silver lining for my family in the ordeal—which really disrupted my family for a good while—was that the son of my grandfather's partner eventually drove the business into Chapter 7 bankruptcy. This meant that my family was the only family to get any wealth out of that company. Karma, I guess.

I wrote this book for you so that you can protect yourself and your family. Now, unrelated business owners of closely held entities also really need the protections afforded by a well-drafted buy-sell agreement. However, I didn't write this book, nor do I intend for it to be used, for you to draft your own buy-sell agreement—that would be a huge mistake. I intend for you to use this book to educate yourself (and many professional advisors) on buy-sell agreements so that you can assist your lawyer in crafting the right buy-sell agreement for your situation.

Some of the material in this book is complex. Why? Because the tax laws are unnecessarily complex. However, I have labored long and hard to make it as simple and as painless as possible. But where it is complex, you can thank your federal elected officials for enacting such byzantine tax laws.

I'd be remiss if I didn't thank Bublish, particularly Kathy Meis, Shilah LaCoe, Nick Newton, and everyone else at Bublish for guiding me through the editorial process. They're amazing to work with!

CHAPTER 1

WHY YOU NEED A BUY-SELL AGREEMENT NOW

If you're reading this book, chances are you either own an interest in a closely held business or are thinking about starting, buying, or inheriting one. A closely held business or corporation has shares held by a small number of people. While these shares may be owned by traditional investors, they may also be held by family members, friends, or other insiders associated with the business. Closely held businesses can be small, mom-and-pop shops or large Fortune 500 companies. Either way, closely held businesses are the economic backbone of the United States.

Being a firm believer in the late Stephen R. Covey's *The 7 Habits of Highly Effective People*, I think that habit number two, "begin with the end in mind," is important for stakeholders in closely held businesses. Many people expend lots of time and money thinking about how to go *into* business, but few think about getting *out* of a business—the exit strategy. As Michael E. Gerber made clear in his books about the *E-Myth*^{SM}, you should work as hard *on* your business as you do *in* your business! When it comes to closely held businesses, an exit strategy is often overlooked. A buy-sell agreement can be a key piece of not only an exit strategy, but a harmonious transition from one set of business owners to another.

A buy-sell agreement is a legally binding contract that stipulates how a partner's share of a business may be reassigned if that partner dies or otherwise leaves the business. This type of agreement is also known as a buy-sell agreement. One expert wrote that failure to implement a buy-sell agreement is the number one reason why small businesses fail, and I don't disagree. The principal reason why businesses that don't have buy-sell agreements fail is due to good old human greed: when a triggering event occurs, the owners' interests diverge, and everyone protects his or her own interests. This can be, and often is, fatal to the ongoing business operations.

Every business with more than one owner should have an *effective* buy-sell agreement. If you think your business is too small in value or size or too young for a buy-sell agreement, I hope to convince you to reconsider. Why? Because the best time to implement a buy-sell agreement is at the beginning of the often bumpy ride of building a closely held business. You want a solid agreement in place *before* you begin to scale and grow. You never know whether your fledgling company could become the next Microsoft, Facebook, or IBM. It's wise to spend a little time and money on the front end to put together a solid buy-sell agreement while everyone is in the same financial boat. When business owners put off this important work, they often face hurdles down the road.

In this book, you'll learn the basics of a rock-solid buy-sell agreement and explore real-world examples to illustrate the importance of these basics. For my first example, let me introduce you to three work friends, Al (age 35), Betty (age 28), and Charlene (age 43). They have left a large employer to start their own company, which will design, sell, and service computer software. Enthusiastically and energetically diving into their new venture, the three friends seek legal advice about forming a business entity. They decide on a corporation in which each will have a 25 percent stake. An investor named Dave (age 38) is financing the start-up. Al, Betty, and Charlene will work full time in the business, while Dave will serve on the board of directors and as the treasurer. While they were in the lawyer's office forming the corporation, which they named MythiCo, the lawyer asked if they wanted to create a buy-sell agreement. Al asked, "What's a buy-sell agreement?"

"A buy-sell agreement," the lawyer explained, "is a legal contract between the owners, and often others, concerning the future transfer of ownership and the management and operation of a business. Sometimes the business entity is also a party to the agreement." Betty asked, "Do we need a buy-sell agreement?" The lawyer said yes and explained further that a buy-sell agreement can do a great many good things at a critical time in the business's life. Charlene then asked, "But do we truly need a buy-sell agreement? Please tell us more about the reasons for having a buy-sell agreement."

Why Have a Buy-Sell Agreement?

The list of things to do as a new business owner can seem endless. The business entity must be formed, business plans must be written, permits must be obtained, signs and business cards must be purchased, and on and on. Very few owners are thinking about selling their business at this stage. But life doesn't typically get calmer after the business is up and running, so the work of creating a buy-sell agreement gets pushed off. Often, it never becomes a priority.

Unfortunately, the value of a buy-sell agreement often isn't clear to business owners until *after* something happens—a co-owner gets sick, divorces, or dies. When such big life events happen—and inevitably they will—how will they be handled? Without a buy-sell agreement in place, there's no road map for such scenarios. Partnerships and relationships can deteriorate quickly in such a void, and often they do. If you're still unsure of the value of a buy-sell agreement, consider how the following scenarios might unfold without the clear direction of a buy-sell agreement.

What if:

- you are a co-owner and are the first to decide you want to leave the company?
- you're the last remaining original owner?
- someone with whom you do not want to be a co-owner becomes a co-owner?
- one of your co-owners dies, divorces, or goes bankrupt?
- you're the first co-owner to die and your family depends on your income?

If one or several of these scenarios become realities, how would each be handled? Having played out a few of these "what if?" scenarios in your head, the importance of a buy-sell agreement starts to become clearer, doesn't it? Wouldn't it be beneficial to be prepared for such scenarios in advance, rather than be forced to react after the fact?

Without proper scenario planning, ownership and other organizational transitions can disrupt or even kill a profitable business. A buy-sell agreement keeps your business stable during rough times because it spells out the rules in advance. Moving forward without the road map provided by a buy-sell agreement significantly increases the likelihood of acrimony, hurt feelings, and even litigation between business stakeholders. Moving forward with a buy-sell agreement alleviates this likelihood.

If you're still saying, "I'll get to the buy-sell agreement next week… I'm too busy," take a quick look at some of the costly scenarios that can unfold without a buy-sell agreement in place:

- Your business partner could sell their stake to a new co-owner like a child or spouse whom you neither trust nor like.
- Your heirs might get stuck with a nonmarketable interest in a closely held business that doesn't pay dividends or make distributions to people who don't work for the entity. This

means that there would be no money available to pay death taxes, support heirs, pay estate expenses, or even cover your own funeral bill.

- You might get stuck in a situation where you and your co-owners are hopelessly mired in a deadlock over an issue, thereby crippling and possibly killing your business.
- A disgruntled minority owner could end your company's status as an S corporation by transferring stock to an ineligible shareholder.
- A present or former owner could compete with the business entity, or even use confidential information that belongs to the entity to compete with and financially harm the business using the entity's intellectual property such as processes and customer lists.

Benefits of a Buy-Sell Agreement

Buy-sell agreements do more than prevent problems; they also have many benefits for a company. The following is not an exhaustive list, but it does cover some of the most important reasons to have a buy-sell agreement in place from the start of your business. A buy-sell agreement:

- provides a market for and orderly transfer of interests in closely held businesses, jointly owned real estate, or other assets owned outside of an entity that are related to the business
- establishes a way to determine a price for future buyouts
- provides a source of liquidity or equitable financing terms for business owners or their estates and survivors, heirs, legatees, and beneficiaries
- ensures that control of the business remains with specified persons so that continuity in management and control is maintained

- restrains or regulates subsequent competition
- ensures against deadlock and disputes over the activities of the entity by providing a mechanism for their resolution
- protects remaining owners against sale or transfer to unwanted persons, including ensuring that the right family members end up with the entity interests
- allows the entity to retain key employees
- guards against loss of S corporation status
- preserves partnership tax treatment through transfer restrictions
- provides for distributions of cash and property to owners
- provides for supermajority votes of owners in certain situations
- provides for minimum requirements to be an owner of the business
- binds future owners to the terms of transfer, operation, and management

In the next chapter, I set out the principal reasons why every business needs a buy-sell agreement. In my view, the buy-sell agreement is as advisable as a last will and testament is to anyone, if not more so. I could tell you war story after war story about failed closely held (and often family) businesses due to either not having a buy-sell agreement or, worse yet, having a defective buy-sell agreement. I implore you to consider whether you really want to be in business with your fellow owner's ex-wife or surviving spouse. That's but one of the horrors of not having a buy-sell agreement.

CHAPTER 2

GENERAL ELEMENTS OF AN EFFECTIVE BUY-SELL AGREEMENT

N ow that you understand the importance of a buy-sell agreement, and the unsettling consequences of putting off the creation of one, it's time to explore the elements of an effective buy-sell agreement. First, it's important to understand that buy-sell agreements are activated by "triggering events"—specific circumstances mentioned in the agreement that trigger its terms. The death of an owner or the sale of a company are examples of triggering events. Second, a buy-sell agreement is only as useful as the terms and provisions it offers in response to specific trigger events. That is to say, having a buy-sell agreement is not necessarily protective in and of itself. Rather, it is the effectiveness of the agreement's terms in helping you achieve your goals that defines the success of a buy-sell agreement.

Topics Covered in a Buy-Sell Agreement

Because buy-sell agreements are legal contracts, they are divided into separate sections or paragraphs. Since every buy-sell agreement is different, let's identify a few topics and sections that should be covered in most agreements. Not every buy-sell agreement will have the provisions in the same place in the agreement or even include all these parts. In fact, some buy-sell agreements may have additional sections. What is most important in a buy-sell agreement is that the various parts of the agreement work seamlessly together and complement each other. Few things are worse in a buy-sell agreement than conflicting provisions. Unfortunately, they happen a lot. Here are some basic and important sections of a buy-sell agreement.

Identification of the Parties

The first thing that a good buy-sell agreement will do is define the parties—the persons or entities that will actually sign the agreement. Parties to a good buy-sell agreement should include *all* of the present, known, and expected future owners of the entity. It's also a good idea to have the spouses of the owners be parties to the buy-sell agreement, even if they have no current ownership interest in the entity. A spouse could acquire an interest in the entity as the result of a divorce. Given that approximately half of all marriages end in divorce, it is very conceivable that a divorce court could award a spouse an interest in the entity in the judgment. Therefore, a good buy-sell agreement should address this possibility.

A court may find that a buy-sell agreement is not binding on a former spouse unless he or she was aware of the terms of the buy-sell agreement, even if the person signed some form of waiver of rights. A buy-sell agreement is more likely to be binding on an ex-spouse if he or she is an actual party to the agreement and signs it. This is because it is more likely that any argument by the ex-spouse that he or she was not aware of the agreement will fail. It is important to give a nonowner spouse adequate time to review the drafted buy-sell agreement and to have it reviewed by separate, independent counsel before asking him or her to sign it. I've had clients who refused to take my advice on this point and didn't have their spouses sign their buy-sell agreements. This later caused problems when they got divorced. Don't make this mistake. Get your spouse to sign the buy-sell agreement. I've had former clients who, despite grousing about having their spouses sign the buy-sell agreement, thanked me years later when they got divorced.

Purposes of the Buy-Sell Agreement

A good buy-sell agreement should contain the reasons for the agreement—the goals to be achieved by creating the buy-sell agreement. It is important to make certain that the ultimate effects of the buy-sell agreement are in accord with its stated purposes. What use would a buy-sell agreement with an intent to provide a market for the company's interests have, if it only gave an option to purchase or a right of first refusal instead of a mandatory purchase or sale? What value could result from a buy-sell agreement triggered by a divorce, if that agreement is silent on what happens in the case of that same event? Unfortunately, these types of disconnects occur in buy-sell agreements more often than you might think.

Definition of Terms

It is not unusual for a buy-sell agreement to contain a section with a definition of terms. For example, the term "disability" might be defined, or what will constitute "cause" for termination of an owner's employment. Many other terms might be defined in this section of the buy-sell agreement. When I create a buy-sell agreement for my clients, I collect all of the terms that are specifically defined throughout the buy-sell agreement and put them into an opening section. For easy reference, I also cite where each definition is located in the buy-sell agreement. The terms defined in the agreement should be consistently used throughout the document. Some lawyers get sloppy with defined terms and unintentionally use terms in ways that conflict with the definition that was given to the term. Another pet peeve of mine is when a lawyer defines a term and then never uses it in the agreement.

Legend for Ownership Certificates

A buy-sell agreement typically contains a paragraph or two that will be placed on every certificate of ownership that is outstanding when the buy-sell agreement is triggered. These paragraphs alert reviewers of the existence of the buy-sell agreement. Whether or not it is stated in the buy-sell agreement, such certificates evidence ownership and should have a reference to the buy-sell agreement included on the face. This alerts future holders to the existence of the buy-sell agreement.

Restrictions on Transfers of Ownership Interests and Exceptions for Permitted Transferees

A well-structured buy-sell agreement contains a general prohibition regarding transfers of interests in the entity, except those expressly authorized in the buy-sell agreement—and even then, only pursuant to the procedures outlined within the agreement. The purpose of such a provision is to prevent end runs around the buy-sell agreement. It is not unusual for a buy-sell agreement to permit certain transfers, mostly related to an owner's estate planning or to a set of permitted transferees, without causing a triggering event under a buy-sell agreement.

Identification of Who Can Buy and Sell

It is not enough for a buy-sell agreement to merely identify the parties to an agreement. The agreement should clearly identify who is allowed to buy and sell and under what specific circumstances. It is not unusual for a well-drafted buy-sell agreement to have a pecking order of buyers after a triggering event. For example, a hybrid buy-sell agreement (which we'll discuss in more detail later) may give owners who are higher in the pecking order the first right to buy, followed by a right or obligation of the entity to buy if other owners don't purchase the interests for sale.

Identification of Triggering Events

A buy-sell agreement should specify the events that will trigger each right or obligation. As mentioned earlier, this might include the death, disability, divorce, or bankruptcy of an owner, or an offer to buy an interest in the entity that's currently owned by a present owner. There are many possible triggering events, which we'll address in more detail in chapter 9.

Responses to Triggering Events

It is not enough for a buy-sell agreement to contain a list of triggering events. The agreement must also clearly state what the specific response should be for each and every event. Suppose that the death of an owner is a triggering event. What is the response to this death? It might be a mandatory sale by the estate of the deceased owner. It could be an option to purchase by the surviving owners or by the entity. It might even be a call option. In another case, the response might be the right to sell by the estate of the deceased owner or a mandatory purchase by the entity and mandatory sale by the estate of the deceased owner. The point is, there must be detailed responses outlined for every triggering event.

Value and Purchase Price for Ownership Interests to Be Sold

A good buy-sell agreement will specify the price at which a stake in the company can be sold. Preferably, the agreement also states how the price of that stake has been determined. There are a number of ways to calculate this—something I will discuss in later chapters.

The Manner in Which Payments for Purchased Interest Will Be Made

A buy-sell agreement would be deficient if it did not carefully detail how purchasers should pay for the stake in the company that they are acquiring. Will the payment be made with a cashier's check or a bank wire? Is a lump sum expected or can payments be made in installments? If the latter, what are the terms for those installments? Will interest be charged? Will there be security required for the loan? All such questions should be answered in the buy-sell agreement.

Timing of Purchase of the Interests

Like the other important elements of an effective buy-sell agreement, it is critical that the agreement specifically address when the purchase and sale are to take place as well as what date they will go into effect. This is referred to as the "as of" date. For example, a buy-sell agreement might provide that, in a death-of-an-owner scenario, the as of date is the end of the month immediately preceding the date of death. The sale, on the other hand, might take place within ninety days of the date of death.

Governing Law

A buy-sell agreement should expressly provide for the jurisdiction under which the agreement is to be interpreted and governed. This provision can be critical, particularly in cases when the owners reside in different jurisdictions.

Termination of the Buy-Sell Agreement

While not every buy-sell agreement will contain a section for when the agreement will terminate (other than upon the mutual agreement of all of the parties), many do contain this provision. A buy-sell agreement might be made to automatically terminate for the following events:

- sale of all or substantially all of the entity's assets
- merger with or acquisition by another entity
- liquidation
- bankruptcy
- dissolution
- the simultaneous or near simultaneous death of owners
- public offering of the entity's stock
- reduction of the ownership to only one owner
- mutual consent of all owners

S Corporation Provisions

Every buy-sell agreement for an S corporation and for any entity that could become an S corporation (including limited liability companies that elect to be taxed as corporations), should contain a section that has a number of specific tax-driven provisions that are unique to S corporations. For example, S corporations can only have one class of stock, although the stock may be divided into voting and nonvoting stock.

Entity Governance

Not every buy-sell agreement will contain provisions relating to how the owners will run the entity. Nevertheless, I strongly recommend that a buy-sell agreement cover as many issues as possible relating to governance, such as the following:

- who will manage the entity or serve on its board
- who will have access to entity records
- who is eligible to work for the entity (this can be very important in family businesses)
- the plan regarding regular distributions to owners (minority owners will want this protection against the majority owner)

Miscellaneous Provisions

Just about every buy-sell agreement that I've reviewed contains a series of provisions under the category of "miscellaneous." This section is almost always at the end of the agreement. While it may be tempting to ignore the type of boilerplate provisions included under miscellaneous, especially if the buy-sell agreement is long and arduous, some of these provisions are very important. For example, a provision stating how notice will be given after a triggering event or whether violation of the buy-sell agreement will give rise to a claim for a specific performance. Some examples of miscellaneous provisions are:

- How words can be used. For example, words in the singular also represent their plural form unless clearly stated otherwise.
- Severability—meaning if a court of law determines that one provision of a buy-sell agreement is invalid, the rest of the buy-sell agreement remains valid and enforceable.

- The agreement supersedes all prior agreements and understandings between the parties. This prevents owners from dredging up provisions from prior buy-sell agreements and from arguing about things that might have been orally agreed to outside of the agreement.

CHAPTER 3

TYPES OF BUY-SELL AGREEMENTS AND ALTERNATIVES

There are three basic types of buy-sell agreements. Why three types? Because each differs only in the identity of the buyer of the interests. In a cross-purchase buy-sell agreement (aka a "criss-cross" agreement), an individual owner is the buyer. Contrast that with a redemption buy-sell agreement, where the entity is the buyer. In a hybrid buy-sell agreement, either the entity or a co-owner could be the buyer, depending on which triggering event occurred. Before we dive into the details of each type of buy-sell agreement in the following chapters, let's start with an overview.

Cross-Purchase Buy-Sell Agreement

In this type of agreement, one or more of the owners agree to buy or to have an option to buy the interests of a co-owner upon the occurrence of a triggering event.

Redemption Buy-Sell Agreement

This type of agreement is made between the owners and the entity itself. In this case the entity, not the owners, agrees to purchase or to have the option to purchase the interests of an owner upon the occurrence of a triggering event.

Hybrid Buy-Sell Agreement

This agreement is a mixture of both the cross-purchase agreement and the redemption agreement. It allows for a "wait and see" approach when the agreement is being structured. A hybrid buy-sell agreement permits the entity and the owners to decide at the time of the triggering event which route makes the most sense from a tax and financial standpoint. Hybrid buy-sell agreements are popular because they provide the most flexibility.

Drawbacks of Buy-Sell Agreements

Even though buy-sell agreements have many more advantages than disadvantages, there are certain implications worth considering as an owner. There are also alternative types of agreements available if you find that a buy-sell agreement isn't right for you and your company.

One of the advantages of a buy-sell agreement is that the terms of the agreement apply to *all* owners. However, as an owner bound by these restrictions, you might find some limitations on your personal estate planning. For example, a buy-sell agreement may prohibit you from gifting loved ones some or all of your ownership interest during your lifetime, although some buy-sell agreements contain exceptions for such transfers. Similarly, a buy-sell agreement could impede a plan to leave your ownership interest to your family at your death because it requires your estate to sell your ownership interest at your death.

Restrictions on Financial Planning

A buy-sell agreement can also adversely impact your financial planning by restricting to whom you can sell your ownership interest and when you can sell it. Suppose you get into a financial bind and need to sell your ownership interest to solve a financial problem, but your buy-sell agreement requires you to offer your ownership interest first to your co-owners, who don't want to purchase your interest or don't want to offer you a fair price for your ownership interest. In this scenario, the likelihood of finding a third party to buy your ownership interest is slim to none. This leaves you stuck between a rock and a hard place because of your buy-sell agreement and could force you into a fire-sale price of your interest, especially if your financial position is dire. Additionally, if a buy-sell agreement prohibits the use of your ownership interest as collateral, you might be prevented from obtaining a loan that you need, particularly if the lender is inflexible and is demanding that you put up your ownership interest as collateral.

Loss of a Special Election to Defer the Federal Estate Tax of a Deceased Owner

Most estates are not subject to the federal estate tax under current law. However, if you expect that you may have a taxable estate, there is a complex provision of federal estate tax law in the Internal Revenue Code, Section 6166, that allows you to defer the federal estate tax on certain types of property such as interests in businesses. However, a purchase of your interest from your estate may cause the loss of the right to defer the estate tax. It is beyond the scope of this book to describe Section 6166, which is a lengthy section that could be the subject of its own book, in full. But suffice to say, if I had to choose a mandatory buy and sell arrangement on behalf of my loved ones in a buy-sell agreement versus deferring estate tax, I'd choose the buy-sell agreement every time.

Sale of Corporate Interests May Result in Losing the Entity's Loss Attributes

There is another complicated tax provision that limits an entity's right to use its own carrybacks (net operating losses that can be applied to a previous year's tax return) and carryforwards (tax losses that can be applied toward future year's returns) on a significant change in ownership. This provision is frequently included in buy-sell agreements. Make sure that your tax advisor structures an effective business continuation plan and reviews your buy-sell agreement so as to not lose your entity's right to use those losses in the future.

Cost of an Effective Buy-Sell Agreement

Cost is probably the most significant drawback of a buy-sell agreement. It costs money to hire competent legal counsel and tax advisors. But if you're going to go to the trouble of putting together a buy-sell agreement in the first place, it ought to be done professionally. You should expect to spend at least $1,500 to $5,000 for a well-done buy-sell agreement, although prices vary in different parts of the country.

Having practiced law and consulted on estate and tax planning for more than thirty years, I have drafted and reviewed hundreds of buy-sell agreements. They are the most challenging agreements to draft because everyone's situation is different. There is no one-size-fits-all approach when it comes to buy-sell agreements. That's why inexperienced lawyers often make mistakes in drafting buy-sell agreements. They try to apply a template where none exists.

I have had lawyers admit to me that they regularly used forms that they did not fully understand. I am always amazed by the number of business owners who admit they signed their buy-sell agreement without understanding the details. This is why so many deficient buy-sell agreements are put in place. Having a buy-sell agreement in place that doesn't support your business goals can actually be worse than having no agreement at all.

Alternative Places Buy-Sell Agreement Language Can Be Found

There really are no alternatives to buy-sell agreements. The following types of scenarios are essentially different documents in which buy-sell agreement language can be found.

Buy-Sell Provisions in Governance Documents

Governance documents (e.g., articles of incorporation, partnership, and organization; bylaws; and operating agreements) frequently have buy-sell provisions. It is critical that they be reviewed when you are creating or altering a buy-sell agreement. The general rule in many jurisdictions is that if there is a conflict between the governing documents and your buy-sell agreement, the governing document provisions win, unless they expressly state otherwise. My preference is to keep buy-sell provisions in a separate contract. However, that's not always the case because a separate agreement can protect the privacy of the LLC operating agreement or the corporate bylaws if a signatory to the buy-sell provisions isn't an owner at the time. I also believe that keeping the buy-sell provisions in their own separate contract allows each document (e.g., the LLC operating agreement or corporate bylaws on the one hand and the buy-sell agreement on the other) to perform their separate functions.

Compensation-Based Plans

Another alternative to a buy-sell agreement is a compensation-based plan, which includes consulting agreements and salary continuation plans. Consulting agreements can be used either in conjunction with a buy-sell agreement buyout provision for an employee-owner or more commonly by C corporations. There is a tax law prohibition against owners having continuing interest in a family-owned C corporation, other than as a creditor, if the owner's shares have been redeemed. The benefit of a compensation-based plan is that the compensation payments—assuming they are reasonable—are deductible by the entity for income tax purposes. The disadvantage to such an arrangement is that the recipient is treated as receiving ordinary income instead of capital gains. However, if there is little or no difference between ordinary income tax rates and the capital gains tax rates, it really doesn't matter to the recipient. Salary continuation plans are frequently used in service businesses and for professional entities like doctors, lawyers, and architects, where much of the value of the retiring professional's interest is in accounts receivable and in their book of business.

Entity Recapitalization

It is possible to recapitalize the ownership interests of an entity in order to change ownership interests, though family-owned businesses are subject to some tight tax restrictions in this regard. For example, a retiring owner can be given a preferred ownership interest compensation for the ownership interest he or she retains while also reallocating some of the owner's salary earned for other activities within the business. However, it is harder for family-owned entities to set up such qualifying preferred interest because of Section 2701 of the Internal Revenue Code. Doing so requires real tax expertise and is not a job for the inexperienced practitioner.

Gifts of Ownership Interests

A simple alternative to a buy-sell agreement is to make gifts of ownership interests to loved ones.

Defined Benefit Plans

Establishing a qualified defined benefit retirement plan is a possible alternative to a straight buy-sell agreement, although there is nothing that would prohibit the use of both a defined benefit plan and a buy-sell agreement.

Charitable Gift of Ownership Interests

It is also possible to make charitable gifts of ownership interest in place of a buy-sell agreement. However, very few charities want an interest in a closely held entity unless a quick sale of that interest can be reasonably assured or unless the interest pays regular dividends.

Private Annuities

In a private annuity, ownership interests are transferred to someone else in exchange for a promise to make payments to you for the rest of your life. These payments are purely a function of your age and are intended to essentially pay off the interest by the time of your expected death. The greater your age, the higher the payment, as determined by an actuary. One big difference between a private annuity and a sale of ownership interest is that the annuity payments are not capped by the purchase price. Annuity payments only stop when you die. The longer you live, the better off you are. In this scenario, payments could easily exceed the sale price. Of course, if you do not live as long as expected, you would come out worse than from a sale. For this reason, as well as some adverse income tax consequences, a private annuity is not typically an attractive alternative.

Employee Stock Ownership Plans

Employee stock ownership plans (ESOPs) are an alternative to buy-sell agreements. They are quite often a sale of the company to its employees on a tax-advantaged basis. The use of an ESOP allows for tax-deductible loan principal payments, which generally are not tax-deductible.

Nonqualified Deferred Compensation Plans

Nonqualified deferred compensation plans (NQDCs)—in other words nonqualified retirement plans such as 401(k) plans or defined benefit plans—can be established primarily in corporations and used to allow an owner to save for his or her own retirement by deferring current salary until retirement. At retirement, these sums could be paid out in a lump sum or over time, essentially in lieu of a buyout. These can be popular plans for service businesses. Nonqualified deferred compensation plans require real tax expertise, especially when it comes to navigating the treacherous waters of Section 409A of the Internal Revenue Code and the tax doctrines of economic benefit and constructive receipt.

Qualifying for Section 6166 Deferral

It is almost always preferable to have a buy-sell agreement and to not rely upon Section 6166 of the Internal Revenue Code to defer federal estate taxes. However, Section 6166 deferral is a possible alternative to a buy-sell agreement. This is because, instead of coming up with the cash needed to pay the estate tax on a business interest, the decision is made to simply defer that tax so that it can be paid in installments. Section 6166 is complicated, and qualifying for it is not easy. You should always consult competent tax counsel for assistance in both qualifying for Section 6166 deferral and making that election on a federal estate tax return.

Division of an Entity

Sometimes owners—for a variety of reasons—simply want to divide a business between themselves. If, for example, it is unlikely that the current owners or the next generation will be able to work together, division of an entity might be preferable over a buy-sell agreement. Section 355 of the Internal Revenue Code permits many types of businesses to be divided without tax consequences. Dividing a business requires serious knowledge of the tax code and should only be done with the assistance of competent tax counsel.

Confidentiality and Noncompetition Agreements

In lieu of or in conjunction with a buy-sell agreement buyout provision, a former owner could be paid to not compete with the entity. Such payments could also compel the former owner to keep secret and confidential the entity's trade secrets, customer lists, and other proprietaries. This type of payment can be very useful—assuming it is reasonable and deductible by the entity. Often, however, such payments must be capitalized and amortized under Section 197 of the Internal Revenue Code for a period of time, rather than being fully deductible in the year of payment to the departing owner. This has the financial effect of reducing its benefit to the entity.

Installment Sales

Through buy-sell agreements, installment sales are frequently used in retirement buyouts. Alternatively, it is possible to have the retiring owner sell his or her stock in exchange for a promissory note that is payable over time.

Sale to Outsiders

Sometimes it is easier and more profitable to sell an entity to outsiders rather than arrange for a buyout by an existing ownership group. An outside group may pay more for the business while the existing ownership group is still involved in the business. This might change after one or more of the owners has left the entity or has died. The senior generation may well decide that the best time to sell the business is now rather than later. This is particularly true if the younger generation is neither interested nor well equipped to run the business at the same level of efficiency and profitability as the current owners.

In my opinion, one of the biggest mistakes that family business owners continue to make is failing to give serious consideration to selling their business. Too many erroneously believe that the business is their legacy and that their children will want it. All too often, this is not the case. The inability to view either themselves or their company objectively can cause the loss of more wealth than you can imagine.

Public Offering

While the prospect of a public offering payday is entertained by many closely held entities, it is realized by few. Nevertheless, a public offering can be a very good alternative to a buy-sell agreement. In fact, it's not unusual for buy-sell agreements to terminate upon a public offering of ownership interests.

New Generation Opens a Similar Type of Business

The current generation of business owners might decide to wind down a business while the next generation desires to open a similar business. In such cases, it is sometimes preferable to allow the younger generation to open a similar or even identical business and to let the existing business wind down and go out of existence. For a variety of reasons, this solution might be better than forcing the younger generation to buy ownership interest in a lightly capitalized, existing service business.

CHAPTER 4

WHICH TYPE OF AGREEMENT IS BEST FOR YOU?

H ow do you decide which type of buy-sell agreement is best for you, your family, your business stakeholders, and your business entity? Which factors are important to consider when formulating a buy-sell agreement with tax and legal counsel? We'll cover the answers to these questions in the following pages as well as discuss the types of transfers and restrictions that are used in crafting buy-sell agreements.

As mentioned in earlier chapters, there are three types of buy-sell agreements: cross-purchase, redemption, and hybrid. The following section outlines some of the most important considerations in making your decision about which type of buy-sell agreement is best for you.

Number of Owners

As a general rule, the greater the number of owners, the more likely it is that the buy-sell agreement will be of the redemption variety, because cross-purchase buy-sell agreements generally become unwieldy and impractical when there are more than three or four owners. That's not to say that you can't have a cross-purchase buy-sell agreement with a large number of owners, but it's just not as common.

Nature and Size of the Entity

The financial size of the entity can have a significant impact on the type of buy-sell agreement that is best to use. Generally, a buy-sell agreement for an operating company where the owners also work part time or full time will be different from that of an entity where income is earned passively. As a general rule, a larger company will call for a redemption buy-sell agreement or a hybrid buy-sell agreement because the ownership interests will probably be worth more. Additionally, the type or nature of entity—corporation, LLC, or partnership—can influence the selection of the buy-sell agreement due, in part, to tax reasons.

Value of the Entity

Generally, the higher the value of the entity, the greater the likelihood that the buy-sell agreement will be a redemption buy-sell agreement or a hybrid buy-sell agreement. This is because the entity is most likely generating income and cash flow that could be used to fund a buyout. This approach will probably be necessary because the interests will be expensive, due to the entity's high value. When there is a disparity between the fair market value and the book value of an entity, this disparity impacts not only the type of buy-sell agreement required but how the entity interests are valued for purposes of the agreement. Under these circumstances, the likelihood of valuation by appraisal is higher.

Relative Ownership Interests

The larger the ownership interest of a business entity, the greater the likelihood that the buy-sell agreement will be a redemption or hybrid buy-sell agreement—all other things being equal. This is because value generally follows the size of the interest. A bigger interest is worth more than a smaller interest, and the more an entity interest costs, the greater the likelihood of a redemption or hybrid buy-sell agreement, because the entity usually has the most money and wherewithal to buy an interest.

Relative Ages of the Owners

When there is a disparity in age between the owners of an entity, there is a greater likelihood of a redemption or hybrid buy-sell agreement, because the senior generation usually owns more interests. This ends up costing the younger owner, often necessitating the entity's cash flow to assist in the buyout.

Financial Condition of the Owners

Generally, the shakier or more questionable an owner's finances, the more likely a redemption buy-sell agreement is necessary, because the entity usually has more money. This is because in a cross-purchase buy-sell agreement, the owner with the shakier finances may be unable to pay the purchase price for an interest he or she is obligated to purchase under the terms of the agreement. This, in turn, could undermine the other owners' original expectations for the buy-sell agreement, leading to potentially bad news for the owners relying on the owner with the shakier finances to purchase their interests.

Enforcement of Buy-Sell Agreement Concerns

The greater the owners' concern about one of them reneging on the purchase or other terms of the buy-sell agreement, the more unlikely the chances for a redemption buy-sell agreement or a trusteed/escrowed cross-purchase buy-sell agreement.

Desire for a New Basis for the Purchasing Owner

If the purchasing owners want a new basis in their ownership interests, this favors the cross-purchase buy-sell agreement, because the purchasing owners will get a cost basis in the acquired interests that is equal to the purchase price. This is not true in the redemption buy-sell agreements because the entity is the buyer of the interests.

Health and Insurability of the Owners

When one owner has low life insurance liability due to good health and another is uninsurable due to poor health, a redemption buy-sell agreement is often preferable, in order to handle the disparity in insurance and health payment obligations between the owners. This tends to adversely affect the other owners, who are often younger, in better health, and without as much in the way of financial resources because they are bearing the cost of the older owner's insurance.

Commitment of Owners to the Business

If some of the owners are not committed to long-term participation in the business, consider either a cross-purchase or a hybrid buy-sell agreement. These agreements can allow the interests of the uncommitted owner to be purchased directly by an owner who is interested in staying long-term.

Availability of Assets inside of the Entity for Redeeming the Interest

The availability of an entity's assets often dictates the form of the buy-sell agreement. Some types of businesses—for example, general construction contractors—have minimum asset and performance bond insurance requirements that may give rise to the use of a cross-purchase agreement if the arrangement cannot be covered with life insurance. This is because using entity assets to buy out an owner could cause a default under a performance bond or reduce the size of jobs the entity may bid on going forward.

State Law with Respect to Entity Redemptions

In the case of a corporation or of distributions to members of an LLC or partnership, especially if the entity is lightly capitalized (e.g., a service business), consider a cross-purchase buy-sell agreement or hybrid buy-sell agreement, because the entity may not have enough legal or stated capital to do a redemption.

Existence of Restrictions under Loan Agreements on the Use of the Entity's Assets to Redeem Equity Interests

The existence of onerous terms under entity loan agreements may make stock redemptions difficult because lenders often will not consent to use of their collateral to buy out an owner. This would militate in favor of a cross-purchase buy-sell agreement.

Family Relationships among Owners

There may be more than one family involved in the ownership of an entity, or a family may be into its second or third generation of ownership. For example, the ownership interest might now be held by cousins instead of siblings or even by the children of cousins. In other words, ownership of the interest has become quite removed from the original owner. In these instances, there is a significant chance that a cross-purchase buy-sell agreement will be used—unless the business is recapitalized to have different classes of ownership for each set of families. With a cross-purchase buy-sell agreement, redemption of the interests has a chance of changing the relative ownership holdings of each family. Many buy-sell agreements go to great lengths to maintain equal ownership interests between each family.

Professional Licensing and Other Qualification Requirements

Some types of businesses, like those run by doctors, architects, and lawyers, require the owner to possess licenses or other certifications or qualifications. These requirements could have a bearing on the choice of buy-sell agreements.

Type of Entity

The very form of the entity can influence the choice of buy-sell agreements. For example, if the entity is a family-owned C corporation and there is concern about a redemption being treated as a dividend, the owners may opt for a cross-purchase buy-sell agreement.

Potential Conflicts

Buy-sell agreements engender a host of potential conflicts of interest for advisors, particularly for lawyers. Savvy lawyers will often address potential conflicts in their engagement letter before the buy-sell agreement is drafted. However, even careful lawyers may not be able to successfully negotiate the rapids of conflicts of interest, particularly when a lawyer has previously represented one of the parties to the agreement. Sometimes accusations of favoritism are made against the lawyer after the owners fall out with one another. In these scenarios, things can get messy fast.

Let's return to our set of characters from the introduction section of this book: Al, Betty, Charlene, and Dave, along with their company, MythiCo. This time, they sign a cross-purchase buy-sell agreement whereby the owners agree that each will purchase an equal interest from the estate of a deceased owner—which in this example will be Betty.

In their cross-purchase buy-sell agreement, Al, Charlene, and Dave buy Betty's stock in MythiCo from her estate in equal shares. After the purchase transaction, the three will each own one-third of MythiCo's stock. Note that in the purchase of Betty's interest, Al, Charlene, and Dave end up as equal one-third shareholders. This does not have to be the case. Suppose that the buy-sell agreement gives Dave, the investor (who probably has more money), the obligation to buy the interests of a deceased owner upon the owner's death. If Dave is called upon to buy out the stock of a deceased owner, then he would become a 50 percent shareholder, with the two other surviving shareholders remaining at 25 percent apiece.

This is one of the differences between a cross-purchase buy-sell agreement and a redemption buy-sell agreement: in the cross-purchase buy-sell agreement, the owners can cause disproportionate ownership shifts; in a redemption buy-sell agreement, the increases in the shares of the remaining owners will always go up proportionately. That is not to say that redemption buy-sell agreements cannot cause shifts in control—they can. Let's suppose that our shareholders in our mythical group are not equal shareholders, but that Dave, the investor, owns 40 percent (which is more likely since he's the one putting up the money), with Al, Betty, and Charlene owning 20 percent each. Now let's kill off Charlene. In that instance, in a redemption buy-sell agreement, MythiCo would purchase Charlene's shares from her estate.

The ownership interests increase proportionately, just like they always will in redemption buy-sell agreements. However, this time, there will be a shift in effective control of MythiCo to Dave because his ownership percentage after the redemption of Charlene's shares will increase to 50 percent, while the interests of Al and Betty will increase to 25 percent. Note that Dave's percentage interest went up twice as much (10 percent) as that of Al and Betty (5 percent apiece) because Dave owned twice as much stock as the two of them, considered separately. Al and Betty may not like the possibility of Dave becoming a controlling shareholder and may negotiate for a put option right. This will allow them to force Dave to purchase their shares if he becomes an owner of 50 percent or more of the stock of the corporation. I define and discuss put option rights in chapter 5.

Trusteed Cross-Purchase Agreement

A trusteed cross-purchase agreement is a cross-purchase buy-sell agreement that uses a third party—referred to as a "trustee" or "escrow agent"—to ensure that the buy-sell agreement is carried out upon the occurrence of a triggering event. In this case, the trustee or escrow agent—not the owners—conducts the purchase and sale transaction. These arrangements usually happen when life insurance is used to fund the buy-sell agreement.

In a basic cross-purchase buy-sell agreement, there's always a risk that an owner who holds a life insurance policy on the lives of the other owners may not go through with his or her purchase obligation or even fail to keep the life insurance in place by neglecting to pay the insurance premiums. Just like in a basic cross-purchase buy-sell agreement, the owners are obligated to buy, and the seller (or the seller's estate) is obligated to sell the selling owner's interest when a specified triggering event occurs, such as death.

However, unlike a basic cross-purchase buy-sell agreement, a trusteed or escrowed cross-purchase buy-sell agreement requires the payment of the insurance premiums on all of the life insurance policies. The purchase and sale of the interest is then overseen by the trustee or escrow agent, who should be a neutral party responsible for seeing that all obligations are carried out. The use of a trustee or escrow agent frees an owner of the entity or that deceased owner's estate from having to deal directly with the buyer. The role of the trustee or escrow agent is almost like that of a regular escrow agent in a real estate transaction. However, the trustee or escrow agent will ensure that the life insurance policies are maintained with timely premium payments. They will also ensure that the sale goes through by taking it out of the owners' hands.

Use of a Partnership or LLC as Funding Owner and Source of Buyout Funds

In this technique, the owners use an existing entity to own and hold the life insurance for the cross-purchase buy-sell agreement funding obligations. It is similar to the trusteed or escrowed buy-sell agreement in that a disinterested third party, often a commercial trustee, serves as the manager of the entity and is responsible for the purchase of life insurance policies and payment of premiums, which are covered by mandated capital contributions from the owners.

It differs from the trusteed cross-purchase buy-sell agreement in that the entity is a freestanding entity, separate from the main business entity. Generally, this technique is only used for operating corporations where life insurance will be used to fund purchases. Unlike the trusteed or escrowed cross-purchase agreement, transfers of life insurance policies between partners or owners of the insurance entity enjoy an express exception to the transfer for value rule, which makes certain life insurance policies taxable when they normally aren't.

Redemption Buy-Sell Agreements

In a redemption buy-sell agreement, the entity and some or all of the owners are parties to the buy-sell agreement. The entity then agrees to buy out the interests of an owner upon the occurrence of a triggering event.

For example, suppose Al, Betty, Charlene, and Dave, who are equal 25 percent shareholders, enter into a redemption buy-sell agreement where the entity, MythiCo (in this example, a C corporation), agrees to buy the stock of a deceased owner from the estate of a deceased owner, which is obligated to sell to MythiCo under the redemption buy-sell agreement. Now let's kill off Al. In that event, MythiCo buys Al's stock from his estate, and Betty, Charlene, and Dave are now equal one-third owners, their interests proportionately increasing when MythiCo redeemed Al's 25 percent of the stock. This proportional increase in ownership percentages across the board always occurs in a redemption buy-sell agreement.

Hybrid Buy-Sell Agreements

The hybrid form of a buy-sell agreement combines aspects of both the redemption and the cross-purchase buy-sell agreements. In a typical hybrid buy-sell agreement, both the entity and other owners have a right—one usually subordinated to the other—to acquire the interests of an owner on the occurrence of a triggering event. Additionally, a hybrid buy-sell agreement often has different potential acquirers based on different triggering events. For example, a hybrid buy-sell agreement might have a cross-purchase option for the owners in the event of the death of an owner, but a redemption option in favor of the entity for all other triggering events. A hybrid buy-sell agreement may also provide for the entity to buy some of the interests while allowing the other owners to buy the other interests of a selling owner. It is very flexible.

Related or Ancillary Documents

The following sections describe some related or ancillary contracts that often are associated with or are created in conjunction with buy-sell agreements.

Noncompete and Nondisclosure Agreements

It is somewhat common to have a freestanding noncompete and nondisclosure agreement in conjunction with a buy-sell agreement, although it is just as common to require these agreements on a sale of interests. I often include these types of clauses in buy-sell agreements.

Employment Agreements

It is not unusual for owners to have employment agreements alongside their buy-sell agreements, since they can be tied together. For example, the term "cause" might be defined in the employment agreement and also used in the buy-sell agreement. However, if both the buy-sell agreement and the employment agreement define "cause" then it is important that the definitions of the term are the same in both documents. Otherwise, an owner may be terminated for cause under one agreement but not necessarily under the other.

Deferred Compensation Agreements

Though somewhat rare, a deferred compensation agreement could be entered into in conjunction with a buy-sell agreement. In a deferred compensation agreement, a person voluntarily defers a certain amount of salary or bonuses, or both, in the present in exchange for payments to be made at retirement.

Death Benefit Only Agreements

In a death benefit only agreement, an entity and an employee-owner enter into an agreement whereby the entity will make a payment, of an amount that is set by a formula, to the heirs or surviving spouse of an employee-owner who dies before retirement. The formula for the amount is often a multiple like three times the final base salary, although the payment can also be for a fixed amount such as $100,000. The owner cannot own more than 50 percent of the interests of the entity for this type of plan to work.

Consulting Agreement

It is not unusual for owners who retire and whose stock has been acquired in a cross-purchase buy-sell agreement to have a consulting agreement with the business entity they once owned. It's also not unusual in a nonfamily-owned business redemption buy-sell agreement. In this case, the retired owner agrees to consult to the business entity for a period of years. Such consulting agreements are often tied to noncompete and nondisclosure agreements.

CHAPTER 5

RESTRICTIONS, TRANSFERS, RIGHTS, AND OPTIONS

A buy-sell agreement can control future transfers of entity interests and can have a direct impact on the owners' and the entity's succession planning. You should always define the term "transfer" very broadly in buy-sell agreements. This way you can cover all possible contingencies. A solid buy-sell agreement will forbid transfers that are not covered by the agreement and only permit transfers to be made in accordance with its terms. This prevents end runs around the agreement's restrictions. An effective buy-sell agreement also clearly defines who has the right or obligation to buy or cause to be bought or sold.

It's probably time to underscore the differences between a "right" and an "obligation" since we're about to discuss both of them. For our purposes, whenever you see the term "option" in the book or the accompanying Interest Transfer Agreement, think "right" because the person who possesses an option has the right to do or to pass, so to speak. This is contrasted with an "obligation," in which the person who has an obligation to do or not to do something must do it, unless there are express exceptions. A buy-sell agreement is an interconnected web of rights and obligations.

Some buy-sell agreements have an exception that permits owners to transfer interests to other owners, but this can be very risky, particularly to minority owners, because such a transfer might shift control to the acquirer. If you are going to permit intra-owner transfers, consider coupling such a transfer with a put option right in favor of a minority owner to force the acquirer to buy out him or her.

Consider the following language for a broad prohibition of transfers:

General Prohibition against Transfer; Absolute Nullity

Except as expressly provided in this Agreement, Owners and Spouses shall not transfer, bequeath, barter, alienate, assign, option, sell, mortgage, pledge, hypothecate, donate, or in any way dispose of or encumber ("Transfer") all or any part of the Interests owned by each such Owner and/or his or her Spouse, directly or indirectly. Any attempt to Transfer Interests or, on the part of the Entity, to issue any additional Interests, in any manner other than as expressly provided in this Agreement, shall be considered an absolute nullity and shall have no legal effect whatsoever, and the parties to this Agreement expressly acknowledge and agree that the Entity and the Owners shall be able to ignore the Transfer on its books and records. Except as provided herein, Owners and/or their Spouses may only make valid transfers of Interests to Eligible Owners pursuant to the terms and conditions of this Agreement.

Restrictions on Transfers

All transfers should be made subject to and in accordance with the buy-sell agreement. Transfers outside of the buy-sell agreement process and procedure should be made null and void ab initio (from the beginning) and of no legal effect, giving the transferee no rights to be an owner or to have any voice in the entity's governance. Alternatively, transfers outside of the buy-sell agreement process and procedure could cause the transferred rights to be converted to nonvoting, and the transferred rights could be subjected to a call option right on favorable terms, including a sharply reduced price.

Absolute Prohibition

Provisions in buy-sell agreements that absolutely prohibit all transfers have been held by courts in many jurisdictions to be unenforceable on public policy grounds because such a prohibition unduly restrains commerce. However, minimum rights of first refusal in favor of current owners or the entity, or both, are valid in virtually every situation.

Exceptions for Permitted Transferees

It is not unusual for a buy-sell agreement to cull its term "transfers" to certain named or otherwise identified people in a buy-sell agreement—for example, other shareholders, revocable trusts over which an owner has the right to revoke, children or other descendants of an owner, certain trusts for the benefit of a spouse and descendants of an owner, or persons who possess certain minimum education or outside work experience qualifications. Caution is still advised before making too many permitted transferees, particularly those who are separate and apart from the owner (e.g., children or a spouse) unless you are willing to be in business with those people.

Options

An option is a right to do something. It can be absolute and possible at all times, or it can only come into play after a triggering event.

There are several different types of options, which I will discuss in the following sections.

In a buy-sell agreement, an option is generally worthless to an owner who lacks the resources to exercise it. For example, suppose that in our fictitious entity, MythiCo, each of the equal shareholders (Al, Betty, Charlene, and Dave) have options to purchase (as opposed to obligations to purchase, as in the case of a mandatory purchase) the interest of an owner upon death for cash. However, suppose that Al, Betty, and Charlene all lack the resources to purchase interests for cash at this time and that there is no life insurance on the lives of any shareholder.

Now, let's kill off Dave. In this scenario, Al, Betty, and Charlene have options to purchase Dave's interest from his estate. However, they all lack the resources to pay cash for Dave's interest. Since no one will lend money to people who have no way to pay it back, Al, Betty, and Charlene will be stuck with worthless options and will have to let Dave's estate, which ultimately will pass to Dave's petulant son, Eric, become a fellow owner. This should demonstrate the importance of either funding a buy-sell agreement with life insurance or allowing a purchasing owner the option to pay for a purchased interest in installments over time.

Put Option Right

A put option is an owner right in a buy-sell agreement that can force the entity, other owners, or both to purchase an owner's interests for a price that is either set in the buy-sell agreement or determined pursuant to a method spelled out in the agreement. The put option right can be absolute and in effect at all times, or it can be only triggered by the occurrence of an event such as a shift in control. For example, suppose Al, Betty, and Charlene—all wary of Dave's son, Eric—negotiate a put option right that will give each of them the right to make Eric buy them out for cash if Dave dies first. When Dave dies, Al, Betty, and Charlene have no way to prevent Eric from becoming a fellow owner, but the put option right offers some comfort. They know they won't have to be co-owners with Eric for very long because they can force him to buy their shares for cash.

Call Option Right

A call option is an owner right—not an obligation—to buy an interest at a price specified in the buy-sell agreement, generally within a specific time period. A call option right may be held by either the entity, the owners, or both. It can be absolute and in effect at all times, or spring into existence after a triggering event. For example, suppose Dave has agreed with Al, Betty, and Charlene that he has a right to purchase their interests for cash if they don't meet certain milestones, such as gross sales or the development of a specified piece of software. Now let's assume that Al, Betty, and Charlene fail to meet those milestones. Dave has a call option right to buy their stock, but this is not an obligation; Dave doesn't have to buy their interests.

Use of Cross-Existing Puts and Calls

It is possible for the owners to have cross-existing puts *and* calls. Suppose that instead of requiring a mandatory buy and sell in the event of an owner's death, the estate, the entity, and the surviving owners have cross-existing rights. The estate of the deceased owner would have a put option right, exercisable for a period of time after death, to put the deceased owner's interest to either the entity or the surviving owners. In that case, the entity or the surviving owners would then be obligated to purchase the deceased owner's interest pursuant to the buy-sell agreement. At the same time, or upon the end of the estate's put right, the entity or the surviving owners have a right to call the interests of the deceased owner, which would then obligate the estate to sell the deceased owner's interest pursuant to the buy-sell agreement. This arrangement gives each group a right to force the other to buy or to sell, but it affords flexibility since it doesn't automatically *obligate* both to buy and sell, as is the case with a mandatory buy-sell arrangement.

Mandatory Sale

It is customary to require a mandatory purchase and sale upon an owner's death unless family succession is contemplated. However, it is not unusual for a buy-sell agreement to require an owner to sell, without necessarily requiring the other owners or the entity to buy. This is often the case with what I call a "bad boy" triggering event. These are events such as termination of employment for "cause"—as defined in the buy-sell agreement or in a separate employment agreement. For example, cause can be:

- competing with the entity
- disclosing confidential entity trade secrets to a competitor
- theft
- misappropriation of entity property
- conviction (or a plea of guilty or no contest) for a serious crime that negatively impacts the business of the entity or prohibits the "bad boy" from continuing to be an owner, such as loss of a professional license

Gift or Testamentary Transfer

In many buy-sell agreements, owners are permitted to transfer interests to a list of permitted transferees identified in the buy-sell agreement. This list might include revocable trusts, family members, other owners, or in the case of S corporations, qualified trusts that can hold S corporation stock. In many permitted transferee clauses, the transfers are conditioned upon the following:

- Transferring owner should continue to be the family's sole voice in company control and management.
- Transferred interests should remain subject to various provisions keyed to the status of the transferring owner.
- Transferred interests should not be subject to retransfer by the transferee.
- The transferee (and his or her spouse) is required to acknowledge and consent to the terms of the buy-sell agreement.

Pledge, Hypothecation, and Mortgage

Typically, owners are not permitted to pledge or in any way encumber their interests, because this could risk a transfer on default of the debt. However, this may not be practical if the entity requires outside financing in which the lenders may demand a pledge of all the ownership interests. In that case, a buyout trigger upon seizure or foreclosure is used to prevent the creditor from being a co-owner for very long. This probably will appeal to the creditor, who likely just wants cash or to be paid over a certain period of time for the seized interest versus being involved in the business.

Seizure

A seizure, or any type of involuntary transfer of an ownership interest, typically calls for a mandatory sale by the seizing creditor, including a bankruptcy trustee, to the entity or to the other owners, who have a call option right, but not an obligation, to buy—often either at a reduced price or on very favorable payment terms, or both. Such a provision can be an effective creditor repellent, although a decent lender to the entity will require subordination of the buy-sell agreement rights to the loan, so this will likely only come into play when a lender doesn't require subordination or when the creditor is the holder of a lawsuit judgment.

Right of First Refusal

This is a contractual right often contained in buy-sell agreements. It gives its holder the option to enter into a business transaction with the owner of something, in accordance with specified terms, before the owner is entitled to enter into that transaction with a third party. The right of first refusal is similar—but not identical—to a call option right.

As a practical matter, a right of first refusal can severely affect the marketability of an interest because an outside purchaser may be unwilling to go through the evaluation and preliminary due diligence phases of an acquisition. This can be costly even if no sale occurs, especially where it is likely that either the entity or the remaining owners will simply swoop in and buy the interest out from under him or her. In so doing, the inside purchasers simply allowed the outsider to do their valuation and due diligence work for them. A buy-sell agreement can include a right of first refusal that is triggered by an attempted sale of the entity assets, which may also include, at a minimum, tag along rights (defined later in this chapter) for the holder's interest in the entity.

Let's hearken back to MythiCo and its four equal owners: Al, Betty, Charlene, and Dave. Suppose that a man named Earl approaches Dave with an offer to purchase his interests at an attractive price. Dave is inclined to accept. However, if the buy-sell agreement contains a right of first refusal, then Dave would be forced to first offer his interests to Al, Betty, Charlene, and even MythiCo, either for the price contained in Earl's offer or a price determined under the buy-sell agreement.

It is imperative that the buy-sell agreement clearly stipulates the price to be paid in the exercise of a right of first refusal. Often, buy-sell agreements allow the owners, the entity, or both, to purchase the offered interests for the lesser of the prices—whether that's the offer price or the price determined under the buy-sell agreement.

Right of First Offer

Right of first offer is a contractual obligation sometimes included in a buy-sell agreement. It requires an owner to negotiate in good faith with other owners for the sale of interest. The other owners or the entity have the right of first offer before offering the interest for sale to third parties. If the holder of such a right is not interested in purchasing the interest or cannot reach an agreement with the selling owner, then the selling owner has no further obligation to the rights holder and may sell the asset freely, unless there also is a right of first refusal, a right to last look, or another such restriction in the buy-sell agreement.

For example, suppose that the buy-sell agreement for our hypothetical corporation MythiCo gives every shareholder and MythiCo a right of first offer if any shareholder wants to transfer shares during his or her lifetime. It should be reemphasized that a right of first offer, similar to the right of first refusal, is worthless if the holder of the right lacks the financial resources to follow through on a purchase. A possible way to protect owners who lack the resources to exercise a right of first refusal is to give the impecunious owners a put option right to put their interest to the entity or to the other owners if a right of first offer is triggered and results in a sale of an owner's interest to an outsider.

Going back to MythiCo, suppose that the buy-sell agreement provides for a right of first offer for lifetime transfers other than to a group of specifically named permitted transferees. However, if Dave sought to sell his shares, neither Al, Betty, nor Charlene could exercise the right of first offer because they lack the resources to purchase Dave's shares, meaning that Dave is free to assign his rights to his shares to virtually anyone.

However, Al, Betty, and Charlene were wise and negotiated a put option right in the buy-sell agreement. This effectively only applies to Dave, without necessarily naming him. It's worth noting that this strategy might limit Al, Betty, and Charlene's rights to sell if they were obligated to buy when the put option wasn't limited to Dave. The put option forced either Dave, the entity, or the purchaser of Dave's shares, to buy all the remaining shares from Al, Betty, and Charlene if Dave successfully sold his shares to a third party that was not a permitted transferee.

Right to Last Look

The right to last look clause is rarely seen in a buy-sell agreement. It gives the entity or other owners the right to match other offers. This clause is useful if an owner who wishes to sell his or her interest receives a superior proposal from either an outsider or a current owner. The right to last look can be structured as a one-time matching right or as a right to match each offer made.

Suppose MythiCo's buy-sell agreement gives each owner a right to last look. Further suppose that Al, Betty, and Charlene have a bona fide offer from an outsider to buy their shares. Dave can exercise his right to last look by requiring the group to allow him the opportunity to match the outside offer.

Tag Along Put Option Right

The tag along put option right is also referred to as a "co-sale right." It prevents majority owners from selling their interests alone and leaving the minority owners with a new majority owner that they may not like or of whom they may not approve. It achieves this by allowing the minority owners to join in the purchase of the majority's interest on the same terms and for the same per share consideration as the majority's shares through exercise of a put option right.

For example, suppose that Dave owned 70 percent of MythiCo until the company met certain milestones—which is commonplace in venture capital type investments. At this point, his ownership would shrink to some lesser percentage. Until that happened, Al, Betty, and Charlene would each own 10 percent. Dave receives an offer to buy his 70 percent from an outsider who isn't negotiating with the minority owners—Al, Betty, and Charlene—and who may intend to freeze them out of MythiCo after purchasing control from Dave.

A tag along put option right would give Al, Betty, and Charlene the right to force Dave or the outside purchaser, or both, to buy their interests for the same price per share as the outsider is willing to pay Dave. Tag along rights can be very effective, although they often coexist with the so-called drag along rights (described below) that majority owners will often want as well.

Drag Along Call Option Right

A drag along call option right in a buy-sell agreement prevents a minority owner from holding up a sale of the company. It does this by giving the majority owner who receives what he or she views as a favorable offer the ability to force the minority owners to sell on the same terms as the majority owner, through the exercise of a call option right.

For example, let's assume that Dave owns 70 percent of MythiCo, with Al, Betty, and Charlene each owning 10 percent. Further suppose that an unrelated third party comes to Dave with a really good offer to buy 100 percent of the corporation's stock. Without a drag along provision, Dave might have to forego his big payday if Al, Betty, and Charlene decide not to sell. If Dave has a drag along provision included in the buy-sell agreement, though, he can force his business partners to sell on the same terms and for the same price that he's getting per share.

Transfer Alternatives

The next three reciprocal rights are transfer alternatives that only apply effectively to two-owner entities. Known by many different names, these all are reciprocal rights that are vested in both owners, usually at all times, instead of just being applicable after a triggering event. These transfer alternatives are designed to separate owners who simply cannot be in business together any longer. In all three of the following alternative types of transfers, either owner may end up being the buyer or the seller.

Russian Roulette

This is a draconian solution used to break a deadlock between two owners. A Russian roulette provision requires one of the two deadlocked owners to serve a notice on the other owner in which the serving owner gives the price and terms for buying the other owner's interest. The owner who receives the notice then has the option to either buy out the other owner or sell out to the other owner at that price and on those terms.

While this type of provision may sound interesting, in my opinion, it should be sparingly used, and generally not included in a buy-sell agreement. This is because an owner who has more resources than the other may be able to force the other owner to sell at a cheaper price, because that owner may not have the resources to buy the wealthier owner out, even at the less expensive price. Of course, one won't know this for certain until the Russian roulette provision is triggered, hence the name. That is not to say that there isn't a place for this sort of agreement—there is. However, they are best used as proposals outside of the buy-sell agreement. This ensures that neither owner is required to act on the offer, which they would be required to do if this term were part of the buy-sell agreement.

Let's vary our hypotheticals and bring in two new characters, Frank and Gordon, who each own half of the interests in an entity. Let's assume that the two have been at loggerheads for some time regarding the direction of the entity, and they are hopelessly deadlocked and have decided that the business is not big enough for the both of them. Frank could decide to trigger the Russian roulette provision in their buy-sell agreement by setting a price for which he'd buy or sell and send notice of that price to Gordon, who would have the right to decide if he was going to be the buyer or the seller at that price.

Texas (or Mexican) Shoot-Out

Another somewhat harsh solution to a deadlock between two owners in a two-owner entity is a so-called Texas (or Mexican) shoot-out. This involves each owner sending a sealed all-cash bid to an independent third party, stating the price and terms at which they are willing to buy out the other owner. The sealed bids are opened together, and the highest sealed bid wins. The winning bidder must then buy, and the loser must sell, the other half share in the entity at the winning bid price. Again, it is my opinion that this sort of provision should not be included in buy-sell agreements but should instead be saved as last-ditch proposals that can be made outside of a buy-sell agreement. I believe the Texas (or Mexican) shoot-out is fairer than the Russian roulette alternative. However, it still favors the owner with the deeper pockets.

Let's return to Frank and Gordon, who are still hopelessly deadlocked. Each wants out if the other owner stays. Frank and Gordon could each prepare a last best offer to buy the other's interest, seal the offer, and then submit it to an independent third party. This third party would then collect the bids and inform the highest bidder that he was going to buy the other out for the price that he bid. Suppose Frank submitted the highest bid. Frank would be forced to buy Gordon's interest, and Gordon would be forced to sell his interest, at the price offered in Frank's sealed offer.

Dutch Auction

A slight variation on the Texas (or Mexican) shoot-out, a Dutch auction is when the two owners send in sealed bids indicating the minimum price and terms for which each would be prepared to sell his or her interest. The highest sealed bid wins and the winning bidder then buys the loser's share based on the price and terms indicated in the loser's sealed bid. In the case of Frank and Gordon, each would submit sealed bids representing the minimum price and terms for which they would be willing to sell their interest in the business. Suppose Frank submits the highest minimum bid. In that case, Frank buys Gordon's interest for the price that Gordon set in his sealed bid.

Other Transfers Consented to in Writing

Frequently not included in buy-sell agreements, the transfers consented to in writing provision permits transfers that would not otherwise qualify under a buy-sell agreement. With the use of this provision, owners can go forward with a transfer if all of the owners give their consent to it in writing. In essence, this is a waiver to override certain terms of the buy-sell agreement.

In my opinion, waivers of buy-sell agreement terms should be rare. If the owners make it a point to repeatedly waive their buy-sell agreement rights and permit nonqualifying transactions to occur with regularity, there is a risk that an owner could successfully convince a court that the buy-sell agreement had been modified or even repealed by the owners since no one was following it anyway. This would allow the complaining owner to enter into a transaction to which the other owners don't consent. Moreover, the IRS may take this position as well.

CHAPTER 6

REDEMPTION BUY-SELL AGREEMENTS

Redemption buy-sell agreements are contracts between the owners of an entity and the entity itself whereby the entity (not the other owners) purchases or redeems the interests of an owner. For whatever reason, most people view redemption buy-sell agreements as simpler to use and more direct than cross-purchase buy-sell agreements. Perhaps it is the fact that there is only one buyer, whereas in a cross-purchase agreement, there may be as many purchasers as there are owners.

There are also fewer life insurance policies required for a redemption buy-sell agreement, since in this type of agreement the entity only requires one policy per owner. This assumes, of course, that the entity purchases life insurance for its owners. In a cross-purchase buy-sell agreement funded by life insurance, more policies are usually required, unless the owners adopt a trusteed buy-sell agreement or have an entity such as an LLC own the life insurance. This is important because every purchasing owner will require a policy on the lives of every owner other than himself or herself.

For example, suppose that MythiCo and its four equal shareholders—Al, Betty, Charlene, and Dave—entered into a redemption buy-sell agreement whereby MythiCo was obligated to redeem the stock of a deceased shareholder at his or her death. Let's pick on Charlene this time and kill her off. In this instance, MythiCo would redeem the shares of Charlene's estate at whatever price per share and on whatever payment terms the buy-sell agreement provided.

As you should be able to glean from this chapter, as well as the next, redemptions can be far more complicated than cross-purchases, particularly in the area of tax consequences.

Advantages of a Redemption Buy-Sell Agreement

Where the number of owners exceeds more than two or three, the redemption agreement form is often selected. The following sections describe the many advantages of using a redemption buy-sell agreement.

The Entity Usually Has the Money

The assets or income stream used to fund the purchase of interests or to make life insurance premium payments, or both, is more readily available inside the entity when a redemption buy-sell agreement is used. It may be harder to get enough cash out of an entity, especially a C corporation, to allow the owners to do the purchasing (as in a cross-purchase buy-sell agreement). This is due to the rules denying income tax deductions for unreasonably high compensation and to the fact that C corporations get no deduction for paying dividends.

Owner Preference on Source of Premium Payments

The entity is responsible for the premium payment on any life insurance that funds the buyout, thereby personally removing the direct burden of the payment of premiums from the business owners. This is why many business owners prefer the redemption structure. Often, it is preferable from a tax standpoint of a C corporation if the shareholders—who are often in a higher income tax bracket than the corporation—allow the corporation to purchase the life insurance. This will not matter to an entity that is taxed either as a partnership or as an S corporation.

No Transfer for Value Problems

Normally, a beneficiary of a life insurance policy receives the death proceeds income tax–free. This is because of an exclusion in the Internal Revenue Code in Section 101. However, similar to just about every general rule in the overly complex US income tax law, there are exceptions that are often complicated. If an exception to the general rule of being tax-free applies, then the life insurance policy beneficiary will have taxable income when he or she receives the death proceeds. The exception that gives rise to concern is when a life insurance policy is transferred for valuable consideration—for example, where someone purchases an existing life insurance policy from someone else. Valuable consideration can include anything of value; it does not require a cash outlay. In fact, it doesn't even have to involve an actual transfer of the life insurance policy; it need only involve an obligation to maintain a beneficiary designation on a life insurance policy.

A transfer of a life insurance policy to the insured is an exception to the exception, which means the proceeds will be income tax–free to the beneficiary of the life insurance policy death proceeds. For example, suppose Al owns life insurance policies on the lives of Betty, Charlene, and Dave in order to fund his purchase of their stock at their deaths. Betty decides to move on to a new job and sells her shares in MythiCo to Al, Charlene, and Dave. The problem arises when considering what to do with Al's life insurance policy on Betty's life, since it won't be used to fund a buyout of her stock at her death. Since Al has been paying for that policy, it is only reasonable that he should be paid for surrendering the life insurance policy to Betty—who probably would like to buy the policy from Al for her family's needs.

When Betty buys the policy from Al, the policy proceeds become subject to income tax at Betty's death unless an exception to the exception applies because Betty paid Al for the policy transfer. While there are exceptions that would allow MythiCo to transfer the policy to Betty, there also is an exception for transfers to the insured, which is Betty.

In a redemption buyout, there should be no transfer for value issues because the entity continues to own all insurance on the lives of the owners that will be used for the buyouts. Moreover, assuming that Betty buys the policy from MythiCo when she sells her stock back to MythiCo in the redemption, Betty's life insurance beneficiary will not have to pay income tax on the death proceeds because an exception to the exception applies for transfers of a policy from a corporation directly to the insured. Therefore, there really is no transfer for value issue in a redemption buy-sell agreement because the transfers of life insurance policies will almost always be to the insured.

Self-Executing

A redemption may be more self-executing when the entity itself is the purchaser of the selling owner's interest rather than one or more of the other owners. While there is always a risk that even an entity will renege on a buy-sell obligation, the risk is usually lower if you are relying on only the entity to purchase the interests, as opposed to having to rely on all of the other owners to make the purchase. Moreover, there is less of a risk that the entity will not pay the life insurance premiums on time. If the entity begins to make late payments, the insured owner will be in a better position to find out sooner than if an individual fellow shareholder owned the life insurance policy.

Increased Ownership Percentages

A redemption buy-sell agreement will result in all the remaining owners' ownership percentage increasing proportionately. Generally, this is not a problem and is what equal owners want. However, a problem can arise when ownership of the entity is not equal between the owners—as in the case that at least one owner owns more interests than another owner prior to the redemption.

May Be Fairer

A redemption buy-sell agreement can even the playing field by allowing less affluent owners who have access to limited resources to be purchasers. This is because the entity, not the individual owners, must raise the cash to pay the life insurance premiums and to purchase the interests. Of course, the flip side of this is that it takes away any advantage that the wealthier owner may have when a fellow owner cannot buy because he or she lacks the financial wherewithal.

Less Negative Estate Tax Payment Effects

Redemption buy-sell agreements generally have less of a negative impact on the loss of estate tax deferral under Section 6166 of the Internal Revenue Code than cross-purchase buy-sell agreements do. This is due to the fact that redemptions that also qualify under Section 303 of the Internal Revenue Code don't count for purposes of losing the right to continue to defer the federal estate tax. A buyout under a cross-purchase agreement at death would generally cause the loss of continued estate tax deferral under Section 6166.

Possible Lower Income Tax Bracket

Insurance premium payments are not typically deductible by a policy owner. However, if the entity is a C corporation, the corporate tax marginal income tax bracket may be lower than the individual shareholders' marginal income tax bracket—meaning that it will cost less after-tax money for the corporation to buy the insurance than for the shareholders to do so personally.

This advantage is nonexistent in entities that elect to be treated as S corporations for income tax purposes. This can include partnerships, limited liability companies that make an S election, and limited liability companies that don't elect to be treated as corporations for income tax purposes. The owners' brackets will apply to the life insurance premiums because the life insurance premiums are not tax-deductible by the partnerships or S corporations.

Asset Protection from the Owners' Creditors

In a redemption buy-sell agreement, life insurance policies and insurance death proceeds are protected from the owners' creditors because the entity, not the owners, owns the life insurance policies. It may well be that the owners have more creditor risk than the entity. However, this isn't always true, which could convert this to a disadvantage.

Disadvantages of a Redemption Buy-Sell Agreement

While redemption buy-sell agreements have many advantages, the following sections describe some of the disadvantages of using this type of agreement.

Possible Control Shifts

Redemptions can cause shifts in control by virtue of the fact that each of the remaining owners' shares goes up. This is particularly true if the ownership is not equal between the owners prior to the redemption. Let's take a look at our example. Assume that Dave owns 50 percent before redeeming Betty out of the ownership of the MythiCo stock. Betty owns 15 percent before her redemption. If Betty's shares are redeemed—instead of Al and Charlene buying her shares—then Dave becomes a controlling shareholder. He will own almost 59 percent after the redemption of Betty's shares. Here's the calculation: 50 percent divided by 85 percent, because Betty's 15 percent goes away in a redemption. Instead of being a 50 percent owner—where Dave could be blocked on decisions by Al, Betty, and Charlene acting together—Dave now has a majority stake in the company. Al and Charlene might not want Dave to become the controlling shareholder, but they would be powerless to stop it if the buy-sell agreement was a redemption buy-sell agreement.

Nondeductibility of Life Insurance Premiums

Premiums on life insurance are nondeductible for income tax purposes, no matter who pays the life insurance premiums.

Possible Exposure to the Entity's Creditors

In many states, the cash value of life insurance policies and the life insurance death proceeds are subject to the entity's creditors. There are states in which the cash value and death proceeds are exempt from all creditors, so you will have to ask your lawyer what the law is in your jurisdiction. If the entity has greater creditor risk than that of its owners, consider a cross-purchase or hybrid agreement.

Insufficient Assets to Redeem Interests

When life insurance is not used to fund an entity's redemption of its interests, there's always a risk that the entity will not have enough nonoperating assets to distribute to satisfy the redemption price. It is also possible that the entity will not have sufficient capital surplus for state law purposes to complete its redemption purchase. This will depend on the applicable law in the entity's jurisdiction, but ask your advisor about this, especially in the case of lightly capitalized businesses like service businesses. You may be better off with a cross-purchase agreement under these circumstances.

Negative Working Capital Impact Caused by Life Insurance and Redemption Payments

To the extent that the entity either pays the life insurance premiums or makes payments for redemptions, there will be that much less operating money left in the entity. This could necessitate a loan for necessary working capital. On the other hand, if the life insurance policy is a cash accumulation policy—for example, a whole life policy—then it is an asset of the entity.

No Effect on Other Shareholders' Stock Basis in C Corporations

When an owner of a C corporation dies, the value of the redeemed owner's interest is increased by the purchase price that the corporation pays to the deceased owner's estate—as long as the federal income tax law provides for a new basis at death, and as long as the redemption is a capital transaction rather than being treated as a dividend.

The stock basis of the other shareholders is not adjusted in a redemption, and there is potentially more taxable gain to be recognized on the subsequent sale of their stock. This is not a problem for S corporations (including limited liability companies that elect to be taxed as S corporations), partnerships, or limited liability companies that are treated for tax purposes as partnerships, if the entity is the owner and beneficiary of a life insurance policy on the life of a deceased owner. This is because the bases of all of the owners in their entity interests will increase by a pro rata share of the insurance death proceeds.

If a C corporation redeems shares, the payment to the selling shareholder will be treated as a dividend for income tax purposes. This can be bad news if it's taxed at ordinary income rates instead of capital gain rates. The transaction must be carefully designed to qualify for one of the five exceptions to dividend treatment. Otherwise, the redeemed shares could lead to wasted stock basis. It's worth noting that stock basis is irrelevant to dividends—as you can't offset your redemption proceeds with your stock basis if the transaction is deemed to be a dividend. The exception to this rule is an S corporation. Doing so will also result in the loss of the right to report your gain in installments as you receive installment payments for your shares.

This could be really bad news if the dividend is deemed to have occurred for income tax purposes. In this case, the dividend income would have to be recognized by the redeemed shareholder in the year of the redemption, even though the entity is not obligated to pay out the entire redemption price at once and can opt to pay for it over a period of several years.

Accumulated Earnings Tax Exposure for C Corporations

The accumulated earnings tax under Section 537 of the Internal Revenue Code that is applicable to C corporations may make it difficult to raise money inside of the corporation to fund redemptions, because the proposed use of the funds in this manner may be deemed to be for private rather than corporate use. The accumulated earnings tax only applies to C corporations and does not apply to entities that are taxed as S corporations or partnerships.

No New Basis to the Remaining Owners

Generally, a redemption provides no new basis to the remaining owners, because they didn't buy anything—the entity did. There are no exceptions for redemptions by C corporations. However, for death redemptions in partnerships and LLCs that are treated as partnerships for tax purposes (although limited liability companies can elect to be treated as corporations and can make S elections) as well as in S corporations that are funded with life insurance that the entity owns and receives at the insured owner's death, the ownership basis of all of the owners will go up by each owner's allocable share of the life insurance proceeds.

For example, suppose that MythiCo is an S corporation and that it owns separate $1,000,000 life insurance policies on the lives of all four equal shareholders—Al, Betty, Charlene, and Dave. If one of them dies and MythiCo receives the $1,000,000 in death proceeds that it then uses to redeem the stock of the deceased shareholder, the stock basis of all four shareholders will increase by $250,000 apiece. This is the $1,000,000 life insurance death proceeds, divided by four.

Family Attribution Rules Can Cause Dividend Problems for Family-Owned C Corporations

In a family-owned C corporation, there is a greater potential for dividend treatment to the selling owner due to the family attribution rules of Section 318 of the Internal Revenue Code. For purposes of determining whether the redemption is a capital transaction or taxable dividend, those rules treat a redeemed shareholder as still owning all stock that is owned by the former shareholder's spouse, children, grandchildren, or parents. Interestingly, stock owned by siblings is not counted for this purpose, which means that if a business makes it down to the second generation (i.e., owned by siblings only and not by their parents), the chances are good that a redemption agreement will qualify as a capital transaction instead of as a taxable dividend.

To demonstrate this, let's assume that the stock of a corporation is owned solely by members of the same family in the following amounts: dad (50 percent), son (25 percent), and daughter (25 percent). Assume that the son dies, and the buy-sell agreement provides that his estate's 25 percent stock be redeemed in full. Unless there is an exception to the family attribution rules, the son's estate will (unfortunately) be deemed to still own 50 percent of the stock because of the father's 50 percent interest. This means that he can't qualify for the exception to dividend treatment where a shareholder has all of his or her stock redeemed by the corporation.

Now, assume that the dad has given his 50 percent interest to his son and daughter *before* the son dies, so that the son and daughter are equal 50 percent shareholders at the time of the son's demise. In this instance, the son's redemption under the buy-sell agreement will qualify as a capital transaction, because the son's estate will not be deemed to own any of his sister's shares. Of course, like all complicated tax rules, there is an important exception to the family attribution rules that allows family attribution to be waived, but only if the following occurs:

- The shareholder whose stock is being redeemed has no continuing interest or involvement in the corporation's affairs except as a creditor—such as in a redemption that is partially paid for with an installment note—for a period of ten years following the redemption.
- The selling shareholder cannot have acquired the stock less than ten years prior to the redemption. Inheritance does not count.
- The estate and its distributees (essentially, those who will receive the estate) agree to maintain records demonstrating that they will have no continuing interest in the corporation

for a period of ten years, other than as creditors. Distributees are required to notify the IRS if they acquire an interest in the corporation in any capacity other than as a creditor. This means that the redeemed shareholder (or any of the distributees of the redeemed shareholder's estate) can't be employed by the corporation, consult for the corporation, sit on the board of directors, or serve as a corporate officer. No capacity other than as a creditor means exactly that— none. This is not palatable to many family businesses, but if they want to avoid dividend treatment, then this route may be the only one available.

Section 303 Redemptions

There is another important exception to family attribution rules, and it is contained in Section 303 of the Internal Revenue Code. The family attribution rules don't apply to redemptions that fall under this section of the federal tax code. This sometimes-helpful section applies to certain redemptions to cover state and federal death taxes and estate administrative expenses. Section 303 can be especially helpful to family-owned corporations. However, these rules are very complicated and require competent tax advice. There are several requirements the situation must meet for Section 303 to apply. It is limited to redemptions of corporate stock. Section 303 does not apply to partnerships or LLCs. Of course, since the historic expansion of the amount of estate tax exclusion each person gets, very few people will find Section 303 of significant help—at least while the exclusion is high. However, the exclusion is subject to the winds of political change, so one must pay attention to current events regarding federal estate and gift taxation.

Unfortunately, Section 303 doesn't apply to lifetime redemptions. You actually have to die for it to apply. The stock also must be at least 35 percent of the value of your estate. Additionally, the only stock that can safely be redeemed is the amount of stock necessary to cover state and federal death taxes and estate administrative expenses. The good news is that if you qualify for Section 303 redemption treatment, this is not only an exception to the family attribution rules, but also an exception to the dividend general rule. Therefore, even Section 303 redemptions from family-owned corporations will qualify as capital transactions.

Let's return to MythiCo and our four familiar shareholders. Charlene's estate is principally comprised of her MythiCo stock, so when she dies, she meets the 35 percent minimum. Let's assume that Charlene's stock is worth $500,000 and her death taxes and estate administrative expenses total $50,000. In this case, MythiCo could redeem $50,000 of Charlene's stock under Section 303. The remaining balance of Charlene's stock, $450,000, will have to qualify for another exception to dividend treatment in order to offset her stock basis (i.e., qualify for installment gain treatment and capital gain taxation). The most common exception is where a shareholder has his or her entire stock holding redeemed. Since none of the MythiCo shareholders are related to each other, Charlene's estate won't have to worry about the family attribution rules.

Tax Consequences

The tax consequences of any transaction should be known in advance of choosing a buy-sell agreement or an alternative structure. The decision should also be examined from the standpoints of all stakeholders in the transaction. We will examine the tax consequences of a redemption from the standpoints of the redeemed owner, the entity, and the other owners. Because the tax consequences can be different if life insurance is used to fund the buy-sell agreement, we'll also analyze situations where life insurance is used and where it isn't.

The tax consequences to the entity first depend on the type of entity, since corporations have different tax rules than partnerships and LLCs that opt to treat themselves as partnerships for tax purposes. Moreover,

C corporations have different tax considerations than S corporations (which can include LLCs that make an S election). You should consult with a tax advisor or lawyer for more information.

Tax Basis

In this book, I will talk about "basis" a lot and in several different contexts, so I should explain the nature of income tax basis. Your basis for income tax purposes (hereafter referred to as "basis") is the value of a property in your hands for purposes of calculating your taxable gain or loss upon the sale or exchange of that property for cash or other property. Knowing this number is critical, as the IRS will expect you to keep up with it. Basis starts with what you paid for the property, including your current basis in any property that you exchange for the new property.

Over time, basis can go up (such as if you improve the property or have income) or it can go down (for example, if you have to depreciate the property or take deductions or distributions). Most people call the basis of the property that an entity owns "inside basis" and the basis of an owner's interest in the entity (e.g., corporate stock, partnership interest) the owner's "outside basis." I'll use these same terms to eliminate confusion. For a view of what this looks like in actual numbers, let's revisit MythiCo, a C corporation with four equal shareholders (Al, Betty, Charlene, and Dave). Assume each shareholder puts up $25,000 for his or her stock in MythiCo. Their individual stock basis is then $25,000. Further assume that in five years, Al decides to sell all of his shares back to MythiCo for $100,000. Al's gain is equal to what he received for the shares ($100,000), less his basis in those shares ($25,000), for a capital gain of $75,000.

Now, let's explore how their buy-sell agreement behaves from a tax perspective in different corporate structures with or without insurance involved.

Tax Consequences in a C Corporation without Life Insurance

There are very few appreciable income tax effects to the C corporation, whether the redeemed shareholder recognizes a dividend or a capital gain (or loss) on a capital transaction on a redemption. One tax consequence is that the corporation cannot deduct principal payments on redemptions. However, if the redemption payments are being made pursuant to an interest-bearing note and the corporation pays interest, it may be able to deduct that interest. You should consult your tax advisor with the specifics of your situation.

The only other impact is that if the transaction is taxed to the redeemed shareholder as a dividend or as a capital transaction, it will carry out or reduce "accumulated earnings and profits" from a separate income tax account. However, you don't really need to worry about this, and it is beyond the scope of this book.

Suffice to say that life insurance death proceeds, even though generally tax-free, do increase accumulated earnings and profits, and it may mean that there are no earnings and profits left in the shareholder account to be taxed for the next redemption. It also means that the life insurance premiums that have been paid decrease earnings and profits.

The C corporation can run into an obstacle in the form of the accumulated earnings tax under Section 537 of the Internal Revenue Code if the corporation attempts to raise cash inside of the corporation in order to fund redemptions. This can become an issue if the corporation attempts to raise more than $150,000 for most service businesses, or $250,000 for all other corporations, for redemption purposes. There are some exceptions to this rule, so consult your tax advisor. The bottom line is to simply be aware of the accumulated earnings tax under Section 537 of the Internal Revenue Code so that you and your tax advisor can plan around it.

There also is a trap for C corporations that attempt to funnel money to the shareholders to use for cross-purchase or life insurance obligations where the amount of those distributions exceeds the highly subjective "reasonable" level of compensation. What is reasonable in one situation may not be in another. Consult your tax advisor if you are concerned about this. If the IRS determines that the compensation—which is usually fully deductible—is excessive, then it will disallow the excessive part of the deduction, which usually will increase the corporation's income and, thus, its corporate income tax.

Tax Consequences to the Redeemed Owner

The tax consequences to the owner whose interests are redeemed from a C corporation depend entirely on whether the transaction will be treated as a capital transaction or as a dividend. If the transaction is treated as a capital transaction, then the redeemed shareholder will realize capital gain or loss to the extent of the difference between the purchase price of the redeemed shares and the shareholder's basis in his or her stock. In some situations, an exclusion of up to 100 percent of the capital gain realized from selling certain types of C corporation stock will apply, but you'll need to consult your tax advisor to see if you qualify.

In a C corporation, a shareholder's basis in his or her stock is almost always what the shareholder originally paid for that stock, as there are no adjusting events. However, if a shareholder dies, that shareholder's stock gets a new basis, which will almost always be fair market value of the stock as of the date of the shareholder's death. Therefore, any redemption that is done shortly after a shareholder's death and that qualifies as a capital transaction usually will have little or no gain to the deceased shareholder's estate, since the purchase price and the fair market value will almost always be fairly close. In a family-owned corporation, getting redemptions to qualify for capital gain treatment is more challenging because of the family attribution rules.

Let's again consider our mythical corporation, MythiCo, and its four equal shareholders (Al, Betty, Charlene, and Dave). Assume that the only person who put out any cash for stock is the investor, Dave. Let's also assume that Dave contributed $100,000 for his 25 percent of MythiCo's stock. When Dave dies, because of the good work of Al, Betty, and Charlene, Dave's shares are worth $500,000. The redemption buy-sell agreement provides for a mandatory redemption and sale at death. Pursuant to the buy-sell agreement, MythiCo pays Dave's estate $500,000 for his shares. In that instance, Dave's estate will have no gain on the sale because what it received in the redemption ($500,000) is equal to its new basis as of the date of Dave's death, which also is $500,000.

Now let's change the facts a little and assume that Dave's shares are redeemed for $500,000 while he's still alive. In this instance, Dave should recognize $400,000 in capital gain, which is computed by subtracting his stock basis of $100,000 from his redemption price of $500,000.

Tax Consequences to the Remaining Owners

In a redemption of a shareholder's stock, there are no direct income tax consequences to the remaining owners. The only indirect tax consequence is that either capital transactions or dividends will reduce accumulated earnings and profits that could apply to future transactions.

Redemption in a C Corporation that is Funded by Life Insurance

We first considered the tax consequences of a C corporation redemption buy-sell agreement where life insurance was not used. Now let's consider a C corporation that owns and is the beneficiary of life insurance policies on the lives of the shareholders that will then be used in a redemption transaction.

Tax Consequences to the C Corporation

The first income tax impact to the corporation is that, despite claims of some so-called "gurus" who believe that they have come up with a "secret way" to deduct life insurance premiums for income tax savings, life insurance premiums are not deductible. Ever. End of story. Refer to Section 264 of the Internal Revenue Code and run from the schemes these "gurus" are selling because they don't work.

The flip side to the nondeductibility of life insurance premiums—and the reason why the premiums aren't deductible in the first place—is that when an insured shareholder dies, the corporation receives the proceeds and doesn't have to pay income tax on those proceeds, under Section 101 of the Internal Revenue Code. This is always the case, with one possible exception: if the insurance policy covers the life of an employee but some notice, record keeping, and reporting requirements are not met and the consent of the insured employee is not obtained, then the death benefits under a life insurance policy could be subject to income tax. The bottom line is that the buy-sell agreement itself should be drafted to give the appropriate notice to the insured employee and to obtain the necessary consent. However, to ensure that the notice and consent requirements are met, a separate notice should be given, and separate consent should be obtained.

The third income tax consequence to the C corporation in a redemption funded in whole or in part by life insurance is that when the corporation receives the life insurance death proceeds, the corporation's earnings and profits account will increase. An increase to corporate earnings and profits can increase the amount of a potential dividend on a stock redemption, if no exception to the dividend rule is found to be applicable. (A discussion of the earnings and profits calculation is beyond the scope of this book.) Paying insurance premiums reduces accumulated earnings and profits, even though the premiums are not deductible by the C corporation. Life insurance proceeds increase earnings and profits. Transactions that are treated as dividends or as redemptions decrease earnings and profits.

The fourth income tax consequence to the C corporation in this scenario is that the C corporation may not deduct any of the principal payments made in a redemption. However, to the extent that the corporation is paying off the redemption over time pursuant to an interest-bearing note, the interest generally will be deductible by the C corporation. Consult with your tax advisor on the deductibility of interest by your corporation.

Tax Consequences to the Redeemed Shareholder

The tax consequences to the owner whose interests are redeemed from a C corporation depend entirely on whether the transaction will be treated as a capital transaction or as a dividend, even where life insurance is used to fund the buy-sell agreement. In a family-owned corporation, you must first get past the family attribution rules, which were discussed earlier. If the transaction is treated as a capital transaction, the redeemed shareholder will realize capital gain or loss to the extent of the difference between the purchase price of the redeemed shares and the shareholder's basis in the stock.

In a C corporation, a shareholder's basis in his or her stock is almost always what the shareholder originally paid for that stock, which often isn't very much. If a shareholder makes a lifetime gift of shares, the recipient of the gift will almost always have the exact same basis as the donating shareholder—in other words, no new basis. So if the recipient sells the stock, he or she will almost always realize a capital gain. If a shareholder dies, that shareholder's stock gets a new basis, and the new basis will almost always be fair market value of the stock as of the date of the shareholder's death. Therefore, any redemption that is done shortly after a shareholder's death usually will have little or no gain to the deceased shareholder's estate because the purchase price and the fair market value will almost always be pretty close to each other.

With MythiCo and its four equal shareholders (Al, Betty, Charlene, and Dave), let's assume that the only person who put out any cash for stock is Dave, the investor, who contributed $100,000 for his stock. Because of the good work of Al, Betty, and Charlene, Dave's shares are worth $500,000 when he dies. The redemption buy-sell agreement provides for a mandatory redemption and sale at death, which is funded by life insurance. Pursuant to the buy-sell agreement, MythiCo receives $500,000 in life insurance proceeds and pays Dave's estate $500,000 for his shares. In that instance, Dave's estate will have no gain on the sale because the $500,000 it received for the redemption is equal to its new basis of $500,000, as of the date of Dave's death.

Now let's change the facts a little and assume that Dave's shares are redeemed for $500,000 while he is still alive. In this instance, Dave should recognize $400,000 in capital gains, which is computed by subtracting his stock basis of $100,000 from his redemption price of $500,000. Given that Dave is still alive in this scenario, the life insurance may not help much or at all to pay off Dave.

Redemption Agreement Involving an S Corporation without Life Insurance

It is beyond the scope of this book to discuss how S corporations are taxed, as that subject alone could be (and has been) an entire book by itself. What you need to know is there are two types of S corporations—those that used to be a C corporation at one point and those that have never been C corporations. I often refer to the latter as "virgin" S corporations.

Unlike the basis of C corporation shareholders, the basis of S corporation shareholders is always changing because the corporation's income automatically and proportionately increases the shareholders' respective stock basis. This works the same as distributions to the shareholders, which reduce their respective stock basis.

All S corporations must maintain a corporate level account named the Accumulated Adjustments Account (AAA), which represents previously taxed but undistributed income during the company's years as an S corporation that can be distributed to the shareholders tax-free. However, AAA really is only important in a redemption where the S corporation used to be a C corporation and has accumulated earnings and profits from its C corporation years. However, if an S corporation that was formerly a C corporation has accumulated earnings and profits from its prior C corporation years, then the taxability of a distribution paid on the redemption will depend on three things: the amount that the company has in its AAA, the amount of the S corporation's earnings and profits during its C corporation years, and the adjusted tax basis of the selling shareholder in his or her stock.

AAA generally consists of the accumulated gross taxable income of the S corporation, less deductible expenses and prior distributions to shareholders. The AAA is essentially a running total of the S corporation's income, losses, deductions, and distributions. However, tax-exempt income—like life insurance death proceeds—does not increase AAA for an S corporation, although it does increase the shareholders' basis in their S corporation stock. This is good news since it can reduce the amount of gain to the shareholder upon redemption of his or her stock but won't matter if the transaction is treated as a dividend.

S corporations that used to be C corporations also may have an account for accumulated earnings and profits from its C corporation years. Accumulated earnings and profits, if distributed or deemed distributed, are taxable dividends that may be taxed at ordinary income rates. AAA represents the amount that an S corporation shareholder may take out of the S corporation tax-free before the distributions become taxable dividends out of the S corporation's accumulated earnings and profits from its C corporation years. Where an S corporation has no accumulated earnings and profits from its C corporation years—which can be the case if it is a virgin S corporation or if it has already emptied that account through prior distributions—AAA is essentially irrelevant to redemptions and is only something that the IRS requires you to maintain on the S corporation's corporate income tax return (Form 1120-S). This is just in case the S corporation ever goes back to a C corporation structure—in which case you'll be glad that you went to the trouble.

Unlike C corporations, S corporations do not have to worry about either the accumulated earnings tax or the alternative minimum tax, so the S corporation can accumulate cash inside the corporation with which to fund redemptions without tax penalty. Of course, the shareholders of an S corporation will pay income tax on the income that the S corporation retains.

Tax Consequences to the Redeemed Owner

The rules for determining the tax consequences of a redemption to the shareholder of an S corporation whose shares are being redeemed in a capital transaction are complicated. The tax consequences to the redeemed shareholder of an S corporation are similar, but not identical, to that of the redeemed shareholder of a C corporation and will depend on whether the redemption is treated as a capital transaction or as a dividend. Additionally, the rules for determining whether a transaction is a dividend or a capital transaction are the same for an S corporation as they are for a C corporation.

Like the redemption of stock in a C corporation, the redemption of stock in an S corporation will be treated as a dividend unless an exception to that general rule applies. An exception can apply if a shareholder redeems all of his or her stock in the S corporation. However, if the S corporation is family-owned, you'll have to waive the rule that treats you as owning all the stock that members of your family (i.e., parents, spouse, children, and grandchildren) still own.

The tax consequences to the owner whose interests are redeemed from an S corporation depend entirely on whether the transaction will be treated as a capital transaction or as a dividend and whether the S corporation has accumulated earnings and profits from its years as a C corporation. If the transaction is treated as a capital transaction and there are no accumulated earnings and profits, then the redeemed shareholder will realize capital gain or loss to the extent of the difference between the purchase price of the redeemed shares and the shareholder's basis in the stock.

In an S corporation, a shareholder's basis in his or her stock is almost always what that shareholder originally paid for that stock, plus that shareholder's allocable share of any undistributed S corporation profits over the years and any tax-exempt income (e.g., life insurance proceeds) that the S corporation recognizes.

If a shareholder dies, then the new stock basis will almost always be fair market value of the stock as of the date of the shareholder's death. Therefore, any redemption that is done shortly after a shareholder's death usually will have little or no gain since the purchase price and the fair market value will almost always be close.

If the S corporation has never been a C corporation or has no earnings and profits from its years as a C corporation, and the transaction is treated as a capital transaction, then the transaction will be taxable to the extent of the excess of the redemption price over the shareholder's original stock basis (what the shareholder originally paid for the stock), plus the shareholder's allocable share of tax-exempt income (for example, life insurance death proceeds) and net undistributed profits. Distributed profits reduce stock basis.

A redemption payment to a selling shareholder of an S corporation that is treated as a capital transaction will be tax-free to the shareholder to the extent that the amount of the redemption does not exceed either the shareholder's stock basis or the allocable share of AAA, which is the percentage of stock being redeemed, if any.

If the distribution to the selling shareholder exceeds the shareholder's stock basis but not the allocable share of AAA, then the excess is treated as a capital gain from the sale of the stock to the extent of the allocable share of AAA. If the distribution to the selling shareholder exceeds the allocable share of AAA, then the excess is taxed as a regular dividend to the extent of the accumulated earnings and profits from its C corporation years. To the extent that the distribution exceeds the amount of the accumulated earnings and profits from its C corporation years, then the excess will be treated first as a tax-free return of any remaining portion of the shareholder's tax basis in his or her stock and then as a capital gain. Your heads are probably spinning. I know mine was the first five hundred times I read and had to learn those byzantine, confusing rules years ago. So, let's consider an example.

Take our now familiar MythiCo and its four shareholders (Al, Betty, Charlene, and Dave) and turn it into an S corporation that used to be a C corporation. Let's redeem Dave's shares for $500,000 at a time when Dave's stock basis is $250,000, AAA is $300,000, and accumulated earnings and profits from MythiCo's C corporation years are $100,000. Further assume that the transaction will be a capital transaction to Dave.

In this instance, the first $75,000 will be a tax-free return of stock basis to Dave due to his allocable share of AAA, which is 25 percent. The next $100,000 of the redemption proceeds will be a taxable dividend to Dave because MythiCo has accumulated earnings and profits, which are taxable at ordinary income tax rates and which will empty and cleanse MythiCo's accumulated earnings and profits account, from its years as a C corporation. The next $175,000 of Dave's stock basis ($250,000 minus $75,000) will be a tax-free return of the rest of Dave's basis. The remaining $150,000 of redemption proceeds will be a capital gain to Dave. To sum things up: Dave realizes $250,000 of income on the redemption, of which $150,000 is a capital gain and $100,000 is a dividend that could be taxable as ordinary income.

However, if the S corporation has no accumulated earnings and profits from its C corporation years, then the tax rules are much simpler. The distribution will be treated first as a tax-free return of the selling shareholder's tax basis and then as a capital gain. Let's consider another example.

Take MythiCo and make it an S corporation. Let's redeem Dave's shares for $500,000 at a time when Dave's stock basis is $250,000, MythiCo's AAA is $0, and its accumulated earnings and profits are $0. Further assume that the transaction will be a capital transaction to Dave. In this instance, the first $250,000 will be a tax-free return of stock basis to Dave, and the last $250,000 (the remainder of the redemption price after subtracting Dave's stock basis of $250,000) will be a capital gain.

If the redemption is treated as a dividend and the S corporation has no accumulated earnings and profits from its C corporation years, or if it is a virgin S corporation, then the rules are slightly different. Counterintuitively, this scenario also gives a better result most of the time, as long as dividends are taxed at a low rate (as has been the case since 2003). The tax consequences to the redeemed shareholder of an S corporation in this situation will depend on the shareholder's tax basis in his or her S corporation stock immediately before the distribution and on the balance of the S corporation's AAA. Unlike the capital transaction situation, the shareholder would get to use his or her entire stock basis (which comes out tax-free) and up to all of the AAA (which comes out tax-free) instead of just the shareholder's allocable share of AAA.

Let's return to MythiCo for an example. Let's redeem Dave's shares for $500,000 at a time when Dave's stock basis is $250,000, MythiCo's AAA is $300,000, and its accumulated earnings and profits are $0. Further assume that the redemption will be a dividend to Dave. In this instance, the first $300,000 will be tax-free to Dave as a result of the transaction emptying the AAA. This is to the detriment of Al, Betty, and Charlene, who won't be able to take any more tax-free distributions from the S corporation until it earns additional income. The last $200,000 will be a tax-free return of basis, resulting in a totally tax-free transaction. Although this sounds too good to be true, it is reality, courtesy of your elected congressmen and senators!

If the redemption is treated as a dividend and the S corporation has accumulated earnings and profits from its C corporation years, then the rules are slightly different. The tax consequences to the redeemed shareholder of an S corporation in that instance will depend on the shareholder's tax basis in his or her S corporation stock immediately before the distribution, the amount of accumulated earnings and profits from its C corporation years, and the balance of the S corporation's AAA.

Taking the above example, let's now assume that MythiCo also had $100,000 in accumulated earnings and profits from its C corporation years in addition to the $300,000 in AAA, but that Dave's redemption proceeds were $750,000 instead of $500,000. In that instance, the first $300,000 of redemption proceeds will be tax-free to Dave out of AAA, which empties the AAA—again to the detriment of Al, Betty, and Charlene. The next $250,000 would be a tax-free return of Dave's stock basis. The next $100,000 would be a taxable dividend, which empties accumulated earnings and profits, and the last $100,000 of redemption proceeds would be a capital gain to Dave. So, in this situation, even though the redemption is a dividend for tax purposes, Dave realizes only $100,000 of dividend income, $100,000 in capital gain, and receives $550,000 tax-free. This represents all of his stock basis and AAA.

Tax Consequences to the S Corporation

Now let's consider the income tax consequences of a redemption for any entity that has elected to be taxed as an S corporation and where the redemption price is not paid for with life insurance. This scenario can also include LLCs that elect to be treated as corporations and then make S corporation elections. The effect to the S corporation will depend on whether the redemption is a capital transaction (think capital gains to the redeemed owner) or a dividend (think often ordinary income to the redeemed owner). It will also depend on whether the corporation was ever a C corporation.

First, if the redemption is treated as a capital transaction and if the S corporation has never been a C corporation or has never merged with a C corporation (no accumulated earnings and profits), then there is no tax consequence to the virgin S corporation.

Let's take the simplest scenario first. Let's make MythiCo a virgin S corporation. Assume that Dave's stock is being redeemed during his lifetime for $500,000 and that the redemption is a capital transaction. Dave's stock basis for his 25 percent of the stock in MythiCo prior to the redemption is $250,000. In this instance, MythiCo will experience no tax consequences on Dave's redemption. We'll consider the tax consequences to Dave and to the remaining shareholders later in this chapter.

Second, if the redemption is treated as a capital transaction and the S corporation has accumulated earnings and profits from its C corporation years, then both AAA and accumulated earnings and profits will be reduced proportionately by the percentage of stock redeemed.

Now let's add a little complexity. Assume that the above transaction is still a capital transaction, but that MythiCo started out as a C corporation and has accumulated earnings and profits from its C corporation years in the amount of $100,000. Dave's stock basis for his 25 percent of the stock in MythiCo prior to the redemption is still $250,000 and AAA is $300,000. In this instance, AAA and accumulated earnings and profits will be decreased by 25 percent, which is the percentage of stock that Dave owned. Therefore, after the redemption, AAA will be $225,000 ($300,000 less $75,000) and accumulated earnings and profits will be $75,000 ($100,000 less $25,000).

Third, if the redemption is treated as a dividend but the corporation has never been a C corporation, then there will be no tax consequence to the S corporation, just as if the transaction were a capital transaction. Now let's add a little more complexity. Assume that the same transaction is a dividend but that MythiCo has never been a C corporation. Dave's stock basis of his 25 percent of the stock in MythiCo prior to the redemption is $250,000. In that instance, MythiCo will have no tax consequences on Dave's redemption, even if it is treated as a dividend, just as if it were a capital transaction.

Finally, if the redemption is treated as a dividend and the corporation has accumulated earnings and profits from its C corporation years, then AAA will be reduced by the entire amount of the deemed dividend dollar-for-dollar—not proportionately to the percentage of stock redeemed as in a capital transaction. This occurs even if it empties the AAA account. Any excess over AAA is treated as a dollar-for-dollar reduction in accumulated earnings and profits, with any excess reducing (but not to less than zero) the accumulated earnings and profits dollar-for-dollar. In other words, this is not proportionate to the stock redeemed as in a capital transaction.

Let's add even more complexity. This time, the same transaction of Dave being redeemed for $500,000 during his lifetime is a dividend and MythiCo has $100,000 of accumulated earnings and profits from its C corporation years. Dave's stock basis for his 25 percent of the stock in MythiCo prior to the redemption is $250,000 and AAA is $300,000. In this instance, AAA will be reduced to zero and accumulated earnings and profits will also be reduced to zero.

Tax Consequences to the Redeemed Owner

The tax consequences to the redeemed owner of an S corporation are similar to those of the redeemed shareholder of a C corporation and depend on whether the redemption is treated as a capital transaction or as a dividend. As discussed earlier, the rules for determining whether a transaction is a dividend or a capital transaction are the same in an S corporation as they are in a C corporation. The redemption of stock in an S corporation will be treated as a dividend unless an exception to that general rule applies. The exception that applies most often is where a shareholder redeems all of his or her stock in the S corporation.

Let's return to our example from earlier. MythiCo is redeeming Dave's stock during his lifetime for $500,000. The transaction is a capital transaction and since MythiCo was never a C corporation, it has no accumulated earnings and profits. Dave's stock basis for his 25 percent of the stock in MythiCo prior to the redemption is $250,000. In that instance, Dave will receive the first $250,000 tax-free and will realize a $250,000 capital gain, which he can report in installments if he is being paid over time via a note.

If the redemption is treated as a capital transaction and the S corporation has accumulated earnings and profits from its C corporation years, both AAA and accumulated earnings and profits will be reduced proportionately by the percentage of stock redeemed. Thus, even if the redemption is not treated as an exchange, which is a capital transaction, the same result will apply. This means a return of capital to the extent of the owner's basis—a gain from the sale of stock to the extent that the amount of the distribution exceeds the shareholder's basis in his or her stock. This is based on whether the amount received by the shareholder is not in excess of the shareholder's allocable share of AAA as of the close of the taxable year and is allocated among all dividend distributions made during the same period. Where the distribution exceeds AAA as of the close of the taxable year, however, any such excess will be a distribution of earnings and profits and therefore taxed as a dividend.

To make things a bit more complex, imagine the same transaction is a capital transaction but that MythiCo started out as a C corporation and has accumulated earnings and profits from its C corporation years of $100,000. Dave's stock basis for his 25 percent of the stock in MythiCo prior to the redemption is $250,000 and AAA is $300,000. In this example, the first $75,000 will be a tax-free return of stock basis to Dave due to his allocable 25 percent share of AAA. The next $100,000 of the redemption proceeds will be a taxable dividend to Dave because MythiCo has accumulated earnings and profits. These are taxable at ordinary income tax rates and will empty MythiCo's accumulated earnings and profits account from its years as a C corporation. The next $175,000 of Dave's stock basis ($250,000 less $75,000) will be a tax-free return of the rest of Dave's basis. The remaining $150,000 of redemption proceeds will be a capital gain to Dave. To sum things up: Dave realizes $250,000 of income on the redemption, of which $150,000 is a capital gain and $100,000 is a dividend usually taxable as ordinary income. However, unless the S corporation used to be a C corporation and still has some accumulated earnings and profits from those days, or the income tax rates for dividends and capital gains are different, the tax consequences to the redeemed owner of an S corporation will be almost the same—no matter whether the transaction is treated as a dividend or as a capital transaction. The big difference is that with a dividend, the redeemed owner would not be permitted to recognize gain in installments. That's right, that's the only difference. So, if cash is being paid for the entire redemption instead of an installment note, then it doesn't matter to the redeemed shareholder of an S corporation, irrespective of whether the transaction is treated as a capital transaction or as a dividend.

If the redemption is treated as a dividend but the corporation has never been a C corporation, then AAA will be reduced by the entire amount of the deemed dividend—not proportionately to the percentage of stock redeemed, as in a capital transaction.

Now, let's assume that the same transaction is a dividend but that MythiCo has never been a C corporation. Assume further that Dave's stock basis for his 25 percent of the stock in MythiCo prior to the redemption is $250,000 and AAA is $300,000. In this situation, Dave will receive an amount equal to his stock basis tax-free and will realize $250,000 of capital gain—which is almost exactly what would happen in a capital transaction. The only difference is if Dave were given a promissory note instead of cash up front. If the redemption is a dividend, then Dave won't be able to report his gain as each note payment is made. He can, however, report his gain if the redemption is a capital transaction. In other words, he must realize all of the gain in the year of the redemption in order to be able to report that gain. This is the only impact on Dave.

If the S corporation used to be a C corporation and the transaction is treated as a dividend, then the redeemed owner of an S corporation will still get to offset his or her interest basis against the redemption proceeds. However, he or she will not get to use installment tax reporting of any gain on the transaction, even if the former owner is receiving the redemption payments over time. The redeemed owner will be taxed at the ordinary income tax rates, which could be higher than capital gain tax rates at the time. The redeemed owner will have to recognize all the proceeds in the year of the redemption, even though the payments will be made over a period of years.

As you can see, avoiding dividend treatment can still be very important but it is not always best, as demonstrated through the above examples. In other words, there are situations where you would want to purposely flunk the capital transaction exceptions so that the transaction is treated as a dividend.

Tax Consequences to the Remaining Owners

Generally, the redemption of an owner's interest—whether it is treated as a redemption or as a dividend—will have few major tax consequences to the other owners. However, like all good tax laws, there are exceptions. The major exception is if the entity redeems the interests of an owner by distributing appreciated property to the redeemed owner instead of paying the redemption price in cash or with a promissory note. In that instance, the other owners will have to realize their respective ownership shares of the gain equal to the difference between the fair market value of the distributed property and the entity's tax basis in that property.

The remaining owners will care about whether the transaction is classified as a dividend or as a capital transaction, as they will be better off if the transaction is treated as a capital transaction. This is due to the differences between how the AAA is treated in a capital transaction as opposed to a dividend. If the redemption transaction is treated as a capital transaction, then AAA is only reduced proportionately to the redeemed owner's percentage ownership. This will always leave some AAA for the remaining owners to be able to take cash out of the entity tax-free. However, if the redemption transaction is treated as a dividend, then the AAA is reduced dollar-for-dollar, which could empty the AAA, leaving no tax-free dollars available for the remaining owners.

Redemption Agreement Involving an S Corporation Funded with Life Insurance

As you will see in the following sections, life insurance adds another layer of complexity to the redemption agreement. There are several tax consequences when life insurance is used to fund a redemption in an S corporation.

Tax Consequences to the S Corporation

The first income tax consequence to an S corporation is that its payment of life insurance premiums will not reduce the taxable income of the S corporation that the shareholders will have to divide among themselves in accordance with their respective share holdings. The second consequence is that it cannot deduct the life insurance premiums. The third tax consequence is that it will not have to recognize any taxable income when it receives the life insurance death proceeds unless the corporation fails to comply with the notice and consent rules.

The fourth tax consequence depends on whether the transaction is taxed as a dividend or as a capital transaction, and whether the S corporation has ever been a C corporation and still has accumulated earnings and profits from its C corporation days. If a redemption is treated as a capital transaction, then the corporation's AAA and accumulated earnings and profits will be decreased in proportion to the number of shares redeemed relative to the total number of shares outstanding. If a redemption is treated as a dividend, then the distribution will reduce the S corporation's AAA on a dollar-for-dollar basis. If the S corporation does not have accumulated earnings and profits from its C corporation days, then the consequences of the redemption not qualifying as a capital transaction—in other words, qualifying as a dividend—are largely irrelevant.

If absent of accumulated earnings and profits from its days as a C corporation, the S corporation will see no portion of the redemption as a dividend and the transaction will result in a tax-free recovery of basis. This will be followed by a capital gain to the extent that the redemption proceeds exceed the redeemed owner's stock basis. If the S corporation has accumulated earnings and profits from its C corporation days, then failure to qualify the redemption as a capital transaction can have adverse consequences to the redeemed owner. The portion in excess of the corporation's AAA will be a dividend to the redeemed owner in an amount that cannot exceed the amount of the accumulated earnings and profits, which will be reduced by the same amount. Additionally, the redeemed owner will not be able to report any gain on the installment method of accounting. This could be bad news for the remaining owners, since these shareholders will have to report the entire gain in the year of the redemption, even though payments are being made over time. Although income from excluded life insurance proceeds passes through to the shareholders and increases stock basis, it does not increase the corporation's AAA because it is tax-exempt income. Likewise, if the S corporation pays life insurance premiums, it will not reduce AAA.

Tax Consequences to the Redeemed Owner

The tax consequences to the redeemed owner of an S corporation when life insurance is used to fund the redemption are similar to those of the redeemed owner of an S corporation when life insurance is not used. Those consequences will depend on whether the redemption is treated as a capital transaction or as a dividend. The rules for determining whether a transaction is a dividend or a capital transaction are the same. The redemption of stock in an S corporation will be treated as a dividend unless an exception to that general rule applies. The exception that applies most often is when an owner redeems all of his or her interests in the S corporation. However, if the S corporation is family-owned, you'll have to waive the rule that treats you as owning all of the interests that certain members of your family still own.

The tax consequences to the owner whose interests are redeemed from an S corporation depend entirely on whether the transaction will be treated as a capital transaction or as a dividend. If the transaction is treated as a capital transaction, then the redeemed owner will realize gain or loss to the extent of the difference between the purchase price of the redeemed shares and the redeemed owner's basis in the interests.

In an S corporation, an owner's basis in his or her interests is almost always what that owner originally paid for that stock plus that owner's allocable share of any S corporation profits over the years that haven't been distributed to the owners. If the scenario involves a death redemption where the corporation owns the life insurance on the life of the deceased owner, the owner's basis would be added to the deceased owner's allocable share of the life insurance proceeds, even though those proceeds are tax-exempt and don't affect AAA. This occurs unless the redemption is done prior to the receipt of the life insurance proceeds and the S corporation is on the cash method of accounting.

If an owner of interests in an S corporation dies when that owner's life insurance is owned by the S corporation, then that deceased owner's new basis will almost always be fair market value of the stock as of the date of the owner's death plus the owner's allocable share of the life insurance death proceeds. Therefore, any redemption that is done shortly after an owner's death will usually have little or no gain, often at a virtually unusable capital loss since the purchase price and fair market value will almost always be close. When you add the owner's allocable share of the life insurance proceeds to that fair market value there will essentially be what I call "wasted basis"— unless you have engaged in some sophisticated advance planning.

If the S corporation has never been a C corporation (a virgin S corporation, as I call them) or has no earnings and profits from its years as a C corporation and the transaction is treated as a capital transaction, then the transaction will be taxable to the extent of the excess of the redemption price over the owner's original interest basis plus the owner's allocable share of net undistributed profits and the owner's allocable share of life insurance proceeds. Distributed profits reduce stock basis. Undistributed profits increase stock basis.

However, if the S corporation used to be a C corporation—and if the income tax rates for dividends and for capital gains are the same—then the tax consequences to the redeemed owner will be almost the same whether the transaction is treated as a dividend or as a capital transaction. If the S corporation used to be a C corporation, still has some earnings and profits from its days as a C corporation, and the transaction is treated as a dividend, then the redeemed owner will not get to use installment tax reporting on any gain from the transaction, even if the redeemed owner may be receiving the redemption payments over time. The redeemed owner will be taxed at ordinary income tax rates, which are sometimes higher than capital gain tax rates. In this instance, the redeemed owner will have to recognize all the proceeds in the year of the redemption even though the payments will be made over a period of years. As you can see, avoiding dividend treatment, even in an S corporation, can still be important.

Tax Consequences to the Remaining Owners

The tax consequences to the remaining shareholders where the S corporation owns life insurance differ substantially from the consequences to those shareholders where no life insurance is owned by the S corporation, or where the redemption occurs during the shareholder's lifetime. When a shareholder dies and the S corporation receives life insurance death proceeds, the stock basis of all the shareholders, including the deceased shareholder, increases by each shareholder's allocable share of the life insurance death proceeds. For example, if MythiCo is an S corporation that has four equal, 25 percent shareholders and Dave dies, the stock basis of each of the shareholders, including Dave's estate, increases by 25 percent of the life insurance death proceeds.

When life insurance is used by an S corporation, the accounting method of the corporation also matters when it comes to the tax consequences for the remaining shareholders. For our purposes, there are two basic methods of accounting: the cash method and the accrual method. In the cash method—which is what individuals almost always use—you recognize income when it is received in cash and you recognize expenses when they are paid out in cash. With the accrual method, you recognize income when it is earned, even if you haven't received payment yet, and you recognize expenses when they are incurred, even if you haven't paid for them yet.

If the S corporation uses the accrual method, then the S corporation recognizes the tax-exempt life insurance death proceeds automatically on the shareholder's death, even though it may take a couple of weeks to receive the check for the life insurance death proceeds from the life insurance company. This almost always will result in "wasted stock basis" to the deceased shareholder's estate and create a loss for a deceased shareholder's estate on any redemption that is treated as a capital transaction.

However, if the S corporation is a cash-basis-method taxpayer (as are the overwhelming majority of small S corporations), it is possible to avoid the wasted basis problem if you're smart and engage in a little advance planning. It is possible for an S corporation using cash-based accounting to divide the basis increase between only the surviving shareholders by doing a redemption of the deceased shareholder's stock in exchange for a short-term note prior to the S corporation receiving the life insurance death proceeds. The S corporation would then pay off all or part of that note with the life insurance death proceeds upon receipt from the life insurance company.

Here's a planning tip: if the S corporation is a cash method–based taxpayer, the redemption transaction should always be done in exchange for a short-term note. This is clearly in the best interest of the surviving shareholders and will not hurt the estate of the deceased shareholder because that shareholder already got a new basis equal to fair market value as of death. The payoff of the note would occur shortly after the corporation receives the policy's death proceeds.

Partnership or LLC Taxed as a Partnership—
No Life Insurance Used

Now let's consider the tax consequences of a redemption in a partnership or an LLC that has opted to be treated as a partnership for federal income tax purposes. These rules can be complicated, even more so than for S or C corporations. For the purpose of this book, I will generalize many of the rules, so you'll have to work closely with your tax advisor in these types of scenarios.

Let me provide some background on the taxation of partnerships and limited liability companies that don't elect to be taxed as corporations, which I'll refer to collectively as "entities." Generally, like the S corporation (but unlike the C corporation), entities that are taxed as partnerships aren't taxpaying entities and don't pay income tax. Instead, their owners, who are partners or members of an LLC, pay the income tax. Entities that elect to be taxed as partnerships file an information tax return (Form 1065), instead of a regular tax return like a C corporation or an S corporation.

For tax purposes, it is helpful to view these entities as falling into one of two categories. The tax law treats each somewhat differently and even the IRS uses these categories for its auditors. The first category is what I'll call "services entity" and I'll call the other "assets entity."

In the services entity category, the primary business of the entity is the rendering of services. Typically, these entities retain few valuable assets inside of the entity, because net profits are distributed to the owners as customers pay for their services. For example, let's consider PDK Pool Cleaning Services, LLC, an LLC owned by Paul, Doug, and Keith, which cleans and services pools for its customers. The hard assets of the LLC consist of five trucks, some pool-cleaning equipment and supplies, a checking account, and office furniture and equipment. In this situation, the LLC is not worth very much when you just look at the value of its hard assets; but when you consider the company's healthy customer list, it's clear that the company does very well financially. The

LLC also may sell pool-cleaning supplies to its customers, but that's not where the real money is made; it's in cleaning and servicing the swimming pools, which someone has to do manually. That's a classic services entity because almost anyone who knows how to clean a pool can do so with relatively little equipment. Does that sound like your business? If so, your entity is a services entity.

In the assets entity category, the primary business of the entity is generating income through the use of the assets, even though some services also may be rendered. For example, let's take Alice & Carol's Laundry, an LLC owned by Alice and Carol, which is engaged in the business of cleaning clothes and running fifty coin-operated washers and dryers. Its assets consist of twenty-five washing machines, twenty-five dryers, five commercial washers, five commercial dryers, a commercial dry-cleaning machine, two delivery trucks, a checking account, and office furniture and equipment. It doesn't take much to see that the assets of this LLC (unlike the pool-cleaning LLC in the previous example) have a lot of value by themselves. This LLC can exist without significant effort of too many employees because it owns the right equipment. Not just anyone can get into the laundry business without spending a lot of money on the front end for the necessary equipment. Does that sound like your entity? If so, your entity is an assets entity.

Almost every item of entity income—gain, loss, deduction, and credit—flows through to the owners, who report them on their respective personal income tax returns through a Schedule K-1 tax form that the entity gives to all owners every year. Each owner reports his or her distributive share of entity income, gain, loss, deduction, or credit on his or her personal income tax return for the year in which the partnership's tax year ends. This is almost always a calendar year, since most of these types of entities are owned by individuals and most individuals are on calendar year reporting for income tax purposes, regardless of when any amounts are distributed to him or her—which is bad news if you're getting taxed on income without getting any cash with which to pay the income taxes.

Like with other entities, every owner has an outside basis in his or her ownership interest in the entity. It is generally equal to what he or she originally contributed to the entity, plus a pro rata share of entity income, less a pro rata share of entity deductions and less distributions to the owner. Your basis in this type of entity rises and falls.

However, unlike with other types of entities, owners of entities that are taxed as partnerships can add their allocable shares of the entity liabilities to their outside basis. This leads to a very big difference (i.e., being able to get basis for third-party debt). Debt rules are complicated, and I've simplified them a lot for the purposes of this book. I'll also point out where liabilities of the entity can create problems for its owners, especially upon redemption or sale of their interests. The flip side of the added basis can become a dark side to an unsuspecting owner, either by redemption or by virtue of being the remaining owner.

I call an owner's basis his or her outside basis so as not to confuse it with the entity's inside basis. You must keep these two basis concepts straight in order to understand the taxation of entities that are taxed as partnerships. Outside basis is very important because it tells you how much income can be distributed to an owner tax-free, how much gain you will have to recognize on a sale or a redemption of your entity interest, and how much of the entity's losses you would generally be able to deduct, subject to some very complex tax limitations.

Tax Consequences to the Entity

The good news is that no redemption can cause termination of an entity for income tax purposes unless the number of owners is reduced to one by virtue of the redemption. The income tax consequences to the entity depend on how the redemption payments are classified. We won't be able to go through all of the details of these complicated rules. What you need to know is—unlike redemption principal payments by either a C or an S corporation—some payments to former owners are deductible by the entity (which passes them on to the remaining owners) and some aren't. The types of assets that can cause problems in this regard are substantially appreciated inventory. This is inventory that is worth 120 percent or more over what the entity paid for it; depreciation on property such as real estate, which causes problems for many entities; and accounts receivable, which causes problems for most services entities. In fact, in services entities, there is little leeway for planning around ordinary income tax consequences on a redemption of an entity interest. This deductible/nondeductible dichotomy creates an interesting negotiations dynamic between the owner whose interests are being redeemed (who prefers capital gains, which the entity can't deduct) and the remaining owners, who want to make as much of the redemption tax deductible as possible, as this is ordinary income to the redeemed owner.

The next tax consequence to the entity is that it almost never recognizes any gain or loss on a redemption, irrespective of what property (cash, note, or other property) the entity gives to the redeemed owner in exchange for his or her ownership interest.

The general rule is that a partnership cannot adjust its inside basis of any asset on a redemption of an entity interest unless the entity (acting through its owners) makes a special election to do so. This election is known by the number of the Internal Revenue Code section to which it refers and is called a 754 election. In general, a 754 election allows adjustments to be made to an owner's share of the inside basis of the entity assets upon the occurrence of certain triggering events, usually the sale or exchange (not a gift) of an interest in the entity. The goal is to align the inside and outside basis of his or her ownership interest so that they are equal. If no 754 election has been made, then no adjustments can be made to the inside basis of the entity's property unless mandatory adjustments are required. The 754 election can really help the remaining owners and, in some situations, the new owners. However, caution is advised in use of the 754 election. It is complicated and, if not executed correctly, can backfire. Work with a tax advisor on this strategy.

If the redemption is for a note of the entity, there is also a tax consequence with the redemption. In this case, the redeemed owner technically continues to be an owner of the entity for tax purposes (but not for state law purposes) until the note is fully satisfied (paid in full). This is unlike the sale or redemption of stock in a corporation where the shareholder's interest ceases even if that owner is paid with a note.

Tax Consequences to the Redeemed Owner

Generally, an owner won't realize any gain on the distribution of cash upon redemption of his or her interest up to the outside basis. He or she will also not realize gain on the distribution of property other than cash, because any amount of cash exceeding the basis will be treated as a capital transaction and thus qualify for capital gains treatment.

Like everywhere else in the Internal Revenue Code, there are exceptions to the general rule. When an entity has substantially appreciated inventory or accounts receivable, the gain realized that is attributable to those types of assets—even if they aren't part of the redeeming distribution—will be treated as ordinary income to the recipient. Additionally, payments made for goodwill (the additional value over and above the value of its assets) will be treated as ordinary income unless the amount allocated to goodwill is expressly stated in the redemption agreement. Even then, the goodwill exception does not apply to most service entities.

Where the entity distributes property other than cash to an owner in a redemption, the redeemed owner generally takes a basis in the distributed property equal to his or her outside basis. The redeemed owner gets to tack on the time during which the entity held that property, just as the redeemed owner always held it in order to determine the nature of the capital gain as either a long-term capital gain (property generally held for at least one year and taxed as capital gains) or a short-term capital gain (which is taxed as ordinary income) when the redeemed partner sells that property. Another income tax consequence to the redeemed owner is that the share of entity debt the owner is allowed to add to his or her outside basis becomes part of the amount realized in the redemption. It is then treated like a distribution of cash.

If the entity has unrealized receivables (accounts receivable awaiting collection from customers), substantially appreciated inventory, or depreciated real estate, then there will be some gain that will not only be ordinary income (as opposed to capital gain). However, the owner won't be able to use the installment method of reporting that income. This risk of ordinary income is far greater in services entities than in assets entities. Therefore, you should seek out good tax advice before taking a note instead of cash up front in a redemption.

For demonstration purposes, let's look at MythiCo as an LLC instead of a corporation. In this scenario, the same four owners (Al, Betty, Charlene, and Dave) plan to redeem Dave's 25 percent interest in the company for $500,000 in cash at a time when Dave's outside basis is $200,000 and MythiCo has $1,000,000 in long-term debt. For purposes of computing Dave's redemption amount, add the $500,000 in cash to his share of the entity's long-term debt, which is $250,000. The total is $750,000. Therefore, Dave's gain is $550,000, which is the total of his amount realized ($750,000) less his outside basis ($200,000)—even though Dave is only getting $500,000 in cash.

Let's change those facts slightly to explore this more deeply. Assume that instead of cash, Dave will receive a piece of real estate called Blackacre in the redemption of his 25 percent interest that has a fair market value of $500,000 but an inside basis of $100,000. MythiCo, still an LLC in this scenario, has $1,000,000 in long-term debt that has nothing to do with Blackacre. Dave's outside basis is $200,000. In that instance, Dave will realize a gain of only

$50,000, which is calculated as follows: his amount realized equals his share of the entity's long-term debt that he is being released from ($250,000, which is treated like a distribution of cash) less his outside basis ($200,000). Dave will take a basis in Blackacre equal to his outside basis ($200,000) reduced by the amount of cash deemed distributed ($250,000) for a basis of $0, even though the fair market value of Blackacre is equal to the value of Dave's 25 percent interest in MythiCo, which is $500,000.

Now let's complicate things a bit further. In this example, assume that at the time of Dave's redemption, MythiCo, LLC has the following attributes:

- accounts receivable: $1,000,000
- substantially appreciated inventory: $500,000
- cash: $500,000
- hard assets (building, office furniture, equipment): $1,000,000
- excess depreciation on building: $500,000
- long-term debt on building: $1,000,000

Dave's redemption price is still $500,000 and his outside basis is $200,000. Assume further that Dave will be redeemed with $125,000 cash and a five-year note for the balance of $375,000. In this example, Dave will have a realized gain that will be a much higher amount in the first year than in years two through five. When all is said and done, and the note is fully paid, Dave will recognize a total gain of $550,000 ($125,000 in cash, plus a $375,000 note, plus $250,000 as his share of the building debt, less his outside basis of $200,000). Of this $550,000 there will be $500,000— which represents his share of accounts receivable ($250,000), plus his share of appreciated inventory ($125,000), plus his share of excess depreciation ($125,000)—that will be ordinary income, and the remaining $50,000 of the gain will be seen as a capital gain.

In the first year, Dave will have to recognize ordinary income of $500,000, even though he is only getting $125,000 in cash up front. This amount probably won't even cover the income tax on the $500,000. The good news is that he'll only have to recognize $50,000 in capital gain over the next five years when receiving the $375,000. I could provide even more complex examples, but what's the bottom line here? The tax consequences of a redemption of an interest in an entity that is taxed as a partnership are complicated and require expert tax advice.

Tax Consequences to the Remaining Owners

In a partnership, the tax consequences to the remaining owners in a redemption are much more complicated than with a C or an S corporation. Generally, the remaining owners will realize no gain or loss on the redemption of an owner. However, like all good tax laws, there are exceptions. The one to watch out for is where the entity distributes a piece of property that has debt on it, and the debt leaves the entity because the redeemed owner assumes it and relieves the entity and its other owners from responsibility for this debt. In this instance, each remaining owner's share of the disappearing debt will be treated as a distribution of cash to that owner, which could be taxable if that owner does not have enough outside basis to cover it.

Let's again look at MythiCo and its four equal owners (Al, Betty, Charlene, and Dave). Dave's interest is being redeemed for $500,000, which will be payable by distributing Blackacre, which has a fair market value of $1,500,000 but has a $1,000,000 mortgage on it. Dave is getting a net $500,000 in Blackacre in exchange for his ownership interest, which is also worth $500,000. Dave's outside basis is $200,000. Dave will be taking Blackacre subject to the mortgage and will be solely responsible for the mortgage payments.

Al, Betty, and Charlene each have an outside basis in their respective ownership interests that is equal to $200,000. In this example, unless something further is done, Al, Betty, and Charlene will each have to recognize income of $50,000 on Dave's redemption because the amount to be distributed, which is $250,000 (their respective 25 percent of the debt on Blackacre), exceeds their respective outside basis of $200,000. This can be a big surprise to the remaining owners, who could be adversely impacted by what someone else is doing.

Another possible tax consequence to the remaining owners after a redemption is that they might be able to add some additional inside basis to entity property by making a 754 election or by already having one. This is usually a good strategy for the remaining owners, as long as the value of the remaining entity property has increased. However, a 754 election is a double-edged sword and can also be bad for the remaining owners, especially where the value of the entity property has gone down. For this reason, caution is advised in this scenario. Suffice to say, a 754 election can get very complicated very fast. It is something that you'll want to discuss with your tax advisor before a redemption or sale of an entity interest takes place.

Partnership or LLC Taxed as a Partnership with Life Insurance Used

The following sections discuss the tax consequences for a partnership or LLC that is taxed as a partnership in cases where life insurance is used to fund the redemption.

Tax Consequences to the Entity

The tax consequences to the entity in a redemption that is funded with life insurance are the same as if the redemption were funded in another way. It should be tax-free to the entity and not cause a technical termination of the entity for income tax purposes. If the life insurance death proceeds are insufficient to fully satisfy the redemption price, then the redeemed owner will technically remain an owner until the note used to cover the balance of the redemption price is fully satisfied. The entity will not be able to deduct the payment of life insurance premiums, which will actually increase the allocable share of entity income for each owner. However, the entity will receive the life insurance death proceeds income tax–free. Those proceeds will, in turn, increase the outside basis of all of the owners.

Tax Consequences to the Redeemed Owner

The tax consequences of a redemption to the redeemed owner where life insurance is used to fund the redemption price are almost the same as the tax consequences where life insurance is not used, with one significant difference. When the entity receives the life insurance death proceeds in a redemption due to the death of an owner— unless other arrangements have been made in the entity's governing documents (for example, a partnership agreement or LLC operating agreement)—the life insurance proceeds will increase the outside basis of all owners, including the estate of the deceased insured owner, by the respective share of each owner in the entity.

Depending on the price at which the redemption will take place, this increased basis may create a virtually unusable capital loss because the estate gets a new outside basis at the owner's death, except as to the decedent's share of ordinary income items such as accounts receivable, substantially appreciated inventory, depreciation recapture, and (sometimes) goodwill. It is possible in the entity governing document to redirect this share of the increased outside basis, which probably won't be used by the estate, to the remaining owners who will have a real use for it. However, you must plan for this result in advance.

Tax Consequences to the Remaining Owners

The tax consequences to the remaining owners of a redemption of an interest in an entity when life insurance is used are almost the same as when life insurance is not used, with one big difference—and this time it's one that is positive for the remaining owners. When the entity receives the life insurance death proceeds, the outside basis of each owner will increase by that owner's share of the entity. Remember that outside basis is the barometer for measuring amounts that can be taken out of the entity tax-free. The higher the outside basis, the more cash that can be taken out of the entity.

CHAPTER 7

CROSS-PURCHASE
BUY-SELL AGREEMENTS

In a cross-purchase buy-sell agreement, the owners have a contract among themselves to agree to buy each other's interests in the entity upon the occurrence of specified triggering events. If you recall, back in chapter 3, we defined a redemption buy-sell agreement as one where the entity—not the other owners—was the purchaser under the redemption arrangement. It is exactly the opposite in the cross-purchase buy-sell agreement: the owners—not the entity—are the purchasers.

Nevertheless, I have always made the entity a party to the cross-purchase buy-sell agreements that I have drafted. I believe that the entity should always be a party to the buy-sell agreement because there are invariably desired provisions that you will want to apply to the entity. This cannot happen if the entity is not a party to the contract. Since entities should always be parties to redemption buy-sell agreements and hybrid buy-sell agreements, they also should always be parties to cross-purchase buy-sell agreements. This is an absolute necessity, for instance, in an S corporation because there are restrictions that you are going to want to put on the entity to preserve the S election.

Consider MythiCo and its four equal shareholders (Al, Betty, Charlene, and Dave). They enter into a cross-purchase buy-sell agreement whereby each agrees to purchase the stock of an owner upon the death of that owner. This time, Betty dies. Al, Charlene, and Dave each buy some of Betty's stock from her estate in whatever amounts they have agreed to among themselves. They buy an equal amount of Betty's stock if they don't or can't agree otherwise, which is fine as long as they buy all of Betty's stock from her estate pursuant to the cross-purchase buy-sell agreement. If they buy equal amounts of Betty's stock, then they would continue to be equal shareholders, just like they would be in a redemption buy-sell agreement. However, if for some reason, the three of them agreed that Dave should purchase more of Betty's stock than Al and Charlene because he has more money, then the cross-purchase buy-sell agreement can be designed to accomplish that goal, either before the triggering event happens or, with enough flexibility, after a triggering event occurs. A redemption buy-sell agreement (by itself) cannot have this type of flexibility.

Advantages of a Cross-Purchase Buy-Sell Agreement

The following sections describe the advantages of using a cross-purchase buy-sell agreement.

Disproportionate Ownership Purchase Obligations

A redemption buy-sell agreement always increases the percentage ownership of the remaining owners proportionately across the board and, in some instances, can cause shifts in control of the entity. It is possible, in a properly structured cross-purchase agreement, to create disproportionate purchase obligations on the occurrence of a triggering event. Let's look at an example. Al, Betty, Charlene, and Dave each own 25 percent of MythiCo's stock. Let's assume a triggering event under a cross-purchase buy-sell obligation requires

Dave alone to purchase Al's shares. The cross-purchase buy-sell agreement can be arranged in such a way that Dave alone is obligated to purchase Al's stock. Therefore, after the sale, Betty and Charlene would each still own 25 percent and Dave would now own 50 percent, meeting the goal of achieving a disproportionate purchase. Compare this to a redemption of Al's 25 percent, in which case each of the remaining shareholders would then own 33.33 percent of the stock because MythiCo would have purchased Al's shares, which wouldn't have met their announced goal of having Dave alone purchase Al's stock.

New Cost Basis

The purchase price provided by the cross-purchase buy-sell agreement increases each purchasing owner's basis in his or her interest in the entity—which can't happen in a redemption agreement since the entity, not the other owners, is the purchaser. This can reduce the capital gain of the purchasing owners on their ultimate sale of the interests since they would each have a new basis in the acquired interests.

Consider MythiCo and assume that an event triggers a buy-sell obligation under the agreement whereby Al, Betty, and Dave must buy Charlene's stock. In this instance, the three purchasers would take a new basis in the stock they bought from Charlene equal to what they paid for that stock.

Contrast that outcome to the result in a redemption buy-sell agreement where the entity purchases the stock. In that case, the ownership interests of Al, Betty, and Dave proportionately increase but their stock basis remains the same since they did not purchase anything—MythiCo did. That does not help the remaining owners with reducing their capital gains exposure on the ultimate sale of their MythiCo stock.

No Adverse Effect on Entity Due to Purchase of Life Insurance

The purchase of life insurance has no adverse effect on the working capital or credit position of the entity since the owners own and pay for the life insurance policies.

No Risk of Reclassification as a Dividend in a Corporation

The purchase transaction of stock in a corporation in a cross-purchase buy-sell agreement transaction cannot be reclassified as a dividend like it can in a redemption buy-sell agreement. Therefore, the selling shareholder should almost always have capital gains treatment.

No Increase in Entity Value by the Insurance

There is no incremental increase in the value of the entity by reason of the incremental increase in cash values or proceeds of an insurance policy on the seller's life owned by the purchaser in a cross-purchase buy-sell agreement, as there can be in a redemption buy-sell agreement.

No Risk of Entity Creditors on Life Insurance

The cash value buildups in life insurance policies and life insurance death proceeds are not subject to the claims of the entity's creditors because the owners own the insurance on the lives of the other owners in the cross-purchase buy-sell agreement.

State Law Limitations or Prohibitions against Redemptions Are Not Applicable

One persistent risk of a redemption buy-sell agreement is that there is always a chance that the entity will be precluded by state law limitations on minimum capital requirements from redeeming interests at the time of a triggering event. This risk is bypassed using a cross-purchase buy-sell agreement since the owners, not the entity, purchase the interests of a selling owner.

Family Attribution Rules Do Not Apply

The family attribution rules of Section 318 of the Internal Revenue Code that are applicable to corporations do not operate in cross-purchase buy-sell agreements. In chapter 6, I explained the family attribution rules that cause a shareholder of a corporation to also be treated as owning the stock of certain family members (i.e., spouse, parents, children, and grandchildren) when determining whether a redemption is a capital transaction or a dividend. Those rules do not come into play in cross-purchase buy-sell agreements because, since the owners sell the stock between themselves, there's no risk of having a purchase treated as a dividend due to the family attribution rules.

Disadvantages of Cross-Purchase Buy-Sell Agreements

The following sections describe the disadvantages of cross-purchase buy-sell agreements.

Multiple Insurance Policies Needed for Multiple Owners

The number of life insurance policies that are required in a cross-purchase buy-sell agreement is computed using an algebraic formula: Number of Policies Needed = $n*(n-1)$, where "n" is the number of owners. Written out, the number of policies needed equals the number of owners, multiplied by the number of owners minus one. In other words, the number of separate insurance policies proliferates algebraically with the increase in the number of owners. For example, where there are six owners, the number of policies needed is 30.

Number of Insurance Policies Required in a Cross-Purchase Agreement

Number of Owners	Number of Required Insurance Policies
2	2
3	6
4	12
5	20
6	30
7	42
8	56
9	72
10	90
11	110
12	132
13	156
14	182
15	210

Table 1 depicts how many insurance policies will be needed for up to fifteen owners in a regular cross-purchase buy-sell agreement that is neither a trusteed cross-purchase buy-sell agreement nor an entity-owned cross-purchase agreement. Both alternatives to the regular cross-purchase buy-sell agreement allow you to use the cross-purchase form when it is more beneficial and simultaneously avoid some of the downsides and disadvantages of cross-purchase buy-sell agreements.

Redemption May Give Better Options

If interests in the entity are highly appreciated and if the owners don't intend to sell their interests during their lifetime, a redemption at death may give better options. It could also give more basis increase as well as qualification for a Section 303 redemption if the entity is a corporation.

Owner Preference that an Entity Pay Life Insurance Premiums

For a variety of reasons, including personal cash flow, owners may prefer that the entity purchase and maintain the life insurance policies.

Inequities in Insurance Costs

A disparity in the ages of the entity owners or in the relative sizes of entity ownership may cause inequities in life insurance premiums where life insurance is being used to finance the cross-purchase obligation. These costs are borne by the individual owners in a cross-purchase buy-sell agreement, while the entity pays life insurance premiums in the redemption buy-sell agreement. Nevertheless, this obstacle is not totally insurmountable. There may be corresponding increases in entity distributions to younger owners in the form of salary or bonus, which can ameliorate or reduce that inequity. With this strategy, one must be mindful of the limit of reasonable compensation, especially in the case of an S corporation, where a shareholder can't be given a non-pro-rata share of corporation profits because that would violate the one class of stock limitation.

The same applies when life insurance is not being used to assist in the cross-purchase obligation, because it is being funded over time by savings of salary, bonus, and profits from the entity. Where one owner holds most of the interests, a redemption buy-sell agreement may mean that he or she is essentially funding his or her own buyout by the minority owners. Therefore, the majority owner may prefer a cross-purchase buy-sell agreement that will force the minority owner(s) to come up with most of the money to pay for the interests of the majority owner.

Potential Transfer for Value Problems

As discussed in chapter 6, any transfer of a life insurance policy for valuable consideration—including naming someone as beneficiary of a life insurance policy in exchange for something of value—triggers the exception to the tax-exempt nature of life insurance death proceeds (absent an "exception to the exception"). There are several exceptions to the transfer for value rule for transfers of life insurance policies, including transfers to any of the following persons and entities: the insured, a partner of the insured, a partnership in which the insured is a partner, and a corporation in which the insured is a shareholder or an officer. Note that there is no shareholder-to-shareholder exception to the exception, which can be problematic for corporation shareholders who desire to use life insurance to fund a cross-purchase buy-sell agreement.

Therefore, the following situation causes a problem with the transfer for value rule. It effectively requires corporate shareholders with a cross-purchase buy-sell agreement who want to finance the buy-sell obligation with life insurance to purchase new life insurance policies. This is preferable to transferring existing life insurance policies between themselves, where a life insurance policy is transferred to any owner other than the insured. Let's look at an example. Al owns insurance policies on his own life that he does not need for other uses. For purposes of a cross-purchase buy-sell agreement, Al proposes to transfer the excess life insurance policies on his life to Betty, Charlene, and Dave to be used in the cross-purchase buy-sell agreement for buying his interest at his death.

If Al does this and specifies that the policies have to be used in the purchase of his stock from his estate upon his death, then the policy proceeds will be subject to income taxation unless the four MythiCo shareholders are also partners in a partnership. Unless this is the case, they will be out of luck. There is no shareholder-to-shareholder exception to the exception that would cause the life insurance death proceeds to be income tax–free again. A transfer of a life insurance policy to anyone other than the insured should be reviewed by a competent tax advisor prior to the transfer.

Life Insurance Policy Cash Values and Death Proceeds Could Be Subject to Owner's Creditors

As discussed in chapter 6, owning life insurance inside of an entity potentially exposes the cash values (if any) of the life insurance policies and the life insurance death proceeds to creditors of the entity in a redemption buy-sell agreement. This is one disadvantage of the redemption buy-sell agreement. In a cross-purchase buy-sell agreement—where the owners themselves own the life insurance— potentially exposes the cash values and the life insurance death proceeds to the creditors of the individual owners, which might be far worse than exposure to the entity's creditors.

The specter of an owner's divorce could cloud the ownership of a life insurance policy on the life of a fellow owner, or at least put its ownership in play in the divorce proceeding. Entities don't get divorced—people do. The entity also may have far greater resources than the individual owners do, which is another consideration for deciding which type of buy-sell agreement is right for you.

No Guarantees on Keeping the Life Insurance Policy Unencumbered and in Force

There is no guarantee that the owner of a life insurance policy on the life of another owner will keep the life insurance in force. They might not continue to pay the necessary premiums to keep the policy active until the life insurance death proceeds are issued when the insured owner dies—or without pledging the life insurance policy as collateral for a personal loan.

It is advisable in a cross-purchase buy-sell agreement to have the owners agree to continue to maintain the insurance in force by paying the premiums and to give notice of payment of every premium to the insured owner. It is also important to secure a commitment from the owner to refrain from pledging the policy to secure a personal loan, which the owner of a life insurance policy has the legal right to do. Moreover, each owner with an insurance policy should commit to using the policy's death proceeds to purchase the interests of a deceased owner, instead of making it in any way optional.

As I mentioned earlier, one way to prevent untoward behavior with regard to the life insurance is to use a trusteed cross-purchase buy-sell agreement, where a trustee holds the policies, pays the premiums, receives the life insurance policy death proceeds, and conducts the purchase of the deceased owner's interests. This approach can come in handy throughout the process. Another alternative to a trusteed cross-purchase buy-sell agreement is to form an entity such as a partnership or LLC to hold the insurance used in the buy-sell agreement purchases.

Owner Lacks the Ability to Buy at the Wrong Time

For a whole host of reasons, which may be unrelated to the entity (for example, personal financial trouble), the owner who has to buy under a cross-purchase buy-sell agreement may not be in a financial position to do so when the triggering event occurs. The owner may have other large financial obligations at the time of a triggering event or a requirement in a personal loan agreement that prevents him or her from using cash to make the purchase. The financial position of owners can be critical in cross-purchase buy-sell agreements. Unfortunately, this can be difficult to gauge since you don't know when the triggering event will occur.

Entity Does Not Have Access to the Life Insurance Policies

Where the owners hold the life insurance that will be used to fund a cross-purchase buy-sell agreement, the policies aren't available to the entity for either loans or as collateral, which is not the case in a redemption buy-sell agreement because the entity owns the life insurance policies. Of course, you may not want the policies to be encumbered by anyone.

A cross-purchase agreement can be an optional purchase or a mandatory purchase and is unfunded, which may prejudice those owners who are not financially able to participate at the same level as the others. At the same time, this can favor those owners who are financially able.

Loss of Estate Tax Deferral

A buyout at death under a cross-purchase agreement generally would cause the loss of continued estate tax deferral under Section 6166 of the Internal Revenue Code.

Nondeductible Life Insurance Policy Premiums Are Paid with After-Tax Dollars

While life insurance premiums are not deductible by anyone, including an entity, an owner of a life insurance policy will have to pay the life insurance premiums with after-tax dollars, which makes them somewhat more expensive. Still, even though life insurance premiums are not deductible by anyone, it is one of the disadvantages of entering into a cross-purchase buy-sell agreement.

Higher Possible Personal Income Tax Bracket than C Corporation Tax Bracket

Since life insurance premiums are not tax deductible, it often makes sense to have the person who has the lowest income tax bracket pay for them. Quite often, a C corporation's marginal income tax bracket is lower than the owners' personal income tax brackets, making individual ownership of life insurance policies to fund a cross-purchase buy-sell agreement more expensive than purchasing those life insurance policies inside of a C corporation.

Tax Consequences

The tax consequences of cross-purchase buy-sell agreements are much simpler than those of redemption buy-sell agreements. In this section, I will analyze the tax consequences of a cross-purchase buy-sell agreement on the buyers of the ownership interests, the entity, and the owners who did not purchase ownership interests when other owners did. Since the tax consequences can differ between the different types of entities (S corporations, C corporations, and partnerships), I'll also discuss the nuances for each entity form, both with and without use of life insurance to finance the purchases under the cross-purchase buy-sell agreement.

Cross-Purchase Buy-Sell Agreement in a C Corporation without Life Insurance

Let's begin with a consideration of the tax consequences of a cross-purchase buy-sell agreement in a C corporation where life insurance is not used.

Tax Consequences to Each Purchaser

In the cross-purchase buy-sell agreement, each purchasing owner takes a new basis in the purchased stock of a C corporation equal to what the owners paid for that stock. However, a cross-purchase will have no effect on the basis of the shares that the owners already own.

Tax Consequences to the Entity

In a C corporation cross-purchase buy-sell agreement, the entity will have no tax consequences.

Tax Consequences to the Selling Owner

In a C corporation cross-purchase buy-sell agreement, the selling owner will realize capital gains to the extent that the selling price received is greater than the owner's basis in his or her shares.

Tax Consequences to Each Purchasing Owner

Each purchasing owner will have a new basis in the acquired shares that is equal to what he or she paid for those shares.

Tax Consequences to Non-Purchasing Owners

In a C corporation cross-purchase buy-sell agreement, the owners who are not the purchasing or selling owners, will have no income tax consequences.

Cross-Purchase Buy-Sell Agreement in a C Corporation with Life Insurance

The following sections describe the tax consequences of a cross-purchase buy-sell agreement in a C corporation with life insurance.

Tax Consequences to Each Purchasing Owner

In the cross-purchase buy-sell agreement with life insurance, each purchasing owner takes a new basis in the purchased stock of a C corporation equal to what the owners paid for that stock. However, a cross-purchase will have no effect on basis of the shares that the shareholders already own. The purchasing owners cannot deduct the principal payments made to purchase the stock. However, if the purchasers buy the stock in exchange for a note, they may be able to deduct the interest. Because the interest deductibility rules are complex, you should consult your tax advisor for this scenario.

As I pointed out previously, although the shareholders don't get to deduct the life insurance premiums on the life insurance policies that will be used to fund the buy-sell agreement, the life insurance death proceeds are tax-free unless there is a transfer for value problem (and without an exception to that exception).

For example, consider MythiCo and its four equal shareholders (Al, Betty, Charlene, and Dave). They entered into a cross-purchase buy-sell agreement that requires the deceased shareholder to sell and the surviving shareholders to buy all of the deceased shareholder's stock for the price and according to the terms set forth in the buy-sell agreement. Charlene dies, triggering the buy-sell agreement at a time when her stock is worth $150,000. In this instance, Al, Betty, and Dave would each purchase $50,000 worth of Charlene's stock from her estate, using the life insurance on Charlene's life to help pay for the purchase. Each would have a basis in the purchased shares equal to what each paid for the stock, which was $50,000.

Tax Consequences to the Entity

In a C corporation cross-purchase buy-sell agreement using life insurance, the entity will have no tax consequences.

Tax Consequences to the Selling Owner

In a C corporation cross-purchase buy-sell agreement using life insurance, the selling owner will realize capital gains to the extent that the selling price received for the stock is greater than the owner's basis in his or her shares.

Tax Consequences for Non-Purchasing Owners

In a C corporation cross-purchase buy-sell agreement, the owners who are not the purchasing or selling owners will have no tax consequence.

Cross-Purchase Buy-Sell Agreement Involving an S Corporation without Life Insurance

The tax consequences for a cross-purchase buy-sell agreement involving an S corporation without life insurance are described in the following sections.

Tax Consequences to Each Purchaser

In the cross-purchase buy-sell agreement without life insurance, each purchasing owner takes a new basis in the purchased stock of an S corporation that is equal to what the owners paid for that stock. However, as I have said before, a cross-purchase will have no effect on basis of the shares that the owners already own.

Tax Consequences to the Entity

In an S corporation cross-purchase buy-sell agreement without life insurance, the entity will have no tax consequences.

Tax Consequences to the Selling Owner

In an S corporation cross-purchase buy-sell agreement without life insurance, the selling owner will realize capital gain to the extent that the selling price received is greater than the owner's basis in his or her shares. Unlike the redemption buy-sell agreement, you don't have to worry at all about possible dividend treatment because the entity didn't purchase the shares—the other owners did.

Tax Consequences to the Non-Purchasing Owners

In an S corporation cross-purchase buy-sell agreement not using life insurance, the owners who are not the purchasing or selling owners will have no tax consequences.

Cross-Purchase Buy-Sell Agreement in an S Corporation with Life Insurance

The following sections describe the tax consequences of a cross-purchase buy-sell agreement in an S corporation with life insurance.

Tax Consequences to Each Purchasing Owner

In the cross-purchase buy-sell agreement in an S corporation with life insurance, each purchasing owner takes a new basis in the purchased stock of an S corporation that is equal to what the owners paid for that stock. However, a cross-purchase buy-sell agreement will have no effect on the basis of the shares that the owners already own. The purchasing owners can't deduct the principal payments made to purchase the stock, although if the purchasers buy the stock in exchange for a note, they may be able to deduct the interest. You should consult your tax advisor as the interest deductibility rules can be complicated. Additionally, as I previously pointed out, although the shareholders won't get to deduct the life insurance premiums on the life insurance policies that will be used to fund the cross-purchase buy-sell agreement, the life insurance death proceeds will be tax-free unless there is a transfer for value problem (without an exception to that exception).

For example, MythiCo and its four equal shareholders (Al, Betty, Charlene, and Dave) enter into a cross-purchase buy-sell agreement that requires the deceased shareholder to sell and the surviving shareholders to buy all of the deceased shareholder's stock for the price and according to the terms set forth in the buy-sell agreement. Al, Betty, and Dave purchased life insurance on Charlene's life for use in the purchase of her stock upon her death. Charlene dies, triggering the buy-sell agreement at a time when Charlene's stock is worth $150,000. In this instance, Al, Betty, and Dave would each purchase $50,000 worth of Charlene's stock from her estate, using the life insurance on Charlene's life to help pay for the purchase. Each would have a basis in the purchased shares equal to what each paid for the stock, $50,000.

Tax Consequences to the Entity

In an S corporation cross-purchase buy-sell agreement using life insurance, the entity will have no tax consequences. Contrast this with the morass of possible income tax consequences to a C corporation in a redemption buy-sell agreement (a topic I discussed in chapter 6).

Tax Consequences to the Selling Owner

In an S corporation cross-purchase buy-sell agreement using life insurance, the selling owner will realize capital gains to the extent that the selling price received for the stock is greater than the owner's basis in his or her shares. Because a selling owner gets a new basis at death equal to the fair market value at that time, there should be little or possibly no capital gains if the purchase occurs shortly after the shareholder's demise.

Tax Consequences to the Non-Purchasing Owners

In an S corporation cross-purchase buy-sell agreement using life insurance, the owners who are not the purchasing or selling owners will have no tax consequences.

Partnership or LLC Taxed as a Partnership Where Life Insurance Is Not Used

Income tax consequences in a partnership setting for a cross-purchase buy-sell agreement are far more complicated than those of either a C or an S corporation cross-purchase buy-sell agreement scenario.

Tax Consequences to the Entity

The tax consequences to the entity in a cross-purchase of an owner's interest used to be the fear that a sale of 50 percent or more of the partnership interests would cause the partnership to terminate for tax purposes, but this is no longer the law.

Tax Consequences to the Selling Owner

Generally, an owner will realize capital gains in a sale of his or her entity interest to other owners to the extent that the purchase price—which includes the amount of entity debt of which the selling owner is being relieved—exceeds the owner's outside basis. However, like everywhere else in the Internal Revenue Code, there are exceptions to the general capital gains rule that can require part of the receipt of sales proceeds to be ordinary income.

Where an entity has inventory of any kind—that is depreciation that is subject to recapture or "accounts receivable"—the gain realized that is attributable to those types of assets (even if they aren't part of the redeeming distribution) will be ordinary income to the recipient. It's as if they were fictitiously distributed to the owner and sold back to the entity for fair market value. This ordinary income must be reported in the year of the sale, even if the interests were sold in exchange for a note that was being paid over a term of years. This risk of ordinary income generally is far greater for services entities than assets entities. Therefore, you should be careful and get good tax advice before taking a note instead of cash up front in any cross-purchase buy-sell agreement context.

The sale of all of an owner's interest in the entity will terminate the entity's taxable year, as for the selling owner. The selling owner will have to recognize his or her allocable share of the entity's income in the last year of his or her ownership. There are two ways that this income can be accounted for:

- The entity could elect to close its books as of the date of the sale and allocate the income between the then owners, which would cap the income of the selling owner.
- The entity could keep the books open all the way through the end of the taxable year and allocate income to the selling owner based on the number of days that the selling owner

owned interests. The buy-sell agreement should address this point.

Let's use some examples to demonstrate how these rules work. Suppose that MythiCo is an LLC instead of a corporation, but with the same four owners (Al, Betty, Charlene, and Dave). Al, Betty, and Charlene are going to purchase the 25 percent interest of Dave for $500,000 in cash at a time when Dave's outside basis is $200,000 and MythiCo has $1,000,000 in long-term debt. For purposes of computing Dave's amount realized in the redemption, add the $500,000 in cash to his share of entity long-term debt ($250,000) for a total of $750,000. Therefore, Dave's gain is $550,000—his amount realized ($750,000) less his outside basis ($200,000)—even though he's only getting $500,000 in cash.

Now let's complicate things a bit further. In this example, let's assume that at the time of the purchase of Dave's interest, MythiCo has the following attributes:

- accounts receivable: $1,000,000
- inventory: $500,000
- cash: $500,000
- hard assets (building, office furniture, equipment): $1,000,000
- excess depreciation on building: $500,000
- long-term debt on building: $1,000,000

Assume that Dave's interest is worth $500,000 (the purchase price for his interest) and that his outside basis is $200,000. Assume further that Dave will be paid $125,000 up front and will receive a five-year note for the remaining balance, $375,000. In this example, Dave will have a realized gain much higher in the first year than in years two through five. When all is said and done, and the note is fully paid off, Dave will recognize a total net gain of $550,000

($125,000 in cash plus $375,000 in a note plus $250,000 as his share of the building debt less his outside basis of $200,000), of which $500,000—his share of accounts receivable ($250,000) plus his share of appreciated inventory ($125,000), plus his share of excess depreciation ($125,000)—is ordinary income, and $50,000 (the remainder of the gain) is capital gain.

In the first year, Dave will have to recognize ordinary income of $500,000 even though he is only getting $125,000 in cash up front, which probably won't even cover the income tax on the $500,000. The good news is that he'll only have to recognize $50,000 in capital gain over the next five years in receiving the $375,000. As you can see, the tax consequences of a sale of an interest in an entity that is taxed as a partnership can be very complicated and require expert tax advice.

Tax Consequences for Each Purchasing Owner

Each purchasing owner will combine his or her existing outside basis with an amount equal to what each pays for the purchased interest, plus a share of the entity liabilities that the owner assumes by virtue of increasing his or her interest and minus a share of any entity debt that is being taken by the selling owner. Note that this is quite different from the result in either a C or an S corporation, where an owner's basis in shares acquired by purchase will be maintained separately from the shares that the owner already owned—in other words, a shareholder's basis in corporate stock is maintained on a share-by-share basis. This is not so in an entity that is taxed as a partnership.

Tax Consequences for the Non-Purchasing Owners

Just like we witnessed earlier, the tax consequences to the non-purchasing owners in a sale of an interest in the entity are more complicated than those with either a C or an S corporation. Generally, the non-purchasing owners will not realize any gain or loss on the sale of an interest. However, like all good tax laws, there are exceptions. The one to watch out for is where the debt of the entity is assumed by the departing owner. In that instance, each remaining owner's share of the disappearing debt will be treated as a distribution of cash to that owner, which could be taxable if the owner does not have enough outside basis to cover it.

For example, Dave's interest in MythiCo is being purchased for $800,000 in cash, plus his assumption of a MythiCo debt of $300,000, which Dave is taking in exchange for his ownership interest, which is also worth $500,000. Dave's outside basis is $200,000. Al, Betty, and Charlene each have an outside basis in their respective ownership interests equal to $200,000.

Al, Betty, and Charlene will suffer a reduction in their outside basis of $100,000 apiece because this is the amount that they are deemed to be distributed. This number is based on their respective 33.33 percent of the debt that Dave assumed less their respective outside basis of $200,000. However, had the debt that Dave assumed been $750,000, Al, Betty, and Charlene would have then had to realize a gain of $50,000 because their respective shares of the debt ($250,000) would have exceeded their respective outside basis of $200,000. This can be a big surprise to the remaining owners, who could be adversely impacted by what someone else is doing.

Another possible tax consequence to the non-purchasing owners after a sale of an interest is that they might be able to add some additional inside basis to entity property by making a 754 election or by the entity already having one. This is often a good thing for the purchasing owners, usually where the value of the remaining entity property has increased. However, a 754 election is a double-edged sword and can also be a bad thing to the remaining owners, especially where the value of the entity property has decreased, so caution is advised. I do not want to delve any deeper into the effects of a 754 election in this book because it can get very complicated very fast. As I noted earlier, the problem with the 754 election is that, once made, it is irrevocable, and the IRS then requires a good reason to revoke it. Suffice to say that a 754 election is something that you will want to discuss with your tax advisor before a redemption or sale of an entity interest takes place.

Partnership or LLC Taxed as a Partnership Where Life Insurance Is Used

The following sections discuss the tax consequences to a partnership or LLC when life insurance is used to fund the cross-purchase buy-sell agreement.

Tax Consequences to the Entity

The tax consequences to the entity in a purchase of an interest by the owners that is funded with life insurance are the same as if the cross-purchase were funded another way. Since the owners hold the insurance, there should be no tax or financial consequences to the entity.

Tax Consequences to the Selling Owner

The tax consequences of a sale of an interest by the owner where life insurance is used to fund the purchase price are almost exactly the same as when life insurance is not used to fund the purchase price. The selling owner will realize gains to the extent that the purchase price, plus the owner's share of partnership liabilities of which the owner is being relieved, less any liabilities that the selling owner is assuming, exceeds his or her outside basis. To the extent that the entity has inventory, accounts receivable, or excess depreciation, that portion of the gain will be ordinary income that is taxable in the year of the sale—as installment sale reporting is not permitted for those items.

Tax Consequences to Each Purchasing Owner

The tax consequences to each purchasing owner under a cross-purchase buy-sell agreement where life insurance is used to fund the purchase transaction are as follows: Each purchasing owner will combine his or her existing outside basis with an amount equal to what each pays for the purchased interest, plus a share of the entity liabilities that the owner assumes by virtue of increasing his or her interest, and less a share of any entity debt being taken by the selling owner. Note that this is quite different from the result in either a C or an S corporation, where an owner's basis in shares acquired by purchase will be maintained separately from the shares that the owner already owned (as shareholder's basis in corporate stock is maintained on a share-by-share basis). This is not so in an entity that is taxed as a partnership. The owners will not be able to deduct the life insurance policy premiums but will receive the life insurance death proceeds tax-free.

Tax Consequences to the Non-Purchasing Owners

There are no tax consequences to the non-purchasing owners of a cross-purchase of an interest in an entity where life insurance is used to fund the purchase price—except to the possible extent that the selling owner assumes an entity debt, in which case the shares of the relieved debt will be treated as a distribution of cash to the purchasing owners. This could result in taxation if the amount of debt relieved exceeds their outside basis.

As I discussed earlier in this chapter, one of the inherent problems with cross-purchase buy-sell agreements is that there is a chance that a co-owner either won't pay the life insurance premiums or won't abide by the agreement to purchase the insured owner's interest. The trusteed cross-purchase buy-sell agreement can solve this problem, but, as you will soon see, this alternative is not problem-free. In a trusteed cross-purchase buy-sell agreement, the owners use a third party (usually referred to as the trustee or escrow agent) to carry out their obligations under the agreement.

The trustee often holds the stock certificates or other evidence of business ownership and would acquire and own one life insurance policy on each owner. Thus, unlike the regular cross-purchase buy-sell agreement, the number of policies is limited to the number of owners when a trustee is used. This overcomes the problem of a multiplication of policies when more than two or three owners are involved in a cross-purchase buy-sell agreement.

This technique also can help involved parties avoid a transfer for value when policies are originally transferred between co-owners— for example, when Al transfers life insurance policies on his life to Betty, Charlene, and Dave to fund the purchase of his stock at death. When Al dies, the trustee collects the life insurance death proceeds of his policy, transfers his shares to Betty, Charlene, and Dave in the agreed proportions, and then pays the life insurance death proceeds to Al's estate.

A potential problem arises when shareholders of a corporation are involved. When a shareholder dies, the surviving shareholders will succeed to the beneficial ownership of the remaining policies by the trustee. While there is no firm guidance on this point, this transfer of rights in policies on Betty, Charlene, and Dave from Al's estate to being held for them in trust may be a transfer for value that would cause the life insurance death proceeds to be taxable (unless an exception to that exception applies). This problem does not arise for transferee partners or members of an LLC, who enjoy an express exception to the transfer for value rule. However, there is no shareholder-to-shareholder exception to the transfer for value rule.

There are also a number of other unanswered questions pertaining to the tax consequences of a trusteed cross-purchase buy-sell agreement. In the next section, I'll discuss an alternative to the regular cross-purchase buy-sell agreement that should solve these problems.

Entity-Owned Cross-Purchase Life Insurance Buy-Sell Agreements

An alternative to both the regular cross-purchase buy-sell agreement and the trusteed cross-purchase buy-sell agreement is the entity-owned cross-purchase buy-sell agreement. This technique involves forming a separate entity, usually an LLC, to own and hold the life insurance policies that will be used in the cross-purchase transactions. A partnership can play the same role, but it should not be a corporation.

Like the trusteed cross-purchase buy-sell agreement, this arrangement permits the purchase of just one life insurance policy per owner. This solves the multiple life insurance policies problem of the regular cross-purchase buy-sell agreement, so it can work when there are more than just a few owners.

This arrangement also solves the "lack of trust" problem that can plague a regular cross-purchase buy-sell agreement. Why? Because an entity—ideally run by someone who is not an owner in the main business entity—handles the payment of life insurance premiums, receipt of life insurance death proceeds, and sale from the deceased owner's estate to the purchasers. In this arrangement, each owner would be obligated to contribute to the capital of the insurance entity sufficient funds to pay the life insurance premiums. Unlike the trusteed cross-purchase buy-sell agreement, the entity-owned buy-sell agreement avoids the transfer for value problem because there is an express exception to the transfer for value exception in Section 101 of the Internal Revenue Code.

This arrangement also solves the life insurance policy transfer problem in a regular cross-purchase buy-sell agreement, when an owner dies owning life insurance policies on the lives of his or her co-owners. Those policies will pass down to the heirs of the deceased owner— and they may not want to part with the life insurance policies. The entity-owned cross-purchase buy-sell agreement solves this problem because the owners of the main business never own those policies directly—the entity does. The buy-sell agreement could include a simple procedure to handle the deceased owner's interest in the insurance entity by providing that it passed to the surviving co-owners when the sale of the deceased owner's interest in the main entity is sold for the life insurance death proceeds.

This arrangement is not without its potential problems. First, it requires a sophisticated, knowledgeable tax counsel. This is because there are some provisions that need to be in the insurance entity's governing documents to honor the intent of the insurance entity and prevent untoward estate tax problems with the insured owner having too much control over the life insurance on his or her life. At a minimum, the governing documents should require the owners to contribute an amount annually to cover the cost of the life insurance premiums. It should also require an amount to cover any shortfall where the life insurance is insufficient in the amount to pay the full sales price, which each purchasing owner should be required to guarantee. Moreover, the insurance entity governing documents should prevent the insured owner from having any say over any policy that insures his or her life.

There is even a benefit where the life insurance death proceeds are never needed to fund the cross-purchase buy-sell agreement. For example, if the main entity itself was sold, the insurance entity documents, together with the buy-sell agreement, could allow for the distribution of the policies to each insured owner for use in his or her own individual wealth management and estate plan. Without this unified ownership of the policies within an insurance entity, the main entity owners might have no obligation to transfer the owned life insurance policies to one another unless the buy-sell agreement itself required it—which it should. Unfortunately, many people don't think this far in advance.

The transfer of policies from the individual insured owners to the insurance entity (for example, life insurance policies that were issued prior to the formation of the insurance entity), the subsequent distribution of unused life insurance policies to the insured owners on termination of the insurance entity, and the cross-purchase buy-sell agreement are all express exceptions to the transfer for value rules set forth under Section 101 of the Internal Revenue Code. This is because transfers to a partnership (or an LLC that is being taxed like a partnership) and terminating transfers to an insured partner are both express exceptions to the transfer for value exception. However, the cross-purchase buy-sell agreement and the insurance entity's governing documents must expressly provide for those results.

CHAPTER 8

HYBRID BUY-SELL AGREEMENTS

I have now discussed both redemption buy-sell agreements and cross-purchase buy-sell agreements in separate chapters. In this chapter, I'd like to discuss a combination of the two. It's called a hybrid buy-sell agreement, and it offers an almost limitless array of possibilities for business stakeholders in need of a more custom solution. I will discuss one possible hybrid buy-sell agreement in particular that has gained popularity. It's called the wait-and-see buy-sell agreement.

Why combine aspects of a cross-purchase buy-sell agreement and a redemption buy-sell agreement? It's all about having the flexibility to react to ever-changing circumstances and laws. It allows owners to tailor a buy-sell agreement to particular situations and needs and to accomplish something that neither a redemption buy-sell agreement nor a cross-purchase buy-sell agreement could accomplish on its own.

Uses of Hybrid Buy-Sell Agreements

A hybrid buy-sell agreement generally employs parts of redemption buy-sell agreements and parts of cross-purchase agreements to satisfy specific objectives or to avoid potential problems. For example, a hybrid buy-sell agreement may be used when stakeholder-owned life insurance is used to fund a purchase obligation for certain triggering events like death, while the business entity is the primary buyer for other triggering events like termination of employment.

You can also use a hybrid buy-sell agreement in situations where the rights of the respective owners and the entity differ due to different types of triggering events. For example, a hybrid buy-sell agreement may give options to an owner who is retiring as an employee in good standing or to an owner who has become disabled. This is not an obligation. However, it allows this owner to sell his or her interests to the entity, the other owners, or both. Likewise, a hybrid buy-sell agreement can be designed to allow the entity, the other owners, or both to call in the interests of an owner who was fired for cause or who has been determined to have been stealing from the entity and the other owners. Such a call option would give the entity and the owners the right, but not the obligation, to call in the interests of the wayward owner and force him or her to sell all interests to the entity, the other owners, or both. The hybrid buy-sell agreement uses pieces of both redemption and cross-purchase buy-sell agreements to accomplish things that one alone could not accomplish. Additionally, a hybrid buy-sell agreement makes it possible to simultaneously have both a redemption (of some of the interests) and a cross-purchase (of the remainder of the interests). This has some unique advantages.

Hybrid buy-sell agreements offer purchasing owners the luxury of determining who should purchase the ownership interests and when. They can make this determination based on current facts, circumstances, and tax laws—which change frequently. For example, if the owners have the first option to purchase, but at the time of the triggering event they don't have the financial resources to exercise this option, it may make more sense for the entity to purchase the ownership interest, particularly if the entity owns the life insurance on the deceased owner. However, it is possible for the entity to lend the life insurance death proceeds to the surviving owners if it makes more sense for them to purchase the interest instead of the entity—for example, if the owners want more basis in their interests (outside basis).

A hybrid buy-sell agreement for a C corporation could also provide that the corporation must redeem any shares that would qualify for capital gains tax treatment under Section 303 of the Internal Revenue Code. This could be accomplished if the agreement required the surviving shareholders to purchase the deceased shareholder's remaining shares under the cross-purchase portion of the hybrid buy-sell agreement. Conversely, if at the time of a shareholder's death, the corporation lacks the minimum capital required to redeem the shares, the surviving shareholders could purchase the deceased shareholder's shares. Alternatively, the remaining owners could purchase some of the interests, and the entity could purchase the rest. This is the type of flexibility provided by a hybrid buy-sell agreement.

Unlike a regular redemption or a cross-purchase buy-sell agreement, a hybrid agreement gives options to all of the stakeholders in the transaction—the selling owner, the other owners, and the entity. The non-selling owners can have the first option to purchase the interest, with the second option going to the entity, or the entity can have the first option to purchase the interest, with the second option going to the other owners. Thus, the hybrid buy-sell agreement's flexibility can come in handy in a wide variety of scenarios. Once a triggering event occurs, the remaining owners can carefully examine the business's capital needs and the existing tax laws to determine the most appropriate choice for themselves and the entity.

Give careful thought to the order of options and to whether a hybrid buy-sell agreement provides the types of options and mandates that are required for the purchase and sale of interests. It is not unusual for hybrid buy-sell agreements to give the remaining owners the first option to purchase the business, generally proportionately.

Life Insurance Policies

One of the key issues in a hybrid buy-sell agreement is who should own the life insurance policies. Should it be the entity? Should it be the owners? Or is a combination of the two the best solution? There is no right or wrong answer, except to say that the person who will be obligated to buy must own and be the beneficiary of the life insurance policies. If, for example, the entity owns the life insurance policies and a decision is made to have the owners buy the interests under the hybrid buy-sell agreement, how does the entity get the necessary cash to the owners to make the purchase possible? There are two basic ways to accomplish this. First, the entity could loan the owners the money to buy the interests with the life insurance death proceeds. The problem with this option is that the entity will have to charge the owners interest at a rate that the IRS issues monthly. That, or they will have to wade through a morass of tax laws and regulations that essentially mimic the charging of interest anyway (with deemed interest income to the entity and a possible interest deduction to the borrowing owners). Conventional wisdom is that it is easier to just charge the minimum required rate of interest and be done with it.

The second way is for the entity to simply distribute the insurance proceeds to the owners so that they can make the purchase. The problem with this approach—and why it usually gives a less satisfactory result than the interest option—is that the owners will probably have to pay income tax on the distribution. This would essentially convert otherwise tax-free life insurance death proceeds into taxable income. This is not a good option. Moreover, depending on the type of entity and the size of the distribution, the entity may or may not be able to deduct that distribution to its owners. Why? Because it's probably a non-pro-rata distribution since the life insurance death proceeds would not be distributed to the deceased owner's estate until the owner purchases the interests from the deceased owner's estate.

If the business owners own the life insurance policies and it is determined at the time of the triggering event that the entity should redeem the interests, the owners can receive the proceeds in two possible ways. First, the owners could loan the money to the entity, which would have to pay interest to the owners at the same minimum required interest rate or suffer the consequences discussed above. In this instance, the owners would have interest income. The second way is for the owners to contribute to the capital of the entity. Generally, this can be done tax-free. The benefit of this arrangement is that no party has interest income because there is no loan—it's a capital contribution, which increases the surviving owners' basis in their respective interests. This, in turn, should reduce their capital gains when they sell their interests. The bottom line is that the person obligated to purchase must own and be the beneficiary of the life insurance. This is true even for regular redemption and cross-purchase buy-sell agreements.

Tax Consequences

Since I have already discussed the tax consequences of both types of buy-sell agreements, there's no reason to duplicate the information here. To the extent that the entity purchases the interests, the tax consequences will be governed by the redemption rules discussed in chapter 6. To the extent that the remaining owners purchase the interests, the tax consequences will be governed by the rules discussed in chapter 7.

It is important to note, that if the arrangement involves a corporation, the corporation should always have the first obligation. This is because if the corporation purchases shares that the shareholders are already obligated to purchase under the hybrid agreement, then the shareholders will be deemed to be receiving constructive dividends, which are taxable as ordinary income. To the extent that the corporation has earnings and profits, this could be an expensive surprise. Don't make this mistake.

Wait-and-See Buy-Sell Agreements

Trying to decide between a redemption buy-sell agreement and a cross-purchase buy-sell agreement can be difficult. As I discussed in chapters 6 and 7, many potential factors must be considered in this decision. Uncertainty as to which route to take can cause procrastination and "paralysis of analysis," which sometimes can cause even more problems than making the decision. The bottom line is that there is usually no perfect answer, but you still have to take action.

What if you could design a buy-sell agreement that would give you the flexibility to defer the decision on which way to go until a triggering event occurs? The good news is that you can. It's called the wait-and-see buy-sell agreement—a specific type of hybrid buy-sell agreement. In a wait-and-see buy-sell agreement, the parties agree to purchase, sell, and set a method of determining the price and the terms based on the occurrence of certain triggering events. With respect to the identity of the purchaser, the agreement makes it possible to "wait and see" (i.e., no decision will be made as to whom the specific purchaser will be until the decision *must* be made and when more is known—at the time of the occurrence of a triggering event).

How a Wait-and-See Buy-Sell Agreement Works

How does a wait-and-see buy-sell agreement work? It usually cites a specified price (or amount determined by formula or appraisal) to be paid for an owner's interests. However, the wait-and-see buy-sell agreement does not specify the identity of the person who is obligated or who has the option to purchase or sell, but instead gives that option to several parties in stages. Then, the party will be determined at a specified date at the expiration of a given period after a triggering event occurs.

In a common version of a wait-and-see buy-sell agreement that involves a death trigger, the following sequence of events is generally set forth in this type of agreement:

- The entity has an option to purchase (a "call right") some or all of the interests of the deceased owner for a specified number of days (e.g., sixty days) at the price and on the terms set forth in the buy-sell agreement.
- If the entity does not exercise its option to purchase all of the interests, the surviving owners have an option to purchase whatever interests the entity didn't elect to buy for a specified number of days (e.g., thirty days), in proportion to their current ownership (or, if desired and specified in the wait-and-see buy-sell agreement, in any proportion to which they agree) at the price and on the terms set forth in the buy-sell agreement.
- To the extent that neither of the previous options have been exercised to purchase all of the deceased owner's interest, the entity is then obligated to purchase the remaining interests of the deceased owner at the price and on the terms set forth in the buy-sell agreement.

This system guarantees the deceased owner's estate a market for the interests of the deceased owner at a pre-arranged price (or according to a pre-established formula or by appraisal) and terms. Warning: if the entity is a corporation, the three-stage wait-and-see buy-sell agreement technique must be used exactly as I laid it out. This is because if the corporation buys the interests after the owners have already obligated themselves to purchase them, the surviving shareholders of the corporation will be treated as if they received a dividend in the amount of the corporation's payment for that stock.

CHAPTER 9

TRIGGERING EVENTS AND RESPONSES TO TRIGGERING EVENTS

This chapter explains many of the triggering events commonly in buy-sell agreements. It also describes what happens when a triggering event occurs, (i.e., the responses in the agreement to the occurrence of a triggering event.

Buy-Sell Agreement Triggering Events

A buy-sell agreement triggering event is an occurrence that gives rise to rights under the buy-sell agreement that didn't exist before the event. For example, let's suppose that Al, one of MythiCo's shareholders, dies. In the redemption buy-sell agreement, if his death triggers a mandatory buy-and-sell redemption of his stock, then death is a triggering event; it was only upon Al's death that his estate was obligated to sell his stock and that MythiCo was obligated to redeem his stock pursuant to the agreement. As you will see in the following sections, death is not the only possible triggering event.

Death

While death is not the only possible triggering event that can be put in a buy-sell agreement, it is perhaps the most common—because it happens to everyone. For all its unattractive aspects, death is at least certain, which is more than can be said for disability as a triggering event. However, a buy-sell agreement that has death as the only triggering event is almost always incomplete. Death triggers can have various responses, from no action (where an owner wants to transmit his or her interests to his or her heirs or beneficiaries), to mandatory buy-and-sell (where the owners want every owner to sell at death), and to all points in between. A buy-sell agreement can give coexistent cross-options to the deceased owner's estate or trust (to put the interest, i.e., force the entity or the other owners to buy the deceased owner's interests) and to the entity or other owners (to call the deceased owner's interests, i.e., to force the estate to sell the interests of the deceased owner), such that each "side" can force the other to act instead of it being mandatory on all sides.

Disability

While not commonly dealt with in buy-sell agreements, from an actuarial standpoint, disability for an extended period (e.g., ninety days or more) is a more likely event than death. The problem with disability being the trigger for a buy-sell agreement is that it is frequently a subjective determination. Some people claim to be disabled when they are not, while others will fight tooth and nail against a disability determination.

Determining how to define a disability triggering event in a buy-sell agreement can prove challenging. While there are no right or wrong ways, it is important to know that there are essentially two types of definitions of disability:

- Social security disability—which means the person is permanently incapable of any work of any kind.
- Own occupation disability—which means that the person is no longer capable of performing the regular duties of his or her occupation, even though he or she could perform the duties of a lesser job. This is used for most disability insurance policies.

The definition of disability chosen should be made clear and should provide for permanent disability. This will ensure that short-term disability won't trigger the disability clause in the buy-sell agreement.

Whichever definition of disability is used, if an owner receives regular disability insurance or disability buyout insurance, the buy-sell agreement should coordinate the definition of disability with that in any disability insurance policy—particularly the disability buyout insurance variety. You would not want to trigger a disability under the buy-sell agreement until the insurance company declares the owner disabled. Until the insurance company determines the owner to be disabled under the disability insurance policy, the other owners (or the entity) will have to go it alone on the purchase of the disabled owner's interest. This is because the insurance company will not pay benefits until it is satisfied that the insured owner is, in fact, disabled under the definition set forth in the disability insurance policy.

Another challenge with disability as a triggering event is specifying who determines the disability. Should it be the entity's management, who may have a conflict of interest? Or should it be a physician's certificate? Though many doctors may not get involved. If a doctor's recommendation is chosen, would it be better to get two opinions? If you have disability insurance, you can put the disability determination on the insurance company. This would be ideal because it is not unusual for someone on the edge of disability to attempt to thwart whatever process to declare him or her disabled that is set forth in the buy-sell agreement.

For this reason, it is good to consider some automatic presumptions of disability, such as failure to submit to a physical or mental examination in a timely manner, or failure to show up for work for a continuous period (such as ninety days). With any type of disability presumption, it is important that, in the buy-sell agreement, you don't trigger a put right in the hands of a shady owner who doesn't show up for work or for a doctor's appointment in order to trigger the put option right purposely. The disability trigger should require an ultimate finding of actual disability and should be a call option right to purchase in that situation. The buy-sell agreement should provide that failure to submit to a physical or mental examination results in temporary disability, which would not trigger the purchase obligation.

It is inappropriate to use a disability trigger where owners who are not actively engaged in work own interests or where the entity's principal activities are passive investments. In that instance, it is irrelevant whether an owner is disabled and will only be used for gamesmanship between the owners who are trying to force another owner out of the entity.

Divorce

The fear of being in business with a partner's former spouse has encouraged many people to act when it comes to getting a buy-sell agreement drafted. No one wants that, and everyone imagines the worst—the "ex from hell." However, sloppy buy-sell agreements often leave the owner with the former spouse in an equally bad position: watching the other owners swoop in and buy the owner's ex-spouse's interest pursuant to the terms of a buy-sell agreement. This makes divorce a triggering event for all owners or for the entity without giving the owner with the former spouse the first right to acquire whatever interest the ex-spouse owns or gets awarded in the divorce decree.

A well-drafted buy-sell agreement should give the divorcing owner the first right to acquire whatever interest his or her ex-spouse has or acquires in the property split. The other owners or the entity would not come into play unless the divorcing owner declines his or her option.

Selling an Interest in the Entity

Sometimes, an owner gets an offer to purchase his or her interests in the entity and is inclined to accept it. This should trigger a right of first refusal under the buy-sell agreement that would give the entity or the other owners the first right to acquire the interest that the owner seeks to transfer to an outsider. In some buy-sell agreements, the other owners only have to match a bona fide offer. In other buy-sell agreements, the other owners or the entity only have to pay the lesser between the price in the bona fide offer and the price set forth in the buy-sell agreement on the terms set forth in the agreement.

In an attempt to separate suspicious offers from real ones, some buy-sell agreements go to great lengths to define a bona fide offer. They sometimes even require proof (in the form of earnest money or a deposit of some percentage of the offer price) to demonstrate the prospective purchaser's willingness and financial ability to consummate the purchase transaction.

My experience tells me that the only real way to stop an owner who wants to sell is to buy his or her interests. The buy-sell agreement should permit the entity or the other owners to buy for an agreed price specified in the agreement rather than match a possibly fictitiously high bona fide offer. Whether you style the trigger response as a right of first refusal, a right of first offer, a right of last look, or as all of the above, the owners who decide to remain will have to purchase the interests of an owner who wants to sell.

Lifetime Gift or Testamentary Transfer by Will or Trust

It is not unusual for a buy-sell agreement to permit estate planning–type transfers (for example, to revocable trusts or even directly to descendants) by creating an exception for such transfers to the "no transfer" or "right of first refusal" provisions in the buy-sell agreement. It really should depend on how the exception is framed and whether the owners have decided to permit children or other descendants to be owners. It is possible (but is uncommon) for owners to make a conscious decision to not permit spouses of owners or decedents to own interests (i.e., a full-fledged anti-nepotism rule). This all depends on the situation.

Some buy-sell agreements even require the owners to provide a copy of their wills or revocable living trusts for the entity's legal department to review to ensure that those documents comport with the buy-sell agreement. However, I don't think that is necessary, or even helpful, as those documents are too easy to change. If the owners do not want any owner to transfer his or her interests by gift, will, or trust, then one should consider triggering an automatic right of first refusal, or even a call, upon attempts to do so. However, I strongly recommend against this for family entities.

For example, some buy-sell agreements require the descendants to be "permitted owners," as defined in the buy-sell agreement, which often limits the ranks of descendants to those engaged in active full-time employment by the entity. It is somewhat rare but usually advisable that "permitted owners" be required to possess minimum education requirements and even to have industry experience with another entity (i.e., one in which the person wasn't a descendant of an owner). Many buy-sell agreements only permit owners' spouses to be beneficiaries of the trusts that own interests and not be direct owners. Moreover, these buy-sell agreements usually prohibit the spouse from serving as a trustee of any trust that owns interests, voting the interests, or having any input in entity management. The entity can call the interests if a spouse attempts to vote the interests or to participate in entity operations in any way other than as a passive beneficiary of a trust.

Retirement

In entities where owners also are employed by the entity, it is possible (but is not common) that retirement from active full-time employment can be a triggering event. There are usually minimum entity service or employment time requirements. For example, a person may be required to have worked at least twenty years and have a clean record. I call these types of triggers "good guy" clauses because they almost always give the retiring owner a put option right. This allows the retiring owner to force a purchase of his or her interests but does not require them to sell. These triggers are distinguished from termination of employment triggers because termination of employment can occur without having met the minimum service or employment time, as noted in the next paragraph.

Involuntary Termination of Employment, with or without Cause

The firing of one owner by another owner is often a triggering event in buy-sell agreements in active business entities. These types of triggers often distinguish, as defined in the buy-sell agreement, between being fired for cause and being fired without cause (i.e., not because of the actions or inactions of the owner). These types of buy-sell agreements often give the owner who is terminated without cause a put option right. It also gives the entity a call option right if the owner is fired for cause.

Competing with the Business or Sharing Confidential Information with a Competitor

While it is not common to include a trigger for competing with the entity or sharing confidential business information with a competitor, these triggers should be considered for entities that have active businesses. Such behavior is a breach of fiduciary duty and is very dangerous to the entity. These types of triggers almost always give the entity or the other owners the call option right to force the competing owner to sell. It is not unusual for these types of triggers to give favorable payment terms over a long period of time and even a discounted purchase price (on behalf of the remaining owners) as a penalty for bad behavior. This action is justified given that the behavior may well have cost the entity money.

Malfeasance or Defalcation

Stealing or misappropriation of entity funds or other property can give rise to a trigger in the form of a call option right in favor of the entity. However, not as many buy-sell agreements have this type of trigger, even though they should. This trigger is not limited to entities with active businesses because stealing or misappropriation is bad, even in passive investment entities.

Bankruptcy or Attempted Seizure of Ownership Interest by a Creditor

Sometimes owners will go bankrupt or experience seizures of property through foreclosure by creditors. A well-drafted buy-sell agreement should provide a triggering event for this possibility. This trigger almost always gives the entity or the other owners a call option right. It should provide favorable payment terms and even a lower price than for other buyouts. However, particularly in bankruptcies, if the terms of payment or discounted price are too onerous, a bankruptcy trustee (the person in charge of a bankrupt property) might attempt to nullify the buy-sell agreement in bankruptcy court. This could cause an unfavorable outcome—if successful, the bankruptcy trustee would then be able to sell to anyone, even a competitor.

Loss of License or Other Qualification to Be an Owner

It also happens sometimes that an owner loses a license or other qualification necessary to engage in the activity of the entity (e.g., a CPA license in a CPA firm). In this instance, where the buy-sell agreement contains such a trigger, the entity would usually get a call option right.

Attempt to Transfer or Encumber Interests in Contravention of the Buy-Sell Agreement

A well-drafted buy-sell agreement should clearly and unambiguously prohibit transfers that do not comport with the dictates of the agreement. Nevertheless, sometimes owners attempt to make such transfers anyway. Not only should those transfers be null and void from the start, but they should also penalize anyone who acquires an interest in this fashion by simply not recognizing them as owners on the books and records of the entity or for any other purpose. Moreover, by putting "belts and suspenders" (a very conservative approach) on the null and void transfer clause, the buy-sell agreement could change the voting status of the transferred interests to nonvoting or give the entity or other owners a call option right, even at a deeply discounted price, which should be okay.

Conviction of a Serious Crime

It is rare to see a conviction of a serious crime as a trigger of a buy-sell agreement. It would be critical to carefully describe the crimes that could cause such a trigger in the buy-sell agreement. Preferably, the crime would in some way be tied to the business entity for it to trigger a buy-sell agreement. An example would be a conviction or plea of guilty or no contest to felony theft in a brokerage business entity that deals with the public and requires public confidence in order to be successful. It is rare to see such a provision in a buy-sell agreement as a direct trigger. However, it is fairly common to include convictions of certain types of crimes in cause for termination of employment, with a corresponding call option right in favor of the entity or other owners.

Attempt to Terminate S Corporation Status

While this particular trigger is limited to entities that elect to be taxed as S corporations, it is common to buttress a null and void transfer clause with a call option right in favor of the entity or other owners of S corporation stock upon any attempted transfer to a person who is ineligible to be a shareholder of an S corporation (nonresident aliens and many types of trusts). In this instance, an owner takes steps to terminate the S election by transferring the interests to someone who is ineligible to be a shareholder of an S corporation or by revoking consent to the S election.

Attempt to Dissolve or Liquidate the Business

While it is rare to see a trigger for attempts to dissolve or liquidate the entity, sometimes a buy-sell agreement will give a call option right to the entity or the other owners. However, it is possible that an owner makes an attempt to dissolve or liquidate the entity by filing a petition in court for such a result. The effect of this provision is to require the other owners to buy the interests of that owner or endure the uncertainty of a lawsuit.

Grant of Proxy or Voting Rights

It is not common to see a trigger in a buy-sell agreement for a mere grant of voting rights or voting proxy to someone (usually someone objectionable to the other owners), but it does happen. Typically, these triggers provide the entity (or all or some of the other owners) with a call option right.

Public Offering

Going public is very rare. However, a public offering trigger is a provision in a buy-sell agreement for minority owners who want to get their money out of the entity when or if the entity goes public. Usually, the buy-sell agreement will give minority owners a put option right to force the entity or the majority owners to buy their interests before the securities laws lock down the sale of entity interests.

Sale or Other Disposition of Related Property

Sometimes, a sale of all or most of the entity's assets and operating business triggers a right on the part of the owners to cause a dissolution of the entity or a put option right against the entity.

Voluntary Termination of Employment

It is not unusual for a buy-sell agreement to give the entity a call option right if an owner voluntarily quits working for the entity for a reason other than retirement or for disability (as defined in the buy-sell agreement).

Responses to the Occurrence of a Triggering Event

The first part of this chapter discusses the common and not-so-common triggering events. Now I am going to take you through possible, common responses to triggering events. It is important to match the response with the triggering event, because a mismatch can create a problem or an opportunity for mischief (for example, if one gave a put option right to an owner who voluntarily quit working for the entity to go to work for a competitor).

Absolute Prohibition against Transfer

Occasionally, I come across a buy-sell agreement (usually in a first-generation family entity) where all transfers, other than those expressly permitted by the owners, are impossible due to an absolute prohibition against transfers or a requirement that all the owners must consent to transfers. One of the problems with such a rule is that courts will almost universally strike it down as an unreasonable restraint of trade—you can't imprison people's property forever.

Mandatory Buy-and-Sell

A mandatory buy-and-sell obligates both sides to act so that there are no options. These are seen most often in death triggering events.

Qualified Prohibition against Transfer

While it is almost always impossible to tie up a person's property interest forever through an absolute prohibition against transfer, it is possible to set forth a group of qualified recipients of interests (e.g., individual family members or current ownership group).

Call by the Entity or by the Other Owners

The exercising of a call option right by the entity or by the other owners is done with the intention of getting rid of an owner. Under the buy-sell agreements I have drafted, this option was exercised after a "bad guy" triggering event such as termination for cause. Exercise of a call option right gives the recipient no option—he or she must sell.

Put by an Owner to the Entity or to the Other Owners

Distinguished from the call option right in the preceding paragraph, typically under the buy-sell agreements that I have drafted, the put option right is exercised after the occurrence of a "good guy" event such as retirement or disability. However, put option rights also can be drafted for use in the situation of death or any other triggering event scenario. However, I would not recommend their use in bad guy triggering events such as competing with the entity or termination for cause. For example, a put option right in the hands of a competitor could force the entity into buying the competing owner's interests. This will do nothing but aid the competitor since the recipient of an exercised put option right has no option either—he or she must buy. A put option right and a call option right can exist simultaneously over the same interest. For example, it is not unusual in a death trigger response to give the estate a put option right and the entity or other owners a call option right over the deceased owner's interests as an alternative to a mandatory buy-and-sell.

Right of First Refusal or Option

The right of first refusal is typically triggered by an owner's attempt to sell his or her interests. This gives either the entity, the other owners, or both, the first right to purchase the selling owner's interests. The problem with only having a right of first refusal without more restrictions is that unless the entity or the other owners are financially capable of purchasing the owner's interests, the exercise of a right of first refusal is meaningless.

Mexican Shoot-Out

This trigger response is known by many different names (e.g., Australian auction and Texas shoot-out) and comes in three types of formats: the Mexican shoot-out, the Russian roulette, and the Dutch auction, each of which is explained in chapter 5.

The basic Mexican shoot-out occurs when one owner, who is fed up with the status quo, is in a hopeless deadlock with the other owner and recommends a price for their interest. He or she then presents it to the other owner (as this trigger response really only works in two-owner entities) with the dictate that the other owner either buys or sells to him or her.

Mere Notice Prior to Action

Sometimes a buy-sell agreement only requires advance notice of action but does not convey a put, call, or mandatory buy-and-sell. A buy-sell agreement sometimes permits transfers of interests to a class of permitted transferees; the agreement requires a transferring owner to give advance written notice to the entity and the other owners.

No Action

Usually, a buy-sell agreement does not affirmatively state that there is to be no action—or even advance notice of one. However, there is an implied existence of this where the buy-sell agreement is silent on a particular action. However, this is rare.

Buy-Sell Grid

Table 2 illustrates the buy-sell grid that I used for clients in order to show the various options in a buy-sell agreement. The possible triggering events take one axis and the responses to triggering events take the other axis.

Buy-Sell Agreements Grid

	Absolute prohibition against transfer	Qualified prohibition against transfer, e.g., only to qualified shareholders	Mandatory purchase and sale	An option or "call" by the entity or other owner(s)	An option or "put" by the owner to sell to the entity or other owners
Death.					
Disability.					
Retirement.					
Termination by company for cause.					
Termination by company without cause.					
Termination by employee with competition.					
Competition by non-employee owner.					
Divorce.					
Gift/other disposition.					
Bankruptcy.					
Action by shareholder to cause Loss of S status.					
Loss of qualification as owner, e.g., professional license, S corp. limitations					
Attempt to dissolve entity.					
Grant of proxy or other voting control rights.					
Public offering.					
Assignment of rights in buy-sell agreement.					
Gift/sale/other disposition of property used in entity operations.					
Voluntary termination of employment for reasons other than retirement or disability.					

	Right of first refusal for owners and/or entity	Coexistent cross options for owner and entity other owners or persons	Drop dead/Gauntlet provision. Ex: "This is the price -- you buy my interest or I'll buy yours"	Mere notice of the transfer or of intention to transfer.	No action by entity, disposing owner or remaining owner(s).
Death.					
Disability.					
Retirement.					
Termination by company for cause.					
Termination by company without cause.					
Termination by employee with competition.					
Competition by non-employee owner.					
Divorce.					
Gift/other disposition.					
Bankruptcy.					
Action by shareholder to cause Loss of S status.					
Loss of qualification as owner, *e.g.*, professional license, S corp. limitations					
Attempt to dissolve entity.					
Grant of proxy or other voting control rights.					
Public offering.					
Assignment of rights in buy-sell agreement.					
Gift/sale/other disposition of property used in entity operations.					
Voluntary termination of employment for reasons other than retirement or disability.					

CHAPTER 10

FUNDING PURCHASES IN BUY-SELL AGREEMENTS

There are several different ways to fund purchases under a buy-sell agreement. There is no right or wrong answer for selecting funding sources, but it is important that the buy-sell agreement clearly defines the particular source or method chosen. The funding method under one triggering event purchase may not be optimal for another triggering event. Therefore, it is advisable to select funding methods on a trigger-by-trigger basis. For example, there are triggers where insurance can be obtained. These insurance proceeds could be paid in one lump sum (as under most life insurance policies and most disability buyout policies), or they could be received (as in a disability income policy) with the balance paid out and with a promissory note calling for payments of principal and interest over a set period of time.

There are four basic methods for paying for interests under a buy-sell agreement: savings, life insurance or disability buyout insurance, third-party debt, and an installment payout arrangement using a promissory note.

Savings

Although it does not happen very often, savings represents a good way for any buyer (entity or individual) to pay for a purchased interest because it saves interest for the buyer. Unfortunately, paying for a purchased interest through savings is easier said than done. For starters, savings almost always must be made after first paying income tax. If the entity (in the case of a C corporation) or the owner is in a 35 percent income tax bracket, it will take $153.85 of income to save $100, which could prove to be difficult.

If the entity is a C corporation, then amassing cash in a sinking fund might be even more difficult due to the accumulated earnings tax in IRC Section 537. Moreover, it might not be able to give enough salary (which the C corporation generally can deduct) to allow the shareholders to save enough money to pay for purchases of interests due to the prohibition against unreasonably high income. In this case, the excess salary would be recharacterized as a dividend, which would not be deductible by the corporation even though the shareholders would have to pay ordinary income tax on the dividend amount.

Life Insurance or Disability Buyout Insurance

Life insurance can be used to finance all or part of a purchase of interests at an owner's death. Additionally, life insurance that has a cash value or investment component that can be accessed to assist in the financing of lifetime purchases as well. However, pure term insurance will not help with lifetime purchases. It is important to coordinate the life insurance with the type of buy-sell agreement, or you might have a mismatch between the person who holds the life insurance proceeds and the person who is obligated to buy the interest of a deceased owner.

Given that life insurance premiums are not tax-deductible, you run into the same problem as you do with debt—you're buying it with after-tax income. When attempting to save enough to finance the purchase of interests, the life insurance premiums are paid after-tax dollars. Therefore, it takes $153.85 in income to pay $100 of life insurance premiums after income taxes, assuming that the purchaser of the life insurance policy is in the 35 percent income tax bracket. If the entity is a C corporation and in a lower income tax bracket than its shareholders, then the C corporation should buy and hold the life insurance. This is less expensive than the shareholders purchasing the life insurance with a higher after-tax cost. For example, if the shareholder is in the 35 percent income tax bracket, it will take $153.85 of income to be able to pay $100 of life insurance premiums. Conversely, suppose the C corporation is only in a 15 percent income tax bracket. In that case, the after-tax cost of the life insurance premiums will be only $117.65 for every $100 of life insurance premiums—a savings of $36.20 per $100 of life insurance premiums, which is a substantial difference.

The prohibition against the deductibility of unreasonably high compensation in a C corporation may prevent sufficient funds from being distributed out to a shareholder to pay life insurance premiums or installment payments on purchases of interests under cross-purchase buy-sell agreements. If the compensation that the C corporation pays to the shareholders is not tax-deductible by the C corporation, then the insurance cost will be much higher because those excess amounts will first be taxed to the corporation and then taxed again when paid to the shareholders. For example, suppose that both a corporation and the shareholders are in the 35 percent income tax bracket. For every $100 of life insurance premiums or installment payments, it will cost the corporation $153.85. It will also cost the shareholders an additional $153.85, for a total cost of $307.70 for every $100 of life insurance premiums or installment payments, which often is cost-prohibitive.

Buy-sell agreements usually use of one or more of three essential types of life insurance policies:

- Traditional single life insurance, which can either be whole life or term insurance, with universal and variable universal life insurance policies being considered as variants of term insurance.

- Second-to-die or survivorship policies, which insure the lives of two people and typically pay their death benefits on the surviving insured's death. This life insurance is typically whole life or term insurance, or a blend of the two, with universal and variable universal second-to-die life insurance policies being considered as variants of term insurance.

- First-to-die life insurance policies, which pay off at the first death among the insured, typically two, although these policies can insure the lives of several owners. The advantage of this policy is a significant premium savings over two separate policies for the same amount of life insurance death benefits. However, these policies are not perfect.

The arguments against these policies are that the premium savings are not sufficient enough to offset the extra benefits and flexibility of having additional policies to fund continuing buy-sell agreement needs. Also, first-to-die policies with extra policy features and options, including paying some benefits on the second death, are likely expensive. This means that their long-term return rates will not compare favorably with the best traditional life insurance policies. Nevertheless, first-to-die life insurance can be a practical and inexpensive route to consider in redemption buy-sell agreements.

As I've discussed on numerous occasions throughout this book, the general rule is that life insurance proceeds are tax-free. However, that law has several exceptions. One significant exception is the transfer for value rules that I discuss at length in chapters 6 and 7. The second exception is for certain life insurance policies that will be used in financing purchases under buy-sell agreements, for purposes of this book. The rule is that life insurance policy death proceeds that exceed the total premiums paid are taxable unless an exception to the rule applies.

As with most other abstruse tax laws, the rules are inordinately complex, and there are some possibly helpful exceptions to these rules. However, I strongly recommend that you follow these rules even if there is an exception because of the severity of the penalty—taxation of most life insurance death proceeds.

What do you need to do to comply with these rules? The first thing is, prior to purchasing a new life insurance policy on the life of an owner, to provide a notice to the insured owner that explains the following:

- The entity or the owners intend to insure their lives by purchasing life insurance policies in whatever maximum face amount of death benefits are being purchased.
- The entity or the other owners will be the owner and beneficiary of that policy and any life insurance death proceeds payable on such owner's death.

Each owner should sign notice to give advance written consent to being an insured under the life insurance policies and the continuation of the policies after the owner ceases to have an interest in the entity, or otherwise terminates employment with the entity. The owners should agree to enter a separate notice and consent containing these terms regarding each new life insurance policy obtained before the issuing of the policy. Just to be safe, I also recommend putting such a notice directly in the buy-sell agreement and having the owner's signature on the agreement constitute consent as well. The last thing that should be done is to file Form 8925 with the IRS every year concerning the life insurance policies. If you don't comply with these rules, the insurance proceeds are characterized as taxable income.

One big issue is whether or not the death proceeds on life insurance policies owned by the entity and earmarked for a redemption buyout are included in the valuation of the entity. This can make a big difference. In my opinion, the buy-sell agreement should affirm that the life insurance that is owned by the entity is not included in the value of the entity if the life insurance policy death proceeds are required to be used as part of the redemption payment. This is because the policy death proceeds will only be in the entity temporarily, as they are earmarked for use in the corresponding obligation to purchase.

However, it is not unusual for buy-sell agreements to provide that the amount of life insurance on an owner that is owned for the purpose of the buy-sell agreement serves as a floor on the value of the interest to be sold. This is because the insurance's purpose was to finance the buyout, not to give the entity or other owners a windfall. One thing is certain—neither the estate of a deceased owner nor a beneficiary chosen by the insured owner should be a beneficiary of the life insurance owned by an entity—especially in a C corporation because the proceeds will be treated as taxable income. According to the IRS, if a redemption buy-sell agreement calls for a C corporation to pay the excess life insurance benefits over what is needed to fund the purchase obligation to the decedent's estate or another person, the excess proceeds will be subject to both estate tax and income tax. The easiest way around this is to make the amount of the life insurance death proceeds the minimum floor value of the interests—meaning that the value of the subject interests can never be lower than the amount of death proceeds from the life insurance.

Third-Party Debt

Debt is another way to finance the purchase of interests by the entity or by the purchasing owners. Like the savings alternative, debt must be paid back with after-tax dollars. This is the only part of a payment that you may be able to deduct the interest, and that is not always true. It is far easier to borrow money than it is to pay it back.

Assuming the interest is not deductible, if a purchaser who has incurred debt has a marginal income tax rate of 35 percent, it will take $161.54 of income to be able to pay $100 worth of debt, plus the interest if assumed at a rate of 5 percent per year—an additional $5 per $100 of debt—for a total annual cost of $166.54 per $100 of debt. If possible, you can deduct the incurring interest at a rate of 5 percent. This will reduce the cost per $100 of debt, inclusive of interest, to approximately $164.79 ($1.75 per $100 of debt—$5.35 for a purchaser who is in the 35 percent income tax bracket). Additionally, debt can crush an owner or an entity by cutting off opportunities to invest more into the business.

Obviously, one method of paying the purchase price is with installments evidenced by a promissory note, which is debt, so the same considerations that I applied to debt apply here.

Disability Insurance

For disability buyouts pursuant to a buy-sell agreement, it is not unusual for people to obtain disability buyout insurance. It is actuarially more likely that someone would be disabled for an extended period than for them to die, which is why disability insurance is so expensive. The same rationale for using a life insurance policy to help fund a buy-sell obligation upon a business owner's death applies to using a disability policy to fund a buyout obligation based on an owner's permanent and total disability. Upon the disability of an owner, the entity may be obligated to continue to carry the disabled owner and pay their salary and benefits for an indefinite period. In addition, the disabled owner often is still entitled to a share of profits and maintains his or her share of the entity.

The disability buyout insurance policy provides a means to buy a disabled owner's interest, generally over a period of years, once it is evident that the disabled owner is not going to return to work. The payment can be a monthly amount or a lump sum. As I discussed in chapter 9, the concept of disability related to an owner's active participation in the business of an entity is often far more challenging to define and describe than most other buy-sell triggering events (e.g., death or termination of employment). Setting forth the conditions under which an individual is deemed disabled can be essential to a successful arrangement. However, I'll caution you again about making a presumption of disability based on the owner's intransigence, because a crafty and amoral owner can easily manipulate a trigger of a put option right in his or her hands.

The success of a buy-sell agreement that has disability as a triggering event may be mostly dependent on the insurance used to fund it. Thus, the most logical definition of disability to use in the buy-sell agreement is likely to be the definition contained in the disability buyout insurance policy that will fund the buyout. This places the burden of determining whether the owner's disability meets the policy's definition of disability on the insurance company, thus avoiding potential disagreements among the owners.

Disability buyout insurance policies may define "total disability" as the inability to perform the duties of the insured's regular occupation or a reasonable occupation based on the insured's education, training, or experience. This is referred to as an "own occupation" definition of disability, instead of being disabled and unable to engage in any gainful employment, which Social Security Disability requires. The owner's ability to contribute in a meaningful way to the entity is what should be insured for a buy-sell agreement that has disability as a triggering event. Even if the owner can work in a different, unrelated business, he or she may still want to continue to be deemed "totally disabled" for purposes of the disability buyout and the disability buyout insurance coverage under the policy, because of the individual's inability to work in the job that he or she had in the entity.

Whether the structure of the disability buyout arrangement is redemption, cross-purchase, or trusteed cross-purchase agreement (which I discussed in chapter 7), the taxation of premiums and benefits under disability buyout insurance policies is the same. The premiums paid are not tax-deductible, but the benefits generally are received income tax–free.

During the early stages of an owner's disability, the owner and the other owners may well expect the owner to recover and return to work. In most cases, total disability is determined only after the injured or sick owner has been incapacitated for some time (time being a proxy for an actual disability determination, such as after a sufficient enough time that the owner's recovery and return to the entity is unlikely). Therefore, it is necessary to establish a definite time after disability first occurs when the buy-sell obligation will be triggered, thereby assuring that no one will purchase the disabled owner's interest until it becomes unlikely that the owner will recover and return to work in the entity.

The appropriate period before the interest of a disabled owner can be purchased under the buy-sell agreement can and will vary from case to case. In determining a reasonable waiting period, consideration should be given to a variety of factors, including the following:

- The available means of support other than the entity that the owner will have during this buy-sell waiting period. (What are the sources of support available to the disabled owner?)
- The length of time that the entity can continue to pay part or all of the disabled owner's salary. (How long can the entity afford to carry the disabled owner?)
- Whether the disabled owner is the beneficiary of any other disability, sickness, or accident insurance policy that could provide benefits during the buy-sell agreement waiting period.
- How long it will be before the disabled owner's absence from the entity's business puts that owner out of touch with the business and woefully behind the other owners.

This last consideration can be especially crucial in establishing an appropriate interim period between when an active owner becomes disabled and the time for the sale of the disabled owner's interest under the terms of the buy-sell agreement. Once an owner sells an interest in the entity because of the owner's disability, the owner should not then have the right to regain the owner's former position in the entity—solely because the owner recovers from the disability—without the consent of the other owners, who have essentially already purchased that disabled owner's interests. A disabled owner's return to work after a prolonged disability absence, especially where the owner was paid for his or her interests in the entity, may not be acceptable to those owners who have remained active in entity's business.

It is important to give a significant amount of thought to the appropriate waiting period before the disability buy-sell triggering event is deemed to have occurred. Suppose the owner manages to recover from the disability before the end of the waiting period. In that case, he or she is free to resume whatever duties were being performed in the business because no triggering event occurred on account of disability.

However, the owner's interest is purchased under the buy-sell agreement because the disability lasts longer than the waiting period and elimination period under the disability buyout insurance policy. However, if the owner recovers after that period, that owner should probably not be entitled to simply resume an active role in the entity unless it is acceptable to all of the other owners due to the mere lapse of time—a time period to which all owners, including the disabled owner, agreed constituted a trigger under the buy-sell agreement. This may not be acceptable to the disabled owner, but it is the fairest result. If an owner has been out that long, the chances are good that the entity has effectively already replaced the disabled owner through a new hire or rearrangement of other owners' and employees' duties.

Disability income insurance policies also contain a waiting period before benefits are paid—this is known in the disability income policy as the "elimination period." Elimination periods for personal disability insurance policies are much shorter (e.g., ninety days) than the elimination periods under disability buyout insurance policies. Disability buyout insurance policies typically come with a choice of one of three elimination periods: twelve months, eighteen months, or twenty-four months.

The premiums for these disability buyout policies usually decrease, often significantly, as the elimination period increases, since it is less likely that the disability will last as long as a lengthier elimination period.

In my experience, the owner who suffers a disabling illness or accident has a higher probability of dying before the disability buyout elimination period is up. The insurance company won't have to pay for any interest since it won't have to pay the disability buyout benefits if the owner dies before the end of the elimination period, unless the policy also has a death benefit rider on top of it (or the insured owner also has a life insurance policy with the same insurance company). Therefore, the buy-sell agreement must have a seamless transition from a disability buyout to a death buyout.

At the end of the elimination period, a typical disability buyout insurance policy pays the benefits in a lump sum, installment payments, or a combination of the two. Whether the policy's elimination period triggers the buyout agreement will depend on the terms of the buy-sell agreement. However, in the typical situation, satisfaction of the elimination period will trigger the disability buyout obligation under the buy-sell agreement.

If the disability buyout insurance policy provides for a lump-sum payment in an amount sufficient to buy the disabled owner's interest in the entity, then the purchase date should almost always coincide with the end of the elimination period. However, if the lump-sum payment is less than the full purchase price of the interests of the disabled owner, or if the disability buyout insurance policy provides for installment payments of benefits, then the buyout will have to be structured as an installment sale. Installment sale payments to the disabled owner will coincide with each receipt of the disability buyout insurance benefits.

Under either circumstance, the parties must coordinate the waiting period before purchase and the elimination period under the disability buyout insurance policy. For example, the buy-sell agreement may provide that the buyout will occur at the end of the elimination period. However, the agreement may also provide a six-month waiting period before purchase, while the funding policy has a twelve-month elimination period. Here, the buyer would have to have sufficient cash on hand to make the payments under the installment sale obligation as outlined in the buy-sell agreement until the disability buyout insurance policy begins to pay benefits.

Once the disability buyout is triggered under the buy-sell agreement, the seller should relinquish all control over the operation of the entity—as well as his or her interests. This is because he or she has sold it, just as in any other sale. However, he or she may retain a collateral interest in his or her interests (or in other security) to secure payments under the installment sale. Payments should continue regardless of whether the insured owner recovers or not, since the buyout obligation was triggered after the end of the time period.

Installment Arrangements

Installment payments often play a significant role in the satisfaction of buy-sell agreement purchase obligations, particularly those that occur during the selling owner's lifetime. However, they are also used in death buyouts, where life insurance is not used or where the life insurance death proceeds are insufficient to pay off the entire purchase price. However, where life insurance is a part of the financing for purchase under a buy-sell agreement, the agreement should require that all the life insurance death proceeds be used to pay down the amount owed on the purchase obligation.

There is no magic period of time for which installment payment periods should last. However, one thing is clear—you need to think about it from the start. Five years (sixty monthly payments) is a frequent starting point, but if the entity's interest being purchased is valuable, five years might not be long enough. However, when in doubt, err on the side of a longer time period of payments. Higher payments over a shorter timeframe could cause cash flow difficulties for the purchaser, which might be the entity and could bring down the financial viability of the entity that is generating the payments. Selling owners won't like this, but they have to understand that if they put too much financial pressure on the entity to make installment payments, they may jeopardize the entity's continuing financial viability or cause the other owners to walk away from the entity and its debts.

One problem comes up somewhat regularly in installment payment arrangements: what to do when the entity is faced with having to redeem the interests of more than one owner at the same time. There is no hard and fast solution here. Still, I believe that all sellers should be treated the same upon the occurrence of a triggering event—the first buyer to hit the triggering event, especially one that is voluntary such as retirement, should not necessarily be given better treatment in the form of being paid first simply for being first.

One possible fix here is to have a payment cutback clause in the buy-sell agreement that provides for reductions in installment payments where two or more triggering events occur within a specified period (e.g., two years). This would require the entity to purchase interests in order to treat all purchasers the same (each would receive a smaller monthly installment payment). Even though the sellers might not like this because their payments may be cut, it strikes me as being the most evenhanded and fair way to go about it.

The buy-sell agreement should contain all of the salient terms of credit for the installment payout arrangement, such that there is nothing left to negotiate, as it is all set out in advance. Consider the following provisions for inclusion in a buy-sell agreement:

- Interest. Any payment over a period of time should bear interest. The IRS will impute interest as if it is being paid if you fail to use a minimum interest rate that the IRS issues monthly— the Applicable Federal Rate (AFR). Although, the interest rate as of the triggering event or the date of the purchase can be locked as the interest rate of the promissory note's life, such that the interest rate doesn't have to fluctuate monthly. Nothing prevents the interest rate from being higher than the AFR, as well as the risk of nonpayment by the purchaser. These factors may necessitate a higher interest rate to compensate the seller for risking being paid in installments. However, the method of determining the interest rate must be set forth, since the parties to the transaction will dispute it if it isn't, with the seller wanting a high interest rate and the buyer wanting a low rate.

- Security pledge of interests or assets. It is customary for a buy-sell agreement to grant the seller a security interest in either the sold interests (in the case of a cross-purchase), or in the entity's interests or in the interests of the other owners (in the case of a redemption) in order to secure the installment payments. These terms should include what constitutes a default and what happens in that event. The security documents should contain default and acceleration provisions that are customary in commercial documents between unrelated third parties and should be subject to the seller's counsel's approval—which should not be unreasonably withheld. The security documents should also allow the seller to have continuing access to the entity's financial position and to have audit rights relative to the entity's financial position or the purchasing owner while any amount remains unpaid.

- Personal guarantees of other owners. In a redemption buy-sell agreement, it is customary for the other owners to personally guarantee the entity's performance on the purchase. In a cross-purchase buy-sell agreement—since the purchaser is already on the hook for the purchase price—you usually only see personal guarantees in cross-purchase agreements where the purchaser is an entity that is owned or controlled by the owner, instead of being the purchaser directly. The parties may decide that in a cross-purchase buyout, the entity will pledge some of its assets to assure repayment, but this can get very tricky and shouldn't be done without assistance from qualified counsel.

- Acceleration of promissory note on sale of all of the company's stock or assets. It is customary for a well-drafted buy-sell agreement to accelerate the remaining principal payments on the note upon the sale of all or most of the assets or stock of the entity. This is because the use of the installment-payout plan was caused by a lack of liquidity (cash) necessary to pay the purchase price in a single lump sum. Upon the sale of the assets or stock of the entity (a liquidity event), the very purpose of and need for the installment payout arrangement goes away.

- Loan type restrictions on entity operations. It is common (but admittedly less so than either of the first two provisions discussed above) for a well-drafted buy-sell agreement to put financial restrictions on the entity for the entire period of the installment payout. These restrictions, which are common in commercial loan agreements, can include a no dividends to owners provision, limits on owners' salaries, acceleration of the note on the occurrence of certain events, selling owner access to entity financial statements and information, and maintenance of minimum financial ratios (profitability, liquidity).

- Release of the owner and the owner's property from all guarantees and security of entity debt. It is only natural that a selling owner expects to be released of any responsibility for entity financing obligations, including personal guarantees and encumbrances on the selling owner's property. A well-drafted buy-sell agreement will take this into account. However, since the decision to release security is in the hands of the lending creditor—over whom neither the entity nor the other owners have any control—the best way to deal with this is to have the entity and other owners agree to get the selling owner and his or her property released from responsibility for entity debts. The entity and the other owners should be required in the buy-sell agreement to agree to indemnify, defend, and hold the selling owner harmless against any such entity debt where the lending creditor won't release the selling owner or his or her property from responsibility.

Clawback Provision

It is rare to see a clawback provision in a buy-sell agreement. A clawback provision is where an additional amount of compensation (as an effective addition to the original sales price) may have to be paid to a previously selling owner if the entity is sold within a specified period of time for an amount per share greater than the buyout price. However, these provisions are usually seen in buy-sell agreements dealing with minority interests, mainly where the entity is the type that might be ripe for purchase by a third party. Controlling owners often owe a fiduciary duty to minority owners not to fail to disclose deals that might have been discussed and possible at the time of the sale of a minority owner's interests.

CHAPTER 11

VALUATIONS IN BUY-SELL AGREEMENTS

One of the most common mistakes made in buy-sell agreements is failing to consider the necessary valuation provisions. In this chapter, I will examine the three principal ways of determining value in a buy-sell agreement and give the pros and cons for each valuation method. I'll also discuss a fourth way that valuation can be determined in special deadlock situations that is usually reserved for two-owner entities.

The three principal valuation methods include the set price (Schedule A) method, the formula method, and the appraisal method. The fourth valuation method that sometimes is used for special deadlock involves an owner invoking a Russian roulette, a Texas (or Mexican) shoot-out, a Dutch auction, or a similar type of clause that I described in chapter 5.

Methods of Valuation

It is imperative that the owners agree to a value or a procedure for determining the value for purchases under a buy-sell agreement when the agreement is negotiated and signed. This is because no one knows exactly who the buyer and seller will be under the buy-sell agreement. Therefore, it is in everyone's best interests to clearly define the applicable valuation process, method, and procedure. Failure to do this could financially affect you or your heirs.

It is possible to have different prices for different triggering events—for example, providing a lower price where someone quits or begins competing with the entity while providing a higher price upon death, disability, or retirement.

One issue that must be addressed in the buy-sell agreement is whether or not to include any life insurance earmarked for buyout in the entity's valuation. For tax purposes, the courts have held that life insurance does not add to the entity's value as long as the entity is required to use all of the life insurance death proceeds to purchase the interest. However, if your buy-sell agreement could be triggered in ways that do not involve a tax controversy, then this must be detailed in the agreement.

The life insurance could either be counted or not counted. The life insurance death proceeds could serve as a valuation floor (the value of a deceased owner's interest could never be less than the value of the life insurance policy death proceeds that covered the life of the deceased owner). In my opinion, the tax court was correct in not counting life insurance that must be used in the redemption of shares, because its inclusion in the entity's coffers is only temporary and shouldn't count as part of the entity's value.

For example, suppose that MythiCo owns $1,000,000 life insurance policies on the lives of each of the four shareholders to assist in financing its redemption obligation in the event that a shareholder dies. The value of MythiCo without counting the life insurance is $4,000,000, but is $5,000,000 if you count the life insurance death proceeds. This directly impacts what the deceased shareholder's shares are worth and, therefore, should be explained in the buy-sell agreement.

Set Price (Schedule A) Method

The set price method is the first method of valuation. I often call this the Schedule A method because the owners usually attach a schedule to the back of the buy-sell agreement with the value on it. For example, suppose that MythiCo and its four equal shareholders use this valuation method and value MythiCo shares at $1,000 apiece. This is the amount they would put on Schedule A.

This method has a host of problems associated with it—so many, in fact, that I have never recommended it to anyone—yet I continue to see lots of buy-sell agreements that use this valuation method. What are the problems? For starters, who says that the owners are good judges of the value of their businesses? Valuing entities and interests in entities is its own profession today, and there's a lot to know.

The skill sets of operating an entity and of putting a value on it, or on any interest in it, are unrelated. It has been my experience that owners have little idea of what their business is truly worth, and the wrong answers vary from too high to too low. The bottom line is that very few owners should attempt to set their own prices in a buy-sell agreement without a qualified business appraiser's assistance.

If that problem alone was not enough to stay away from the set price method, consider this: most of these Schedule A valuations are supposed to be updated every year or every other year by mutual agreement. There are at least two related problems here. The first is that most owners forget to update the Schedule A value until something happens to trigger the buy-sell agreement, which is too late, as that favors either the buyer or the seller, depending on whether the price agreed on is too high or too low. The second problem is that when Schedule A is about to be revisited and one of the owners is near death or disabled, then that compromised owner will be at a distinct disadvantage as the other owners may purposely set the price too low, betting that the teetering owner will soon have a triggering event happen first.

One thing is clear: if you are going to disregard my advice here and use a Schedule A valuation, then you ought to have a fail-safe backup method, such as an appraisal, when the parties either fail to update Schedule A for a period of time (two or three years at the max) or they are unable to agree on the value to place on Schedule A. Otherwise, please do yourself and your loved ones a favor and avoid Schedule A valuation methods like the plague!

Formula Method

The formula valuation method is another method that I don't like. In more than thirty years of working with buy-sell agreements, I've never seen a formula that is capable of producing a satisfactory value in all cases nor one that isn't susceptible to manipulation in any case.

If you are going to disregard my advice and use a formula valuation method, at least engage a competent, qualified business appraiser to design the valuation formula for your business. Then have the appraiser perform an actual valuation of the entity to show you exactly how the formula will work with real numbers before a triggering event occurs. However, if your business changes through expansion or contraction, then your formula probably needs to be revisited and reworked. I have seen some horror stories of valuation formulas that have generated a zero or even a negative number, so heed my warning!

If you use a valuation formula, steer clear of so-called "rules of thumb." A rule of thumb is a quick and dirty way to assign a value to an entity. However, it is unlikely to consider the issues of valuing interests in the entity or the entity's unique features that may make it more or less attractive than the result under the rule of thumb. Moreover, rules of thumb often are outdated or incorrect. Rules of thumb are what they are—quick and dirty valuation methods for an entire entity that might form a starting point for a valuation of an entity or be used as a sanity check against a valuation formula result or an appraisal, but no more than that.

If you insist on trying to confect a formula, consider the following: use a mixed approach formula that considers both balance sheet (assets and liabilities) and income statement (revenues and expense) components. For example, consider having hard assets such as real estate appraised (do not just use book value—get it appraised by a qualified real estate appraiser). Moreover, for the income statement component, consider defining the valuation multiple to be used as well as the time periods that should be examined. For instance, you could consider the last three years of income statements, or the past five, tossing out the high and low years and using the three years in the middle to give a more realistic value of the business in an average year. However, past performance is no guarantee of future performance. Or you could weigh the more recent years greater than the past years. There are many ways to construct a formula, but none of them appeal to me because someone can manipulate the numbers that go into the formula to the advantage or disadvantage of an owner who has to buy or sell.

If your business is cyclical and susceptible to changes in revenue, you should avoid a formula in general, as it could significantly overvalue or undervalue the entity. Also, you need to ensure that your formula addresses whether or not there are to be any valuation discounts for minority interests in a privately held entity. The discounts to which I am referring are discounts for lack of control (for a minority interest that cannot unilaterally control the entity, making that interest worth less) and discounts for lack of marketability (because, unlike publicly traded securities, there is no established market for closely held business interests, which makes the interest worth less).

Other issues and questions concerning valuation formulas include the very base on which a valuation multiple (e.g., five times net earnings) is applied. Will it be net income? Net income before owners' salaries and perks (which could be excessive)? Income before depreciation and amortization? Each of these earnings figures could produce wildly different results, so be careful.

Another question is, who will do the computing under the formula? Who will pay for the computations? Additionally, whose financial data is to be used, and what accounting method is to be used? You should clearly address all of these questions in the buy-sell agreement.

If it seems like I'm trying to scare you away from using a valuation formula method, it's because I am. Valuation formulas tend to foment litigation because, inevitably, someone will be displeased with the result reached by the formula, and accusations of manipulating the data or the results will ensue. If you are still intrepid and desirous of using a valuation formula, at least get a business valuation expert to design one for use in the buy-sell agreement. Also, have that expert revisit the formula every few years, with a default appraisal method if the formula is not updated or reviewed for a specified small number of years (i.e., two or three years).

Appraisal Method

Unfortunately, the downsides to the appraisal method are that it is more expensive to have done initially and that someone will probably not like the value reached by the business appraiser. However, it's been my experience that the appraisal method is the fairest to all parties and is the most economical in the long run because valuation litigation is usually much more expensive than a qualified business appraisal. The term "value" can have any number of meanings. A lower value is typically in the purchasing owner's best interest, thus, they will vociferously argue and posture for using that value. Therefore, further guidance for the business appraiser in the buy-sell agreement is advisable.

Despite stating in the buy-sell agreement that a competent and qualified business appraiser will reach the price to be paid, there are many provisions that you should still include in the agreement in order to provide some guidance to the business appraiser. The following sections describe five such provisions.

Selection of the Business Appraiser

The first issue to address in the buy-sell agreement is who selects the business appraiser. What I see most often—which I don't recommend—is where each side hires its own business appraiser, who each values the interests. If the business appraisers are vastly different in their conclusions of value by more than a specified percentage, the two business appraisers or the parties themselves should select a third business appraiser.

The third business appraiser's conclusion of value either governs or is averaged with the conclusions of value that the other two business appraisers reached. Typically, the parties split the cost of the third business appraiser. However, your buy-sell agreement could provide that the third business appraiser's cost be solely borne by the party whose business appraiser's conclusion of value was the farthest from that attained by the third business appraiser. In my opinion, that's a bit too draconian because valuation can be subjective.

As an alternative to the three-appraiser approach, I suggest that each side select a business appraiser, and then have those business appraisers select a business appraiser to conduct the actual business appraisal, which would be the only appraisal. Typically, I would expressly permit the business appraisers to agree that one of them would perform the business appraisal instead of selecting a third business appraiser to do the appraisal. This one-business-appraiser approach should save substantial amounts of money. This is because instead of each side paying for a business appraisal and then generally having to split the cost of the third business appraiser, you're splitting the cost of only one business appraiser. The business appraiser's conclusion of value will be as binding as the third business appraiser's result in the other way to do this that I described earlier.

The "As of" Date

The second provision is the date on which the valuation is to be made, which I identified earlier in the book as the "as of" date. The as of date should be explicit for each of the various triggering events. The business appraisal date can make a significant difference in the conclusion of value, particularly for cyclical businesses.

One tip for the as of date: use the month-end figure from the financial statements for the month ending immediately before the occurrence of the triggering event, as this makes it easier for the business appraiser and less expensive. This is because particular financial statements then don't have to be prepared for an odd date. However, for tax purposes, the date of death or the date of a donation of interests, for example, is the generally employed as of date.

Standard of Value

The third provision is the so-called "standard of value." There are several standards of value, such as fair market value (which is used for tax purposes), fair value (which is typically used for divorce and minority shareholder actions purposes), and intrinsic value. Clearly state the standard of value to be used in the buy-sell agreement.

Premise of Value

The fourth provision is the so-called "premise of value." There are two possible premises of value. The first is the "going concern" premise of value, which calls for the entity to be valued as an ongoing business concern. The second is the "liquidation" premise of value. The liquidation premise of value calls for the entity to be valued as if it was being liquidated in parts and pieces. Most of the time, the premise of value should be that of a "going concern."

Level of Value

The fifth provision is the so-called "level of value." As table 3 shows, there are several different levels of value, and each level sets forth a vastly different value than that produced by another level of value.

Today, the top level of rational value (there is an irrationally high level of value that sits above all of the levels of value) that is believed by most experts to exist is the so-called "strategic" (also called "synergistic") control level of value. This value level assumes both control and a special buyer who has the synergies to make the entity run differently and better than is presently operating.

The next level is the so-called "financial" control level of value. It assumes that the buyer has control of the entity. It further assumes that the buyer of such an interest in such a situation could make the entity work better than it presently does, but not necessarily any differently than it currently operates. This is the difference between the strategic level of value and the financial control level of value.

Table 3: Level of Value

Classic Levels of Value

© L. Paul Hood, Jr. 2019

Another Depiction
of the Levels of Value

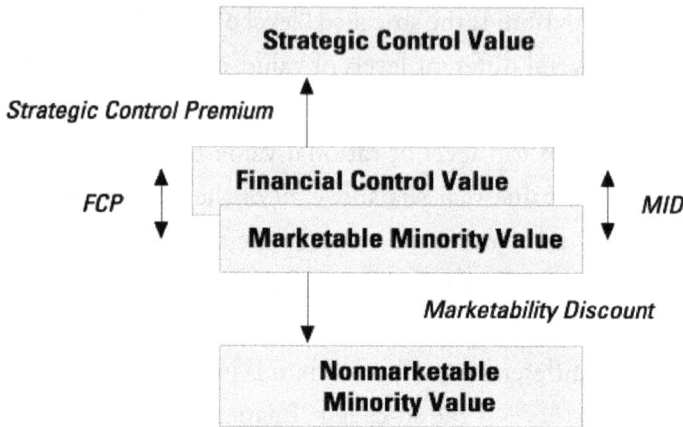

Strategic Control Value

Strategic Control Premium

FCP

Financial Control Value

Marketable Minority Value

MID

Marketability Discount

Nonmarketable
Minority Value

© L. Paul Hood, Jr. 2019

Generally, strategic buyers will pay more than financial buyers because strategic buyers have unique characteristics that enable them to use economies of scale and synergies to transform how the entity operates. The majority of business appraisal experts equate financial control level of value as the top level in the fair market value standard of value used for federal tax purposes.

For example, you are bidding against a company in the same business of the entity you are both are bidding on, but you are not in that same line of business. The competing company could save costs in its acquisition of the entity merely by eliminating duplicate functions that both companies operate (such as an accounts payable department, as only one accounts payable department is necessary). Additionally, the competing company may add to its revenues because the entity provides a "missing piece" or a complementing business that can funnel customers to the competing company. With the ability to both cut costs and add revenues—which you can't do—it should not be surprising that the competing company will offer more for the entity than you can afford to pay because you don't have the same advantages.

The third level of value is the so-called "marketable minority" level of value, which most valuation experts believe is where publicly traded stocks trade on the various stock exchanges every day. This level assumes that the holder is a minority owner, as is the case with just about all publicly traded stock owners.

The bottom level of value is the so-called "nonmarketable minority" level of value, which assumes that the holder of the interest is not in control of the entity and that there is no established market for the interest in such an entity. The lack of a market is what distinguishes publicly traded companies from privately held companies. This is the level that nearly every minority interest in a closely held entity is valued. For example, consider MythiCo and its four equal shareholders. Each of their interests is a nonmarketable minority interest because MythiCo is a private company with no formal market for its stock. Each of their interests is a minority stock holding.

Special Valuation Method for Two-Owner Entity Situations Where There Is a Deadlock

This valuation method should be saved for particular circumstances and should be used in conjunction with the appraisal method. This valuation method would apply in two-owner entities where there is a disagreement on an important issue, where the buy-sell agreement includes this valuation method, and where there is a deadlock. It's simply this: one owner names a price at which their interest could be bought or that he or she would pay for the other owner's interest, and then leaves it up to the other owner to decide either to buy at that price or sell their owner's interest at that price.

This would be a "cutthroat" valuation method unless the offering owner went to the time and expense of having a business appraiser appraise his or her interest and that of the other owner. It is cutthroat because, if the offer price is too high, then the other owner will sell, which might mean that the offering owner overpaid. Alternatively, if it is too low, then the other owner will buy the offering owner's interest, which might mean that the offering owner may have left money on the table.

The only way I know to avoid these two problems is to have a business appraiser appraise both owners' interests. This is because, as I noted early in this chapter, my experience is that frighteningly few owners have any clue as to what their interests are worth. Unless and until someone else makes an offer, they will either accept it, consider it, or reject it because they believe it is too low. Either way, the chances are fair that the owner has no idea of whether or not the offer is good unless and until he or she is assisted by a business valuation professional.

Tax Value for Buy-Sell Agreements

The applicable standard of value for tax purposes is "fair market value." This is defined in Section 20.2031-1(b) of the IRS regulations as "the price at which the property would change hands between a willing buyer and a willing seller, neither being under any compulsion to buy or to sell and both having reasonable knowledge of relevant facts."

The courts assume that the "willing buyer" and "willing seller" are hypothetical people and cannot be identified as a current owner or a likely potential acquirer of an interest. There is a published revenue ruling from the IRS, Revenue Ruling 59-60, that expands on the definition of fair market value of a closely held business interest as involving a consideration of the following factors that are set forth in Section 4 of that ruling:

- the nature of the business and the history of the entity from its inception

- the economic outlook in general and the condition and outlook of the specific industry to which the entity belongs
- the book value of the entity and the financial condition of the entity
- the earning capacity of the entity
- the dividend-paying capacity of the entity
- whether or not the entity has goodwill or other intangible value
- sales of the interests and the size of the block of interests to be valued
- the market price of stocks of corporations engaged in the same or a similar line of business having their stocks actively traded in a free and open market, either on an exchange or over the counter

Many people believe that a buy-sell agreement sets the value of bought and sold interests for all purposes. For nontax purposes, that is probably true. However, for tax purposes, the IRS and the courts have consistently held that the IRS is only bound by the value stipulated in a buy-sell agreement or by a formula set forth in the agreement if all of the following characteristics are satisfied:

- The price must have been fixed or determined by a formula.
- In the case of a death trigger, the estate must be obligated to sell at the price determined under the buy-sell agreement. Mere rights of first refusal in the hands of either the entity or the other owners are insufficient to fix the price for tax purposes.
- The obligation to sell at a price determined under the formula or the price set in the buy-sell agreement must be binding on the owner during lifetime and not just at death.
- The buy-sell agreement must be "a bona fide business arrangement and not a device to pass shares to natural objects of decedent's bounty for less than full and adequate consideration." This quote was taken directly from the case law. It means that the buy-sell agreement must be legitimate and not simply a tool

for an owner to put a lowball value on his or her interest for tax purposes (unless it is a charitable contribution, in which case the roles of the owner and the IRS are "reversed"—the owner arguing for a high value and the IRS arguing for a low value).

Since October 9, 1990, buy-sell agreements for family-owned entities also must satisfy all of the following additional requirements in order for the IRS to respect a fixed price or valuation formula:

- It is a bona fide business arrangement.
- It is not a device to transfer such property to members of the decedent's family for less than full and adequate consideration in money or money's worth.
- Its terms are comparable to similar arrangements entered into by persons in arm's length transactions.

A simple analysis of the first two additional requirements reveals they are almost identical to the last court requirement identified above. The previous requirement is new. This new requirement makes it even harder for family-owned entities to have any fixed price or formula that does not equate to fair market value because you have to know what unrelated parties who are dealing with each other at arm's length are doing, which can be hard to prove. To date, no litigating taxpayer has been able to meet it.

For this reason and many others, many buy-sell agreements use the "fair market value" standard of value for all triggering events because it is well-known and well-developed by case law, even for nontax purposes. Family-owned entity buy-sell agreements generally must use the fair market value standard of value. This is because of the risk that the IRS wouldn't respect the value set forth in the buy-sell agreement and would likely assert that the interest's fair market value is much higher than the value set out in the buy-sell agreement.

Hiring a Business Appraiser

I emphasize that a business appraiser need not be local. Many of my clients did not want a local business appraiser because of the level of detailed information that the appraiser needs about the entity and its business in order to perform his or her work. Some cautious clients were concerned that their companies' confidential information could be inadvertently given to a local competitor if the business appraiser also valued the competitor. I never saw this as a problem.

You can find qualified business appraisers in any of the following organizations by going to their respective websites:

- American Society of Appraisers (ASA). Look for appraisers who do business appraisal work, not real estate appraisal, or any other kind of appraisal work and who have the ASA designation (www.appraisers.org).
- American Institute of Certified Public Accountants. Select a CPA with the ABV certification (www.aicpa.org).
- National Association of Certified Valuators and Analysts. Select CBA or CVA designations (www.nacva.org).

CHAPTER 12

COMMON ERRORS IN BUY-SELL AGREEMENTS

The buy-sell agreement is perhaps one of the most challenging agreements for lawyers of closely held entities to draft. This chapter discusses some of the most perplexing, practical errors found in buy-sell agreements. Failure to discover or address all these problems virtually assures a less than optimal result, and possibly even a lawsuit.

Failure to Coordinate

People rarely focus on the intricacies of buy-sell agreements when forming an entity. Most people usually seek buy-sell agreements after they've already entered into other agreements that can impact buy-sell agreements—articles of incorporation (or organization or partnership), bylaws and operating agreements, loan and security agreements, franchise agreements, and leases. Many of my clients (and many advisors) often do not realize that buy-sell agreements should coordinate with these other agreements and documents. Failure to do so could create needless ambiguity, document conflict, or both. It could even cause a breach of a covenant.

A buy-sell agreement could unintentionally create an event of default, or other triggering event, under another agreement. The consent of a third party, such as a lender or a franchisor, may be required to put a buy-sell agreement into place. It is also possible that local law could provide that another document (e.g., articles of incorporation) could trump the buy-sell agreement to the extent that the two documents are inconsistent. It is impossible for an advisor or a lawyer to draft a buy-sell agreement without a thorough review of the official entity governance documents.

Improper Selection of Type of Buy-Sell Agreement

Most lawyers and advisors are aware that there are essentially three types of buy-sell agreements:

- Redemption buy-sell agreements (where the entity purchases the entity interests)
- Cross-purchase buy-sell agreements (where one or more persons buys the entity interests)
- Hybrid buy-sell agreements (a mix of the cross-purchase and the redemption)

For example, redemption of an owner's interests under a redemption buy-sell agreement, where the remaining owners' interest always increases proportionately, can cause unintended consequences. These consequences can be in the form of a shift in control or giving a parent controlling interest again (often, some neat estate planning had gotten him or her down to an estate tax-saving, noncontrolling position through lifetime gifts of interests). This can happen when a child who already has an interest in an entity dies before the parent. In such a case, the buy-sell agreement provides for an automatic redemption at death of the child's interests, when it was assumed that the parent would die first, giving the child control of the entity after the redemption of the parent's interests.

These out-of-order events happen and must be accounted for in the buy-sell agreement.

Improper Selection of Triggering Events

The number of potential triggering events built into a buy-sell agreement is limited only by the parties' needs and desires. The buy-sell agreement that fails to cover reasonably foreseeable and appropriate triggering events may well have covered those events by not providing for them! However, it may not be productive, or even feasible, to include some triggering events in a situation. For example, a disability buy-sell trigger may have little place in a buy-sell agreement for an entity that generates only passive-type income (e.g., rents), or that produces income that is not dependent on the personal efforts of the owners or where the owners don't work in the business.

I read a court decision where an owner in a passive-income entity was forced to sell at a bargain-basement fixed price in the buy-sell agreement due to an unrelated disability that wasn't in any way affecting or even relevant to the operations of the entity. In my opinion, that disability trigger was inappropriate for that entity's buy-sell agreement since the disabled owner was the investor and never worked for the entity.

As is the case with triggering events, the selection of what occurs upon the occurrence of a triggering event can run the gamut from no action, to mere notice to mandatory buy-and-sell, and all points in between. A mismatch between a triggering event and the rights and obligations that flow from that event can cause serious problems. For example, if an entity is forced to purchase an owner's interest on termination of employment—even if the owner is competing with the entity—the entity will be providing capital to the new competitor.

In that instance, the buy-sell agreement should give the entity, the other owners, or both a call option right (but not an obligation) to purchase the fired owner's interests on favorable installment payment terms that required little, if any, down payment or even at a discounted price. There is nothing that would prevent the entity or the other owners from making a larger down payment to the fired owner for his or her interests. Still, they could take it on a case-by-case basis and not lock into a rigid requirement of always having to put down a sizable down payment.

Vexatious Valuation

The "ostrich" in all of us wants to avoid or defer dealing with problems instead of facing them head-on. This often causes us to gloss over potential hot spots. Valuation in buy-sell agreements is one of these hot spots. I have always suspected that the principal reason people do not focus on valuation when it comes to buy-sell agreements is that, deep down, each sees themselves as the survivor. There are three "ostrich" valuation methods or problems that concern me.

I call the first of the ostrich valuation methods the "crystal ball" or "Schedule A" method: the owners list the agreed value for a buyout sometime in the future on a schedule to the buy-sell agreement. Sometimes these valuation "swamis," who have no valuation experience, agree to update their valuation "prognostications"—sometimes, they don't. But what happens if the Schedule A value is vastly different—either too high or too low—from the fair market value (either when the value is set or when the triggering event occurs)? It is a mistake for owners to come up with their own valuations in Schedule A without a professional business appraiser's guidance.

What happens if well-intentioned but busy owner valuation "swamis" never get around to revisiting the Schedule A value? What if those swamis agree to a Schedule A value method and sign the buy-sell agreement without putting the value on the schedule? These unanswered questions too often get answered by a judge in a courtroom after the parties cannot agree that a set price in the buy-sell agreement is correct and controlling.

The second ostrich valuation method is a gesture toward the positivists in philosophy: an attempt to reduce the valuation determination at some time in the future to a mathematical formula set forth in the buy-sell agreement. The positivists' attempt to conform philosophy to mathematical certitude failed because many philosophical questions cannot be answered with numbers. Likewise, the attempt to reduce the valuation to a mathematical formula almost always produces a similar result. In fact, formula valuations can run an even greater risk of problems than the Schedule A ostrich method discussed above. This is because many formulas can be subject to manipulation or ambiguity as to how the formula is computed or what numbers are used.

As I learned in graduate school, if you torture the numbers long enough, they'll confess to whatever you want them to say. But what happens if the formula is not updated to reflect changes in the business that may have occurred after the ink dried on the buy-sell agreement? What if the valuation formula simply creates a nonsensical number? There have been reported cases where a court has upheld a buy-sell agreement that produced a zero value because that's what the parties negotiated, and the court reasoned that this was what they decided.

A formula valuation method that does not require periodic revisiting with a backup valuation method for disputes or for failures to address the formula presents the same risks as a wayward Schedule A value, or worse. It is a huge mistake to try to develop a valuation formula to put into a buy-sell agreement without either having assistance from a qualified business appraiser or working the formula through before a triggering event occurs to see if the result makes sense.

The third ostrich valuation method is on the opposite end of the spectrum from the other two methods. However, in my judgment, it is an ostrich method because it neglects to consider the commonsense issue of cost. This is the so-called "three-business-appraiser method," where each side picks a business appraiser and the two business appraisers pick a third, all of whom appraise the interest. This can get rather costly. What about considering hiring one business appraiser that is selected by two business appraisers, and then the business appraisers agree that one of them is to value the interests? In my opinion, that makes far more sense than having three business appraisers each value the interests.

However, if you insist on having the classic three-business-appraiser method, then the buy-sell agreement should carefully describe what is to be done with the conclusions of value reached by the business appraisers. Are the findings of value to be averaged? Is it a matter of the third business appraiser deciding whether the conclusions of value that the two business appraisers reached are too far apart? What happens if the two business appraisers cannot agree on the third business appraiser to appraise the interests? Who pays for the work of all these business appraisers? These questions must be clearly answered in the buy-sell agreement that employs the three-business-appraiser method.

Failure to give an appraiser a standard of value in a buy-sell agreement creates several problems. There are standards of value other than fair market value—which probably is the most common—including fair value (often used in divorce cases and certain types of state law corporate lawsuits), and intrinsic value. What level of value is the appraiser to consider? Chapter 11 discusses the levels of value in detail.

What about valuation discounts? Valuation discounts can be a double-edged sword. Frequently, people want valuation discounts when it comes to estate taxes (which is why the IRS frequently attacks valuation discounts) as well as buyers of the interests, who obviously want to pay the lowest price possible. However, this is not universally desired, particularly by those selling their interests and those who want to maximize their profits on the sale.

There's no right or wrong answer on the valuation discount issue. However, if fair market value is the applicable valuation standard, the appraiser will have no choice but to consider valuation discounts for a minority interest (if applicable) and a lack of marketability unless the buy-sell agreement directs the business appraiser otherwise. The best solution to the valuation discount may be to have the buy-sell agreement determine whether valuation discounts are to be used (and which ones are to be considered) on a triggering-event-by-triggering-event basis, such that not every triggering event will take valuation discounts into account.

Life Insurance Issues

It is not unusual for a buy-sell agreement to be funded, at least in part, with life insurance. I often find buy-sell agreements that assume the entire purchase price will be paid with life insurance death proceeds and that make no mention as to what happens if the life insurance death proceeds are insufficient to pay the entire purchase price. This is a deficiency that must be addressed because failure to do so could allow the seller to demand cash up front on the date of selling the interests for the entire purchase price. When a buy-sell agreement is silent on whether or not the seller has the right to pay the balance due in installments, this could cause a hardship for the buyer and even force a default under the agreement.

Another life insurance issue to be addressed is whether or not the life insurance death proceeds relating to life insurance policies that an entity owns are to be counted as an asset of the entity for valuation purposes, even though those proceeds are earmarked for use in the financing of a redemption. Generally, I do not think that the life insurance death proceeds should count, because doing so will inflate the value of the salable interest. They should also not count because their receipt is merely transitory, especially if those death proceeds are required to be paid out to the seller, as they should be in the buy-sell agreement. However, if the buy-sell agreement is silent on the issue, then the death proceeds will most likely count and add value to the interests being sold. The result is that the seller will be paid for an interest with a higher value due to a temporary influx of funds earmarked for the redemption—which doesn't make sense to me.

Failure to Protect the S Election

If the entity is taxed as an S corporation, then the buy-sell agreement should prevent transfers and actions that would cause the loss of the entity's S election. Yet, I often run into buy-sell agreements—that were probably drafted for C corporations—that don't protect the S election. This is a real deficiency in the buy-sell agreement. Moreover, there are several admittedly nuanced, yet important, choices under the law relative to the S corporation that the buy-sell agreement should address.

Failure to Properly Plan for Funding Obligations

It is one thing to have parties agree to take on potential future obligations to purchase. It is quite another to plan how these obligations will be satisfied. As a practical matter, death triggering events can be easier to fund than lifetime triggering events, especially if life insurance is available.

Is funding available on a tax-advantaged basis to the person who is obligated to purchase? For example, suppose that a buy-sell agreement is styled as a cross-purchase, but the insurance or other funding source is within the entity. How will the purchaser get access to the death proceeds to honor the purchase obligation, if the only way to get them out of the entity involves a tax on those otherwise generally tax-free death proceeds? Inquiring minds will want to know. Nevertheless, it is imperative that the parties consider payment sources when putting together a buy-sell agreement. An unfunded buy-sell agreement can be a bigger problem than no buy-sell agreement at all.

Low, Easy Terms

It is usually mere coincidence when the "funding rabbit" pops out of the "money hat" with precisely the right amount of money necessary to consummate the buy-sell agreement transaction. While many buy-sell agreements contain installment payout plans for payments of the purchase price that exceed life insurance (or even life insurance cash values), very few agreements provide much detail or flexibility regarding the amount of installment payouts. In this difficult time of "cut-and-paste," too often, the installment payout period is a vestige from a prior buy-sell agreement.

Sixty months is an installment payout period that I see in a lot of buy-sell agreements. Was any analysis done before picking the installment payout period, or was it also picked out of the "money hat"? Does the buy-sell agreement contain any system for adjusting payments to reflect changed circumstances after the triggering event occurs?

In C corporations, it is important not to tie the installment payments to the corporate earnings. That will cause the redemption to fail as a capital transaction—which means dividends and ordinary income to the selling owner, instead.

One common problem that I see in this respect is that the buyout obligation comes before the first buyout obligation is paid out. The entity can afford to pay for one buyout, but not for two at the same time. What does one tell the heirs of the second owner who died? "Sorry you'll have to wait?" The buy-sell agreement can and should address this situation by reducing by half the payments being made to the first seller to accommodate obligations to the second one, and then by thirds, if a third buyout obligation occurs, and so forth.

Divorce as a Triggering Event

I often run into buy-sell agreements that address divorce as a triggering event, which is fine and dandy. No one wants to be in business with their co-owner's ex, especially if the spouse owner is still an owner after the divorce, as it may make for an uncomfortable workplace. However, to the extent that there is a divorce, what does the buy-sell agreement provide? Does it give the divorcing owner the prior right to acquire the interests of his or her spouse? In my opinion, the answer to this question should be a resounding "yes!" Nevertheless, I see buy-sell agreements that simply call for either the other owners or the entity to be given the obligation or option to acquire the ex-spouse's interest instead of the divorcing owner. This is a deficiency in the buy-sell agreement that frequently gets exposed, especially given the high incidence of divorce.

The Spouse as Potential Owner or Controller of Interests

Many buy-sell agreements permit transfers to permitted transferees, which often include trusts. However, it may not always be wise to permit the spouse, now a surviving spouse in a death transfer, to either own outright or control interests in the entity by virtue of being the trustee or even the executor of the deceased owner's estate that owns interests. You have no real experience with the surviving spouse as a fellow owner, only as the spouse of an owner. It is often prudent to give the entity or the remaining owners an option to acquire those interests, for at least a long enough period to gauge how easy or difficult the surviving spouse is to work with. Not enough buy-sell agreements broach this subject, yet it is always on everyone's mind.

However, prohibiting all spousal transfers can seriously impinge on a common estate tax deferral device: a spousal transfer, which can either be outright or in trust. I recommend that a testamentary QTIP (qualified terminable interest property trust—permitted under Section 2056(b)(7) of the Internal Revenue Code) trust be permitted by the buy-sell agreement to be an owner, provided that

- the principal beneficiaries of the QTIP trust, who will receive the ownership interest on the subsequent death of the surviving spouse, are permitted transferees (e.g., being descendants of the deceased owner) under the buy-sell agreement;

- and the trustee of the QTIP trust is either a permitted transferee (e.g., a descendant of the owner) or is a corporate trustee.

This, of course, may not please the surviving spouse, who is being denied control over what may be their only source of income. Still, I believe that it strikes a fair balance between not wanting the spouse as an owner at all and not forcing an automatic sale of the interests at the owner's death.

Blanket Prohibition of Lifetime Transfers of Interests for Estate Tax Planning Purposes

I have seen buy-sell agreements that go to the extreme and try to prohibit all lifetime transfers by owners, even for estate planning purposes. This type of rigidity usually catches owners by surprise after the fact. Most buy-sell agreements should permit some lifetime estate planning motivated transfers, particularly to revocable living trusts and estate tax savings in the form of gifts to children, especially those who will be working in the entity's business. The failure of a buy-sell agreement to harmonize with the owners' estate planning desires can be a big problem. However, as previously noted, one of the disadvantages of this agreement is the loss of some personal flexibility in transferring your interests as you see fit. However, most people would rather trade the flexibility for assurance of a set procedure for transferring interests, which a buy-sell agreement provides.

A related problem is putting too severe a restriction on lifetime transfers, such as only permitting them with all of the owners' consent. This could cause a gift tax issue if the interests were first given to the donees but then subjected to the harsh no-transfer restriction. Since there is not much that the donees can do with the interests, and if the interests aren't receiving income from the entity, the IRS may successfully argue that the gift was of a "future interest" instead of a "present interest."

This makes a difference on whether the gift qualifies as a tax-free annual exclusion gift. Taxpayers who have put these types of harsh restrictions on transfers have lost several court cases to the IRS on this score.

Subsequent Sales of the Entity

The buy-sell agreement should provide what happens with respect to subsequent sales of all or substantially all of the assets of the entity or all of the interests in the entity to a third party. It is reasonable to provide for acceleration of any remaining installment payments as the reason why the installment agreement was initially entered into was due to a lack of cash liquidity. If a subsequent sale solves that problem, then the selling owner should receive the balance of what is owed to him or her. Yet, I continue to see buy-sell agreements that do not provide for such acceleration, which is a great deficiency.

Although it is rare, the buy-sell agreement should provide an increase in the compensation paid to a selling owner if the entity is sold for a higher price—at some point in the reasonable future—than what the owner sold his or her interests for (e.g., two years after the owner's sale of interests). Or even provide a sliding percentage scale downward as the time gets further away from the date that the selling owner sold his or her interests.

Lack of Trust

Buy-sell agreements frequently permit interests to be held in an owner's trust. However, it is common for there to be restrictions on the trustee. Suppose a disgruntled minority interest owner holds his or her shares in a revocable living trust (a permitted transferee under the buy-sell agreement). The buy-sell agreement doesn't say who may or who may not be a trustee of such a trust. Nothing would prevent that owner from changing the trustee of his or her revocable living trust to an owner of a competing entity, which would be highly undesirable to the other owners.

The buy-sell agreement should consider having both affirmative requirements (e.g., the trustee must be the owner or a descendant of an owner) and negative requirements (e.g., the trustee can't also own interests in a competitor).

Failure to Provide for Methods of Dispute Resolution

The courthouse is not the only place to resolve disputes in buy-sell agreements. This isn't clear as most buy-sell agreements provide no means of dispute resolution other than court, which is very expensive and usually an unsatisfactory experience. Buy-sell agreements should provide for some means of mediation and arbitration of disputes arising out of buy-sell agreements and set out basic rules or guidelines for arbitration and mediation.

Family Issues

Very few buy-sell agreements for family entities address the family and descendants issues that frequently arise in successful family entities. By "successful," I mean those family entities that last past one generation.

A buy-sell agreement should address the issue of children who work in the business and who own interests as well as children who don't work in the business but who also own interests. This can be a continuing thorn in the side of a family entity. Children who work in the business typically do not appreciate the restrictions that their siblings who are owners but don't work for the entity place on them. It would be beneficial for an entity to give the children who don't work in the entity's business nonvoting interests (but still allow them to select management representatives and vote on extraordinary matters) while giving the children who do work in the business the voting interests. Each situation is different. Another family issue that is rarely addressed, but should be, is accounting for the fact that families tend to fan out and become less cohesive over generations. I address this in the following paragraphs.

It is important to maintain equal ownership of interests down a generational line. This way, no branch of a family can gain control over the entity and effectively over the fate of now-cousins' interests. For example, I have three children, Aimee, Belinda, and Chase, who work in the business and co-own interests with me (the "senior generation"). We have a buy-sell agreement that provides for a right of first refusal on attempted transfers to persons outside of the family and the ability to pass interests down to their descendants.

Let's suppose I die and leave the balance of my interests to my three children equally, such that they are now equal owners of all the entity. When my children start their own estate planning and have children wanting to work in the business, should the buy-sell agreement provide for a prior right along, say, Aimee's descendant line for her descendants to have a first crack at purchasing the interests of another member of her descendant line who wants to sell? This is what most people want when asked about it, but the overwhelming majority of buy-sell agreements for family entities that I see fail to provide for that, often because the drafting advisor failed to ask the question about fanning out generations. Moreover, it is usually important to the family's various branches that the relative ownership percentages of the branches be maintained to the fullest extent possible, yet very few buy-sell agreements that I see adequately address that concern.

The best way to handle these issues is to either separate the ownership by branch of the family, such that each branch owns a different class of ownership, or to define the word "family" in the buy-sell agreement to mean a particular branch of the family. I've found that either way works satisfactorily.

Bad Surprise Boilerplate

People often sign what they think are standard buy-sell agreements, but the first mistake is assuming that there is something known as a "standard buy-sell agreement"—it does not exist. These buy-sell agreements are rigid one-purpose buy-sell agreements that are not explained to the signers before the buy-sell agreement is signed.

There's an old Spanish proverb that states "Drink nothing without seeing it; sign nothing without reading it." This saying can apply to buy-sell agreements. You should not sign a buy-sell agreement without first having at least several discussions among your co-owners—and with your advisors—as to your collective concerns and desires.

Table 2, The Buy-Sell Agreements Grid, can be a helpful way to capture what you want to happen on just one page. You can then give the completed page to your advisors for review and comments. Once that is done, your lawyer can then draft a buy-sell agreement that fits your situation.

Failing to Keep a Buy-Sell Agreement Current

Just because you persevere and take the buy-sell agreement to completion does not mean that it is over. I have seen perfectly good buy-sell agreements go stale and out of date. This can happen for any number of reasons. Perhaps some new owners have not signed the buy-sell agreement and somehow acquired their interests without having to acknowledge and agree to the buy-sell agreement terms. Perhaps the funding mechanism changed. Perhaps the installment payout period is wrong under the current finances of the entity. There are lots of other reasons as well. The bottom line is that you must read your buy-sell agreement at least once a year to see if it is current and still aligns with what you all want.

I strongly recommend that every three to five years, your advisors and your lawyer review your buy-sell agreement, as well as upon the occurrence of significant events such as a triggering event, a significant change in the business, or an addition of a new owner.

Too Many People Involved Who Are Not Informed about the Agreement

While not a problem per se with the buy-sell agreement, sometimes the failure of your advisors to work together or communicate with each other can create problems in the buy-sell agreement, particularly in creating the agreement. For example, I've seen situations where the buy-sell agreement contemplated funding purchase obligations triggered by death of an owner with life insurance. Yet, the life insurance agent for each owner wasn't made aware of the need for a policy, the need for a policy restructuring, or the fact that the buy-sell agreement was either being written or revised. I have seen several of these situations. I've seen situations where, had the life insurance agent been made aware of the ongoing buy-sell agreement process, he could have come forward with material information that could have dramatically impacted how the buy-sell agreement was drafted (such as disclosing that an owner is uninsurable when the owner didn't inform the lawyer). Likewise, your accountant needs to be brought into the process, particularly if you are going to tempt fate and attempt to use a formula valuation method.

Forgetting Related Properties

It's one thing to provide for the sale of ownership interests. It's quite another to consider related property. Related property can include life insurance policies on the life of the selling owner, life insurance policies on the other owners which the selling owner owns, interests in affiliated companies, or interests in land or other property co-owned by some or all of the remaining owners (e.g., property on which a business operates), intellectual property, leases, or other contractual obligations.

Relationships, needs, and interests frequently change after a sale of interests in an entity. For example, a former business entity owner may care more about how much the entity pays in rent for the property that he or she continues to co-own after a sale. Failure to address these continuing relationships at the time of the buy-sell agreement can negatively impact operations down the road. It is not always necessary to solve this problem with the required sale of all related property. Sometimes, a lease that ensures that the entity will pay fair market value rent is all that is necessary.

Failure to Carefully Coordinate Triggering Events with Responses to Triggering Events

The last two points pertain to many, if not all, of the preceding points, all of which are interrelated. For example, selecting a triggering event must be carefully coordinated with the rights and obligations that are triggered by that event. Those rights and obligations must, in turn, be carefully coordinated with the terms of installment payout for any purchased interest. For example, suppose any termination of employment triggers a right of the terminated owner to force the entity to purchase his or her interest for cash. In that case, it may be impossible to ever fire that owner, even one who does nothing productive for the entity.

If death is the event that forces the deceased owner and another owner into a mandatory buy-and-sell for cash, it may present the purchaser with a significant, overbearing financial hardship, thereby exposing the deceased owner's estate.

One Size Does Not Fit All

Buy-sell considerations differ from owner to owner, and from triggering event to triggering event. A buy-sell agreement that applies the same triggering events—or rights and obligations flowing therefrom—to every owner runs a serious risk of fomenting controversy. Each owner is different, as is each triggering event. For example, consider a situation where there are two owners, one of whom has a child working in the entity's business and one of whom doesn't. Is it appropriate to force the owner whose child is working in the business to sell at death? Probably not. Is it appropriate to restrict that owner from making lifetime gifts or sales of entity interests to that child? Again, probably not.

As previously discussed, not every triggering event should produce the same rights and obligations even as to the same owner. Remember the termination of employment trigger. There are "good guy" reasons for termination, such as retirement or disability or termination without cause. And then there are "bad guy" reasons, such as competing with the entity, termination for cause, or pilfering.

CHAPTER 13

WORKING WITH PROFESSIONAL ADVISORS

I n this chapter, I discuss working with professional advisors in putting together a buy-sell agreement or reviewing a buy-sell agreement that is already in place. I will also discuss how to find and evaluate professional advisors you may be thinking about hiring to assist you with your buy-sell agreement.

Contrary to what you might read elsewhere, you probably will not be able to create your own buy-sell agreement from scratch without help. This book is intended to provide you with tools to assist in the formulation of a tailor-made buy-sell agreement for your entity. Because of state law and tax considerations involving buy-sell agreements, I know you will need competent professional assistance in this task.

One of my main goals in writing this book is to give you the preliminary education and background on buy-sell agreements so you can make informed decisions in a cost-efficient manner and to help you help yourself. For example, you could simply complete the one-page Buy-Sell Agreements Grid (refer to table 2 in chapter 9) and give it to your lawyer and other professional advisors, together with the documentation listed in the Buy-Sell Agreement Review Checklist (included at the end of this book). Your lawyer, assuming that he or she is competent and knowledgeable in buy-sell agreements, should be able to draft your buy-sell agreement based on your choices and get it close, if not perfect, in just one draft, which should save you significant legal fees. Even if it takes more than one draft, you and your professional advisors will still be better informed about the issues regarding your desires and fears.

Before I developed the Buy-Sell Agreements Grid many years ago, one of the biggest problems I routinely faced with buy-sell agreement clients was that I often had to modify the draft agreement multiple times. The clients didn't know or didn't understand all of the available options for triggering events and responses, probably because I failed to explain them completely or properly. The Buy-Sell Agreements Grid significantly reduced the number of draft buy-sell agreement versions that I had to prepare, which saved my clients significant fees.

How to Evaluate and Select Professional Advisors

Selecting and evaluating professional advisors is always difficult because clients generally start off at a significant knowledge disadvantage. I hope that this book reduces your knowledge disadvantage, as that was my intent in writing it. After reading this, you may find yourself knowing as much (or more) about the workings of your buy-sell agreement as your professional advisor, which is as it should be, in my opinion.

Too often, professional advisors are placed in the difficult position of deciding significant matters for their clients, either because the client lacks the knowledge to make an informed decision or wants the advisor to make the decision for him or her. Of the latter of these reasons, I always tried to avoid that by not permitting clients to abdicate important decisions about their lives and the lives of their loved ones or business partners to me if I could help it.

So, your next question is likely to be, "Well, Paul, how do you select and evaluate professional advisors?" That is an excellent question. I have a lot of personal experience as I have been a client of several other professional advisors. For starters, I tend to select professional advisors based not on what they tell me, but on what they ask me. In my opinion, good pointed and piercing questions usually demonstrate significant knowledge—much more so than a professional advisor who does all of the talking, trying to demonstrate his or her knowledge of the subject matter of your particular problem.

I also evaluate a professional advisor on their ability to listen to what I am saying, in contrast to rehearsing a rote reply in their head while I talk. Professional advisors who listen before talking always make me feel validated. The ones who launch into a "solution" before really listening to me and the problem are a waste of my time.

With respect to selecting professional advisors, I often base my decisions on word-of-mouth experiences from actual clients or persons familiar with those who were happy with their advisor. However, this is not always possible. So, how would you find a professional advisor who knows the ins and outs of buy-sell agreements? I was a practicing lawyer, so that's the profession that I know best, although I've indeed hired professional advisors other than lawyers. Generally, the lawyers who tend to know the most about buy-sell agreements are tax lawyers, estate planning lawyers, or corporate lawyers. This is where I would start.

Bar associations in many jurisdictions recognize lawyers as specialists in taxation and estate planning. Some jurisdictions may even recognize corporate law as a specialty (though I am not familiar with any). Find a few of those lawyers in your geographical area. You also might check with the American College of Trust and Estate Counsel (www.actec. org) for estate planning lawyers, as it is the preeminent organization for estate planning specialists.

For tax lawyers, check with the American College of Tax Counsel (www.actconline.org), the preeminent organization for tax law specialists. From there, you can seek some information from your prospective lawyer about his or her direct experience with putting together buy-sell agreements.

Instead of asking whether the lawyer knows how to draft a buy-sell agreement (all will answer yes), consider asking the following questions:

- How often do you draft or review buy-sell agreements?
- How many buy-sell agreements have you revised or drafted?

You may have to get this information from the lawyer's assistant, since many lawyers will not talk to you until they are hired, for fear of having a conflict of interest from the outset. So, if this happens to you, it's okay and not personal. The lawyer is being cautious and looking out for everyone's interests by trying to avoid a conflict of interests. This is a good sign.

However, you should be given the information if the lawyer is taking on clients and is interested in representing you since buy-sell agreements can be a significant source of future legal business. If the lawyer grants courtesy no-charge interviews (I didn't, and it's okay if the lawyer that you want to interview doesn't), certainly take him or her up on the offer since you can gauge the lawyer's focus on you and on details simply by watching him or her in action. You also can evaluate in person whether you could work with that lawyer.

Your next question probably is: "How much is this going to cost?" I'm a lawyer, so the answer to that question is: "It depends." However, buy-sell agreements are an investment and are considered very important—much more so than mere entity governance documents. Therefore, you can expect to pay a high price. Do not be turned off by a lawyer's hourly rate, especially one that strikes you as high—which it likely will be (they all will seem high, especially if you don't hire lawyers often).

What's more important than the lawyer's hourly rate is how long it will take the lawyer to perform the task. I was a very expensive lawyer on an hourly basis, with some of the highest hourly rates in the area. However, when you consider that I performed tasks in my practice areas in far less time than a lawyer who charges a lot less per hour but who is not as well versed in the subject matter, it actually saved my clients money in the long run.

If you do get an interview with either the lawyer or the lawyer's personal assistant, ask for a range of possible fees that you could expect. An experienced lawyer will usually be able to give you a ballpark range even though a careful lawyer will not tie himself or herself to that range. If the lawyer is being asked to draft a buy-sell agreement where the parties are clear about what they want and where there will be no back-and-forth negotiation, it should cost significantly less than a full-blown, fully negotiated buy-sell agreement. Those can get very pricey because you are not controlling the negotiation process.

I almost always provided clients with a range of estimated time to accomplish a task. I could do this because I had usually done something similar before. It is harder to give a price range when you are working on a fully negotiated buy-sell agreement. I also often requested a retainer in an amount that I estimated was the lower end of the range of expected total fees. This is common. Do not let it deter you from hiring the lawyer who has impressed you as someone who you could work with and who knows his or her stuff.

Who Should Be on Your Advisor Team?

If you are contemplating putting together or revising a buy-sell agreement, you will need a lawyer, since a lawyer is the only person (other than yourself) who can legally help you draft a buy-sell agreement. But there are other professionals you should also have on your team.

For starters, a good Certified Public Accountant (CPA) who is well versed in buy-sell agreements and the taxation of entities such as corporations and partnerships can be an invaluable part of your team. Not every CPA will be knowledgeable about buy-sell agreements and entity taxation. For example, a CPA might do nothing but audit work or only work the individual's taxation. You will want to find a CPA who works in corporate or partnership tax.

Conduct the same experience inquiries with a CPA that I suggested using for evaluating and selecting a lawyer. If you can get a free interview with the CPA, then go for it. Ask the CPA how many buy-sell agreements they have dealt with and exactly what their experience is with respect to the taxation issues and the exercise of rights under buy-sell agreements.

In many ways, a CPA is as valuable as a lawyer, if not more so. A client's relationship with a CPA often is closer and more recurrent than a relationship with a lawyer, particularly one who drafts buy-sell agreements and whose services might not be needed for a long time. This is because the CPA often prepares tax returns every year and might even do bookkeeping work every month.

If you are contemplating using life insurance or disability buyout insurance to assist with the funding of your buy-sell agreement obligations, then you will need the services of a qualified insurance professional who has experience in these matters. Despite my repeated warnings against it, some of you will still contemplate using either a fixed price valuation mechanism or a valuation formula. If so, I implore you, beg you even, to engage the services of a qualified business appraiser who specializes in business valuation and who does that kind of work most of the time, as opposed to merely dabbling in business valuation.

If you are going to use the fixed price valuation mechanism, neither you nor your fellow owners have any experience in business valuation and shouldn't be setting your own price to be used to actually buy and sell interests in the company. To me, doing so is like playing Russian roulette. Sooner or later, someone is going to lose and lose badly. The only question is, will it be your turn when the triggering event happens to you, and you are either forced to buy or to sell at a ridiculous (in either direction) price? You'll have to take my word for it that these types of travesties happen with some frequency, because if someone has an advantage—courtesy of a fixed price that is too high or too low—you can expect that person to force the other side to follow the buy-sell agreement, which is a contract. Courts are loath to rescue someone who made a bad deal for himself or herself.

The Ethical Issues

It is important to recognize that your professional advisors have rules about ethics that will influence their behavior in your matter, often restraining them. If you're like most people, you want all the owners to get just one lawyer to advise and draft the buy-sell agreement. The problem is, right or wrong, that the lawyer sees multiple people (including the entity) in that situation who may have different interests to protect, which may be so pervasive that the lawyer can't or won't represent all of you at the same time. The careful lawyer has no choice but to see the situation that way. If you run into this, it's not unusual. The lawyer is trying to be cautious. The stark fact is that if the lawyer simultaneously represents all of you, he or she may not give your interests the same attention and undivided loyalty that you need and deserve.

The lawyer who takes on more than one client in the same matter may well ask those clients to sign off on waiving any conflict of interest between the parties. This is common and is not out of the ordinary. However, it does not mean that you always should waive the conflict. You might be better off with your own separate lawyer, particularly if your interests are unique and conflict with the other owner's interests.

I drafted many buy-sell agreements where I only represented the entity and not any of the owners individually, even if I represented one or more of the owners individually in different matters. However, I have also participated in putting together buy-sell agreements where every owner had their own lawyer, so the buy-sell agreement was the product of a negotiated, collaborative effort. This is a much more expensive way to proceed, considering that every owner is paying their own lawyer, but is one in which every owner has the luxury of having his or her own lawyer looking out for just his or her interests.

It's purely up to you as to which way to proceed. However, you should know that there is a trade-off choice to be made: less cost or less attention and focus on your unique issues. Even if your entity is just starting, I can't tell you which way is best for you. I can see situations, such as becoming a minority owner where someone else is the majority owner, where you probably should consider having your own lawyer. However, in the end, you will have to make that decision for yourself.

A Final Word about Your Professional Advisors and This Book

I have expressed my opinions on many points in this book, which, even though they are based on my years of experience, are still only my opinions. For example, the buy-sell agreement clauses in this book do not constitute the only way—or even the best way—to draft a particular clause, as your professional advisor probably has his or her own way of putting together or drafting buy-sell agreements. Nevertheless, the book and accompanying clauses and checklist will help your advisor help you and might even help a professional advisor navigate some of the thorny issues that arise in buy-sell agreements.

CHAPTER 14

FOR PROFESSIONAL ADVISORS

You may be wondering why a book that I wrote for the layperson on buy-sell agreements would include a chapter written expressly for professional advisors. I decided to do this because there are many points of consideration in putting together or even reviewing and revising a buy-sell agreement that are technical and thus best suited for the professional advisor. I felt that I had to give my thoughts on those points.

I also wanted to demonstrate to professional advisors how using this book for clients can make their jobs easier in putting together and advising on what is, without any doubt in my mind, the hardest entity document to get right. Moreover, perhaps the professional advisors aren't as up on buy-sell agreements as they need to be to assist their clients with these agreements or may just need a good review of some hot-button issues to watch out for and avoid. I wanted to give professional advisors the benefit of my thoughts that are derived from more than thirty years of experience working with, reviewing, crafting, and even making mistakes on buy-sell agreements.

I believe that even a seasoned advisor could benefit from reading this book, as it is full of practical tips that I've learned over the years, sometimes by making the same mistakes I chronicle here. I will not repeat all the useful tips in this chapter. However, if I had to select only two chapters that a professional advisor should read before assisting a client with a buy-sell agreement, it would be this chapter and chapter 9. They address some of the common errors that professional advisors and clients make in putting together buy-sell agreements and serve as an excellent reminder of which areas to focus on avoiding.

Top Twenty-One Traps

This entire chapter could have easily been titled the "Top Twenty-One Traps" because I'll be discussing twenty-one specific traps to watch out for when drafting buy-sell agreements that are critical to their success.

1. Blowing the Marital Deduction

This error can come back to haunt a professional advisor since it is avoidable and can lead to a malpractice claim against the advisor. It is critical to remember that this error applies to all buy-sell agreements that involve an interest in a QTIP trust or, for the reasons described later in this section, possibly even to an outright disposition to a surviving spouse. It is irrelevant that the entity is not a family-owned entity; this mistake can happen in any buy-sell agreement that permits a decedent to either retain his or her interests for the benefit of loved ones or that requires a sale pursuant to the buy-sell agreement. This mistake is also an excellent reason why the fair market value standard of value should be used in every buy-sell agreement in which a surviving spouse or a QTIP trust may be forced to sell the interest (which is just about every buy-sell agreement that requires sale at death) either to the other owners or back to the entity. This would be at a price other than fair market value (e.g., pursuant to a valuation formula, book value, or at a price set in the buy-sell agreement), where a marital deduction is desired.

In this instance, if the surviving spouse or a QTIP trust is required to sell at a price other than fair market value, the IRS will assert and successfully argue in court that the deceased owner's estate should lose the entire marital deduction. This is because the surviving spouse may have to sell for less than fair market value, meaning that someone other than the surviving spouse will receive part of the property during the surviving spouse's life. This violates the QTIP requirement that only the surviving spouse be entitled to any of the QTIP property during his or her lifetime. Look at Rinaldi's Estate v. United States., 97-2 U.S.T.C. 60,281 (Ct. Cl. 1997), aff'd., 178 F. 3d 1308 (Fed. Cir. 1998), cert. denied, 526 U.S. 1006 (1999). Also refer to TAM 9139001 (book value price per the buy-sell agreement was far less than fair market value of the stock) and TAM 9147065 (fixed price in the buy-sell agreement was less than the fair market value of the stock).

I am also concerned that a marital deduction for even an outright bequest of interests to a surviving spouse will be limited by any such right to force the interests to be sold for less than fair market value to the value prescribed in the buy-sell agreement (i.e., at book value or pursuant to a formula or set price because that is what the spouse is entitled to under the terms of the buy-sell agreement), which could expose the estate to needless estate taxation. My point is that you should use fair market value for all spousal transfers. This is because you will not know when you put together the buy-sell agreement whether the stipulated price or pricing method will equate to fair market value or what the estate tax situation of the owner and his or her spouse will be at the time of the owner's death. Therefore, if you should use fair market value for this purpose, why not make it applicable to all transfers, including spousal transfers?

2. Losing the Right to Defer the Federal Estate Tax under Section 6166 of the Internal Revenue Code

As I discussed in chapter 3, a frequent disadvantage of a buy-sell agreement is that it can cause the loss of the right to defer the federal estate tax under Section 6166 of the Internal Revenue Code. However, I never worried too much about that. For starters, very few owners will have to worry about the federal estate tax. Of the ones who do, many will arrange their personal estate planning in such a way as to create the necessary liquidity.

In my opinion, Section 6166 is far from perfect and really should only be used as the technique for a very last resort. Nevertheless, there are ways to reduce the negative effects of loss of the deferral right in buy-sell agreements. This is done by structuring the purchase of the interests of a particular owner who needs to rely on Section 6166 as a redemption, even being able to tie the redemption to Section 303 redemptions.

3. Loss of Credit Financing

The transfer restrictions contained in a buy-sell agreement frequently foreclose the ability to borrow money or use third-party financing to pay the purchase price. As discussed in chapter 3, this is one of the few disadvantages of a buy-sell agreement. However, I view its loss as a cost of doing business. Nevertheless, the owners may agree, on a case-by-case basis, to waive the "no encumbrances" clause for an owner who demonstrates a need.

4. Excess Life Insurance Proceeds

Most clients want to provide all they can for the benefit of their families. When an entity acquires life insurance on the owners' lives, some clients want to provide that any excess life insurance proceeds (i.e., above and beyond the purchase price for their interests in the entity) would go to their families. This is a nice idea, but it is a really big mistake to do it that way. In this case, the excess life insurance death proceeds will be taxed twice. First, the excess proceeds will be taxed in the gross estate under Section 2038 of the Internal Revenue Code, if the estate is a taxable estate. Then, all of the excess life insurance death proceeds will be taxable income to the recipient heir or the estate because they weren't paid pursuant to the life insurance policy beneficiary designation and covered by the tax-free shield of Section 101 of the Internal Revenue Code. Instead, they were payable by the entity. (Refer to IRS Private Letter Ruling 8943082.)

This is how I dealt with this issue and gave the client exactly what was desired: to simply provide that the floor price for an interest redeemed by virtue of death in the buy-sell agreement cannot be lower than the total life insurance death proceeds owned and received by the entity. This will generally keep the insurance out of the estate and, to the extent permitted by the transaction (i.e., where it is a capital gain transaction), the proceeds will only be taxed if the price exceeds the estate's basis in the interests, which just got reset to fair market value by virtue of the owner's death. Therefore, this should result in little to no gain, which transforms an otherwise doubly taxable mistake into a hopefully tax-free transaction.

5. Inadvertent Bias against the Impecunious Owner

You have to be careful not to inadvertently create bias in the buy-sell agreement against owners who cannot realistically exercise a purchase option contained in the buy-sell agreement (e.g., where an all-cash purchase price is required, and an owner cannot pay it). If you don't draft the buy-sell agreement in such a way as to permit installment payouts at the purchaser's option, then a right in the hands of someone who lacks the resources to exercise it is no real right at all.

6. Inadvertent Cost Bias against Certain Owners

It is almost unavoidable that you will encounter situations where, due to age disparities, insurability, or ownership size differentials between the owners, it's going to cost some owners more to insure or purchase the interests of a fellow owner.

You should be careful not to create or exacerbate bias against certain owners who must incur greater costs under the buy-sell agreement (e.g., a younger, healthier owner who is required to carry insurance on the life of his or her older, less healthy co-owner). This would be the case in a cross-purchase buy-sell agreement where life insurance is owned and paid for by the individual owners. In this event, perhaps recommending a redemption buy-sell agreement (where the costs could be essentially shared between the owners), or, if other reasons still militate in favor of a cross-purchase buy-sell agreement, suggesting that the younger owner's compensation be adjusted upward to assist with the insurance premium burden. However, that solution could create another problem as well as some client pushback if the older owner owns a larger interest and feels that he or is she is asked to pay for his or her own buyout, so you have to take it on a case-by-case basis.

7. Using Buy-Sell Agreement Forms Drafted by Someone Else without Understanding Every Word in the Document

This point drives me insane, yet it happens a lot. I realize that some people will use the model forms associated with this book without reading them and understanding them fully, despite my repeated warnings and explanations. However, these people do not understand that this is probably the number one reason why a buy-sell agreement brings about a suboptimal result. So why do it? I realize that there are time and cost pressures, but a malpractice suit over a poorly drafted buy-sell agreement that you didn't even draft since it was the shoddy work of someone else is no fun and costs a lot of time, money, and heartache.

Every buy-sell agreement is crafted with a specific purpose in mind. Therefore, when you use, for example, specimen buy-sell agreements provided by a life insurance company, the document probably only contemplates a triggering event that involves life insurance (i.e., a death buyout). Every buy-sell agreement form that you find was probably drafted with certain purposes and considerations in mind, and it might not be any good or useful for your client. You just don't know unless you invest the time in reading and understanding every word you intend to use.

8. Failing to Properly Account for the Fact That Owner-Employees and Owner-Nonemployees Often Have Different Objectives

Situations where there are owners who work as employees of the entity and owners who do not work for the entity often create conflict. You should keep in mind that this conflict is due to each having their respective objectives that differ from each other. There are many points in a buy-sell agreement where striking a healthy balance between the owner-employees' objectives and the owner-nonemployees' will need to happen, or the two sides will ultimately clash over those differences.

For example, the buy-sell agreement in such an instance probably should provide for outside third parties to review the compensation of the owner-employees. This is because compensation is so often in dispute, with the owner-employee claiming that their compensation is too low and the owner-nonemployee arguing the opposite. It is critical that you point out to the parties where these potential hot spots are in advance so that the various points of view are heard and considered. This is the only way a true compromise resolution that can be memorialized in the buy-sell agreement can occur.

216

9. Failing to Structure a Redemption to Qualify for Redemption Capital Gain Treatment under Federal Corporate Tax Laws to the Fullest Extent Possible

As a general proposition, you should be intimately familiar with the tax consequences in advance of drafting or making recommendations. If you're unsure of the tax consequences, then consider reading chapters 6, 7, and 8 of this book. In those chapters, I've attempted to describe the particular tax consequences of the redemption buy-sell agreement, cross-purchase buy-sell agreement, and hybrid buy-sell agreement.

One area that I routinely see in redemption buy-sell agreements is the failure to consider whether or not the proposed redemption will qualify for capital gains treatment. Whether you're drafting the buy-sell agreement or advising on an upcoming redemption, you should structure the redemption in such a way as to qualify for capital gains treatment to the fullest extent possible. This is particularly problematic in buy-sell agreements for family-owned entities.

10. Creating a Taxable Dividend in a Hybrid Buy-Sell Agreement

One can create a taxable dividend in a hybrid buy-sell agreement in a corporation where the corporation redeems one owner's stock when the taxpaying shareholder had the primary obligation to purchase the stock.

Be careful when drafting hybrid or wait-and-see buy-sell agreements for corporations and when crafting the cascading options and obligations to purchase. If the shareholders are obligated to purchase (as opposed to merely possessing an option to purchase) but the corporation actually purchases the stock, then the owners who were obligated to purchase will have a taxable dividend because the corporation relieved them of their purchase obligation. (Refer to Rev. Rul. 69-608.)

How should this be done? If you are using a classic wait-and-see hybrid buy-sell agreement, the corporation should have the first call option right, followed by a second call option right (but not an obligation to purchase) in the hands of the shareholders, followed by an obligation of the corporation to purchase whatever shares weren't acquired via exercise of the two cascading call option rights. This will permit the shareholders the luxury of deciding whether to structure the buyout as a redemption or as a cross-purchase, based on the existing financial and tax circumstances.

11. Using a Purchase Price Formula that Is Inappropriate for the Type of Business Being Valued

In my opinion, attempting to concoct a valuation formula for a closely held business interest, particularly without the assistance of a full-time business valuation professional (as opposed to someone who "dabbles" in business valuation), is a fool's errand and is close to malpractice. However, if you disagree and are hell-bent on using a formula in the buy-sell agreement, at least do a little research to determine the proper type formula to use for the entity's business. Some industries are more susceptible to certain types of formulas (but do not use a "rule of thumb," as that is nothing more than a quick and dirty valuation result).

I ran into a lawyer a while back who disagreed with me on this point. He used what he thought was a brilliantly crafted valuation formula for every buy-sell agreement that he drafted, reasoning that all businesses are pretty much the same and this saves business appraisal fees. I asked this lawyer if he'd ever run any numbers through the formula to see how close it came to the actual fair market value or if he had done any research in a real case where the formula result could be compared to the result that a business appraiser reached. He had not done either. My next question to him was: "How do you know, then?" He had no answer for me. He did vociferously defend his beloved formula and the research that he'd done to craft the formula. In my opinion, that lawyer is an accident waiting to happen, followed closely by a malpractice lawsuit.

12. Using a Schedule A Valuation

Sadly, I see so-called Schedule A valuations too often. These are almost always a bad idea for the reasons I expounded on in chapter 11. However, if a client insists on using a Schedule A valuation method, I recommend advising them against it in writing to protect yourself. I've heard of situations of clients suing because a Schedule A conflict led to a conflict and litigation, resulting in a malpractice lawsuit against the drafting lawyer.

13. Failure to Review Other Documents

Failure to review other documents such as the articles of organization, bylaws, operating agreements, loan agreements, and franchise agreements before drafting a buy-sell agreement is, in my opinion, absolute malpractice. However, I continue to run into it all the time. I don't know how many times I've been asked to review an existing buy-sell agreement that is in inexplicable conflict with the entity's governing documents. Although it is a question of applicable state law, many states provide that, to the extent that there is a conflict between the two documents (or in the worst case I ever ran into — three conflicting documents, each of which contained buy-sell agreement provisions), the governing documents trump the buy-sell agreement, even if the buy-sell agreement was executed after the governing documents were put into effect. The $64,000 question is: "Why did it happen in the first place?" This should never happen.

The documents should be coordinated with one another so that they operate seamlessly. Resolve to never make this mistake.

14. Failure to Properly Legend Stock and Ownership Interests

It is unquestionable that a certificated security can be transferred if there are no restrictions on the ownership certificate, even if the transferor was subject to restrictions on transfer in a buy-sell agreement. The other owners probably have a cause of action against the transferring owner who violated the buy-sell agreement restrictions. Still, my position has always been that neither those other owners nor the entity can restrict the transferee from taking the transferor's place.

However, I have encountered many lawyers who either don't understand this or don't follow the project through to completion, which includes placement of a legend concerning the existence of the buy-sell agreement on the face of the certificate. Just because the buy-sell agreement contains the legend language is not enough; that language must make it onto the certificate.

15. When to Terminate a Buy-Sell Agreement

A buy-sell agreement should contain a provision that calls for the termination of the buy-sell agreement upon the occurrence of any of the specified events. Yet, many agreements that I review do not contain such a provision. Although this is an unlikely event, perhaps a buy-sell agreement, or at least its obligations, should also terminate on the simultaneous deaths, or deaths close in time, of all of the owners.

While I've never seen that provision triggered in any buy-sell agreement that I've drafted, I used to put it in all of my buy-sell agreements because of the devastating and unnecessary effects that the obligations to purchase something that no longer existed (at least in its state before the owners' deaths) would have on the estates of those who had to purchase. Plus, you would not have to sort out who died first.

16. Entity Restrictions and Requirements

You must deal with several restrictions on entities within the buy-sell agreement. These restrictions vary depending on the type of entity.

Corporations usually cannot redeem stock if it would put them under the minimum capital requirements under applicable state law. Your buy-sell agreement must account for that possibility. Loan agreements that are in place also may restrict the ability of the corporation to redeem interests. I typically dealt with that by forcing the remaining owners to either guarantee the redemption or purchase the shares themselves. However, there are other ways to deal with this, ranging from recapitalizing the entity to changing the corporate structure. The bottom line is that the buy-sell agreement must deal with this possibility.

It would be best if you also dealt with the S corporation restrictions on both the number of shareholders and the identity of who may hold interests in the S corporation. The buy-sell agreement must account for these restrictions.

17. Spousal Consent and Affirmation of Existence of the Buy-Sell Agreement and Agreement to be Bound by Its Terms

While you can expect a lot of pushback from clients on this one, I believe spouses should be brought in and forced to at least acknowledge the terms of the buy-sell agreement and, preferably, they should be parties to it. This is an absolute necessity in community property states. In my experience, divorce is a prevalent event that occurs with frightening repetition. The professional advisor must be adamant about forcing the owners to deal with their spouses while everything is still copacetic at home.

This is because once all hell breaks loose and the divorce papers start flying around, it is too late. The owner will then be forced to deal with the now ex-spouse and the vagaries of equitable distribution by inconsistent and unpredictable courts with an uncertain (and no doubt unexpected) and often unwelcome outcome. To protect the owners, the buy-sell agreement must give the divorcing owner the prior right to acquire whatever interest the ex-spouse acquires in the divorce proceeding and judgment.

18. Failure to Provide with Respect to Related Properties in Buy-Sell Agreements

It's one thing to provide for the sale of ownership interests in a buy-sell agreement. It's quite another to consider property related to the business of the entity in which the selling owner has an interest. Related property can include life insurance policies on the life of the selling owner and the lives of the other owners, interests in affiliated companies, interests in land or other property co-owned by some or all of the remaining owners (e.g., the property on which a business operates), intellectual property, leases, licenses, and other contractual rights.

Relationships, needs, and interests frequently change after a sale. For example, a former business entity owner may care more about how much the entity pays in rent for property that the entity operates that he or she continues to co-own after a sale of interests. Failure to address these continuing relationships at the time of the buy-sell agreement can upset and negatively impact operations. It is not always necessary to solve this problem with a required sale of all related property, but I do believe this is the route that is best for all concerns (i.e., a clean break on the sale of interests). However, sometimes a lease on the property that ensures that the entity will pay fair market value rent is all that is necessary.

19. Failure to Suggest Need for Funding for Buy-Sell Agreement Obligations

It is imperative to have a frank discussion with the owners about the importance of considering funding for buy-sell agreement obligations. Some professional advisors who are not life insurance professionals shirk this duty because it is not their bailiwick. This is bad practice. The discussion will force the owners to think about whether or not to enter into an unfunded buy-sell agreement and to decide if it is better to shift some of that risk —of early death, for example—to a larger life insurance company. If, after discussing those substantial risks (i.e., taking on potentially mountainous debt, under which many owners crumble and walk away), the owners may decide to consider life insurance as a funding mechanism, and there is no shortage of life insurance professionals who can help. Frankly, I agree with what one life insurance expert said to the effect that an unfunded buy-sell agreement is as risky an enterprise as not having a buy-sell agreement at all.

20. Failure to Consider a Life Insurance Policy Exit Strategy for Lifetime Buyouts in Buy-Sell Agreements

Whether the buy-sell agreement is structured as a cross-purchase or as a redemption, lifetime buyouts—before the life insurance matures—can give rise to the issue of how to handle unmatured life insurance policies. (In chapters 6 and 7, I discussed the potential for transfer for value problems.)

However, there is a practical issue that the buy-sell agreement should address: Should an owner have the right to acquire the life insurance on his or her life on a lifetime buyout? If the answer is "yes," then the buy-sell agreement should give that insured owner a time period in which to exercise his or her option to acquire those life insurance policies by paying the called for consideration in the buy-sell agreement. If the insured owner does not want the life insurance policies, then the buy-sell agreement should affirmatively state that the owners of the policies have the right to either maintain the policies or to dispose of them. This point frequently gets missed in buy-sell agreements that I review.

21. Creating a Mismatch between the Source of Funding and the Person Obligated to Buy

The mistake of creating a mismatch between the person who holds the funding and the person who is obligated to buy interests is easy to make. If the buy-sell agreement is a cross-purchase buy-sell agreement, then the entity shouldn't own the life insurance policies because the death proceeds will be locked up in the entity and won't be able to be distributed without tax consequences, particularly if the entity is a C corporation. Quite often, the funding of a buy-sell agreement and its drafting are two simultaneous processes and must be coordinated. However, in the wait-and-see version of a hybrid buy-sell agreement, it may not be as critical if the mismatch is there. This is because if the owners hold the life insurance (which I prefer in this instance alone) and the entity ends up being the purchaser, the owners can either lend the death proceeds to the entity to make the purchase, or make contributions to capital of the entity, which will increase their respective outside basis in their interests.

Ethical Issues

Buy-sell agreements can create some gnarly ethical issues that are best hammered out at the beginning of the representation. Questions abound after there is a problem. Who did you represent? The group? The entity alone? A single owner? Did you serve as a neutral third-party? The answers to these questions could well dictate whether you can represent anyone in a buy-sell agreement dispute. As Justice Brandeis once answered in his Supreme Court confirmation hearing, did you represent the "situation"? Did you have an engagement letter that spelled this all out, as well as what would happen if there was a dispute between the owners or the entity?

There are only a few safe ways for lawyers to represent clients who are putting together a buy-sell agreement. You could choose to represent one owner alone and let every owner and the entity know that. Or you could represent the entity alone and let the owners know that. Or you might be able to serve as a neutral third-party and not represent the entity *or* any owner and let the owners and entity know that.

Every other way is potentially problematic for a lawyer because either the lines of representation are unclear, or you are simultaneously representing more than one party. What happens if there is an actual conflict of interest down the road? In chapter 13, I address ethical issues for owners to be aware of when working with professional advisors, which could create some questions that you might not have otherwise expected. However, those conversations should be fruitful, as they can cement a safe place for the lawyer's representation at the outset before there are any difficulties.

How to Use This Book to Make Your Job Easier

This book contains a number of tools that I designed and used to help clients work through the various issues that arise in buy-sell agreements and aid in drafting an agreement that closely mirrored their desires. The handiest tool is the Buy-Sell Agreements Grid (refer to chapter 9, table 2). One axis shows the various triggering events chosen for inclusion (which I discuss in chapter 9). The other axis shows the various responses to the triggering events (also discussed in chapter 9) that the clients would like to associate with each event. The best part about the grid is that it allows the clients to associate each triggering event with the desired response on a triggering-event-by-triggering-event basis since these responses will almost always be different for each triggering event.

You also should find the Buy-Sell Agreement Review Checklist and Buy-Sell Agreement Drafting Checklist (located at the end of this book) to be of assistance in reviewing an existing buy-sell agreement.

Outside Buy-Sell Agreement Resources

There is a helpful free buy-sell agreement audit checklist available from Mercer Capital on its website (www.mercercapital.com) that I encourage you to download and use. It is a free download and is well worth having.

Lawyers, CPAs, and estate planning professionals who wish to delve into technical nuances may wish to consult Gorin, "Structuring Ownership of Privately-Owned Businesses: Tax and Estate Planning Implications," a fully searchable PDF with over 2,800 pages that discuss income and transfer tax issues. Steve provides the most recent version through his quarterly newsletter, "Gorin's Business Succession Solutions." For a free subscription and the PDF, complete the form at http://www. thompsoncoburn.com/forms/gorin-newsletter.

For lawyers and other estate planning professionals looking to do a deep dive into buy-sell agreements, I also highly recommend *Structuring Buy-Sell Agreements: Analysis with Forms, Second Edition* by Howard M. Zaritsky, Farhad Aghdami and Mary Ann Mancini. It's pricey ($540) but is excellent. It's available from Thompson Reuters here.

You will find any of these resources extremely helpful in your work with buy-sell agreements. I heartily endorse all of them.

Selected S Corporation Issues

I did not really have a place in this book for some of the technical points about S corporations, but wanted to include a discussion on some of them. Therefore, I decided that this chapter was the best place to do so, because they are nuances and technical points probably better suited for the professional advisor. You can find a layman's description of the various S corporation tax consequences in chapter 6 (Redemption Buy-Sell Agreements) and chapter 7 (Cross-Purchase Buy-Sell Agreements).

Eligible Shareholders

It is important to keep in mind that only certain persons may be shareholders of an S corporation, at least under present law. An S corporation can only have one hundred shareholders (although the attribution rules under IRC Section 1361(c)(1) make it easy for families to stay under the one-hundred-shareholder limit). The eligible shareholders include several different types of trusts (but for only two years following the death of the shareholder) and estates (indefinitely during the period of administration). The trusts that can be shareholders include grantor trusts, qualified subchapter S trusts (QSSTs), and electing small-business trusts (ESBTs). There are several different factors on how to choose the type of trust to make a shareholder of an S corporation. These factors include the marginal tax rate of the beneficiaries (a high rate favors an ESBT and a low rate favors a QSST), the desired distribution provisions of the trust (a desire to accumulate income favors the ESBT while annual distributions favor the QSST), and the number of beneficiaries desired (a QSST can only have one beneficiary).

One Class of Stock Limitation

Most people know that S corporations can only have one stock class that differs in rights other than voting and nonvoting rights. There are three somewhat nuanced issues that involve buy-sell agreements and the one class of stock requirement. The first of these issues is whether or not buy-sell agreements create a second class of stock. Generally, they do not. [Treas. Reg. Sec. 1.1361-1(l)(2)(iii)(B)].

However, I advise caution when fashioning valuation provisions where different shareholders have differing prices for buyouts (i.e., one price for one set of shareholders and another price for another set of shareholders of the same class of stock). The IRS has found that arrangement problematic as it creates a prohibited second class of stock. (e.g., PLR 200632004.) It should be okay to have different prices for purchases of interests under different triggering events in the buy-sell agreement, as long as those prices apply to all shareholders who trigger those events.

The second issue relating to the class of stock pertains to minimum dividends paid to the shareholders. In PLR 200934021, the buy-sell agreement paid different minimum dividends to shareholders who live in different states because of different state income tax rates. The IRS ruled that this difference constituted a prohibited second class of stock, even though it granted the corporation an inadvertent termination ruling. It is perfectly alright to pay a minimum dividend to shareholders based on tax rates that are tied to the maximum federal, state, and local income tax rates applicable to individuals as long as all the shareholders receive the same minimum dividend per share.

The third and final class of stock issue involves debt, which can have many characteristics of equity. The IRS is aware of this—IRC Section 1361(c)(5) prohibits debt other than "straight debt." Do not treat straight debt as a second class of stock for this purpose. It is a written unconditional promise to pay in money a sum on-demand or on a specified date provided that:

- the interest rate and the interest payment dates are not conditioned on the corporation's profits or discretion,
- the debt is not convertible into stock,

- and the creditor is an individual other than a nonresident alien, an estate, a trust that could be a shareholder in an S corporation, or a person actively and regularly engaged in the moneylending business.

Additionally, the buy-sell agreement for an S corporation should prohibit the issuance of any corporation's debt other than straight debt.

Income Allocation

The final issue that I wanted to discuss relative to S corporations is the allocation of corporation income for the year of a transfer of stock. Normally, S corporation items of income, gain, loss, deduction, and credit are allocable between the shareholders on a pro rata basis (the items are averaged and not considered when the item was created, received, or incurred). However, in the year of a complete termination of the ownership of a shareholder, the corporation and all of the affected shareholders (both buyer and seller) can elect under IRC Section 1377(a)(2)(A) to treat the S corporation taxable year of the termination as actually being two years—one year ending on the date of the transfer of stock.

Typically, the pro rata method works out more fairly where a business has a business cycle that is predictable. However, where the business is not predictable and where the shareholders are keen to match the items of income, gain, loss, deduction, and credit to each day that the particular item was generated, then the election to terminate the taxable year of the corporation should be made. The buy-sell agreement should provide for either one method or the other. Point the issue out to the shareholders and then let them decide.

CHAPTER 15

EXAMPLES OF BUY-SELL AGREEMENTS

In this chapter, I'll look at several different situations to give you a feel for what issues are present in the buy-sell agreement and the language that I use to address those issues. Even though everyone's situation is unique, I tried to select situations that are commonly seen. None of these are real-life situations that I worked on.

The following situations involve all three types of buy-sell agreements, but in the interest of full disclosure, I often used the hybrid form in practice because of its flexibility. Nevertheless, I wanted to depict all three types and provide as realistic examples as I could, despite having created them. I also depict all three forms of entities (for tax purposes): C corporations, S corporations (which can include limited liability companies that elect to be taxed as corporations and then make an S election), and partnerships (which includes LLCs, unless they elect to be taxed as corporations).

A few words about the clauses in this chapter, which appear in italics: These are selected provisions that go into a larger document; they don't constitute an entire document and shouldn't be considered as a separate free-standing document. As I've said, these clauses are intended to spur thinking and give you some idea of what I think these types of clauses can look like. I offer no warranties, express or implied, on the various clauses depicted in this chapter or elsewhere in this book. You're on your own if you blindly use these clauses without fully researching your particular situation.

1. Cross-Purchase Buy-Sell Agreement Examples

The following sections provide examples of clauses for cross-purchase buy-sell agreements.

1.1 Equal Owners of Interests in a C Corporation

In this example, the equal owners of the interests in a C corporation desire a cross-purchase buy-sell agreement that contains a mandatory buy-and-sell death trigger. They have decided to have an independent third-party institutional trustee serve as the manager of a separate LLC that will hold the life insurance policies on the lives of each of the owners, which will then be used to fund the purchase obligations under the cross-purchase buy-sell agreement.

1.1.1 Death

Death Trigger. Except for Transfers to Permitted Transferees, upon the death of an Owner ("Deceased Owner"), the Deceased Owner and his Spouse and Representatives obligate and bind themselves to Transfer, and the remaining Owners shall purchase, in amount(s) proportionately to the Interests held by each of the remaining Owner(s); provided, however, that nothing shall prohibit the remaining Owners from purchasing the Deceased Owner's Interests in any proportion between them as long as all of the Deceased Owner's Interests are purchased, all of the Interests owned by or for the benefit of the Deceased Owner and his Spouse upon the terms and conditions contained in this Agreement.

1.1.2 Selected Provisions of the Life Insurance Limited Liability Operating Agreement

Special Allocations of Income.

(a) Life Insurance Policy Death Proceeds. The life insurance policy death proceeds on the life of a deceased Owner will be specially allocated to the contributing Owner; provided, however, that if the deceased Owner is the contributor of life insurance policies on his own life, then the life insurance policy death proceeds shall be allocated to the surviving Owners.

Capital; Capital Accounts; Additional Capital Contributions.

(a) Initial Capital Contributions. The original Owners have made or are obligated to make the Initial Capital Contributions to the Entity in the amounts shown in Annex "A" attached to this Agreement, and the Owners have become the owners of the respective membership interests and voting rights set forth opposite their names in Annex "A."

(b) Maintenance of Capital Accounts. The Entity shall create and maintain Capital Accounts for each Owner in accordance with Code Sections 704(b) and (c) and the Treasury Regulations thereunder, all as more fully described below. The Entity also shall create and maintain separate Capital Accounts for each life insurance policy that an Owner contributed to the capital of the Entity and that insures the life of another Owner, as well as a general capital account for each Owner. The original Owners agree that the Capital Account balances and ownership percentages reflected on Annex "A" are accurate and correct.

"Capital Account" means, with respect to any Owner, the Capital Accounts maintained for such Owner in accordance with the following provisions, all of which are intended to comply, and should be interpreted to comply, with Treasury Regulation Section 1.704-1(b)(2)(iv):

(1) Credits. Each Owner's Capital Account will hereinafter be credited with the Owner's Capital Contributions, the Owner's allocable share of Profits, any items in the nature of income or gain that are specially allocated to the Owner except adjustments of the Code (including any gain or income from unrealized income with respect to accounts receivable allocated to the Owner to reflect the difference between the book value and tax basis of Entity Property contributed by the Owner), and the amount of any Entity liabilities that are assumed by the Owner within the meaning of Treasury Regulation Section 1.704-1(b)(2)(iv)(c) or secured by any Entity Property distributed to the Owner; provided, however, that the separate Capital Accounts for each Owner with the respect to each of the life insurance policies that an Owner contributed to the Entity shall be accounted for separately, such that capital contributions that pay premiums for a particular life insurance policy shall be credited to the capital account for that life insurance policy.

(2) Debits. Each Owner's Capital Account will be debited with the amount of cash and the Gross Asset Value of any Property that is distributed to the Owner under any provision of this Agreement, the Owner's allocable share of Losses, any items in the nature of deduction or loss that are specially allocated to the Owner, and the amount of any liabilities of the Entity assumed by the Owner or which are secured by any Property contributed by the Owner to the Entity; provided, however, that the life insurance policy death proceeds of a particular

life insurance policy that are specially allocated to the contributing Owner and ultimately paid out for that Owner's use in the purchase of interests in [NAME OF ENTITY] pursuant to that certain Interest Transfer Agreement dated [DATE] shall be debited from the Capital Account relating to that life insurance policy.

(c) Additional Capital Contributions. Each Owner shall be required to make additional annual Capital Contributions pursuant to this Agreement in amounts equal to the premiums due on the life insurance policies that the Owner contributed to the Entity on the lives of the other Owners, plus the Owner's share of Entity administrative expenses, including the compensation of the Manager, as determined by virtue of the Owner's membership interests in the Entity.

Manager

(a) General. Management of the day-to-day business and affairs of the Entity shall initially be conducted by one (1) Manager, who shall not be an Owner, and the initial Manager shall be [NAME OF INITIAL MANAGER].

(b) Removal and Replacement of Manager. The Owners may remove or select a replacement Manager by simple majority vote of the Owners by percentage interest. Any replacement Manager must be an institutional trustee or an individual who is bonded, neither of whom shall be a "related or subordinate party" (as defined under section 672(c) of the Internal Revenue Code) with respect to the Owners or their assignees.

(c) Powers of the Manager. The Manager shall be authorized and directed to transact all of the Entity's business in its name, including, without limitation, sole and absolute power over life insurance policies on the Owners' lives that the Entity owns; provided, however, that the Owners shall have the right to vote on matters other than on life insurance that the Entity owns that insures the lives of the Owners by either a simple majority vote or, in the case of certain enumerated events, by a supermajority of [PERCENTAGE EXPRESSED IN WORDS (NUMBER%)] of Owners by percentage interests owned on the extraordinary events described below. With respect to the life insurance policies on the lives of the Owners that are targeted for use in that certain Interest Transfer Agreement dated [DATE], the Manager shall take any and all steps to insure that those policy death proceeds are fully used to purchase Interests in [NAME OF OPERATING ENTITY] pursuant to said agreement.

Owners

(a) Owner Voting. Except as otherwise expressly provided in this Agreement, where applicable, Owners shall be entitled to voting rights equal to each Owner's ownership percentage interest in the Entity, as set forth on Annex "A," which the parties agree reflects the accurate and correct ownership percentage interests.

(b) Required Vote of Owners. Except as otherwise expressly provided in this Agreement, where applicable, all actions requiring the vote of Owners shall be decided by a simple majority in interest, i.e., by percentage interests, of the Owners.

(c) Actions Requiring Super Majority Consent. The following matters shall require the vote or consent of not less than two-thirds (2/3) in interest of all of the Owners in order to authorize such action:

   (1) New Owners. The admission of a new Owner;

   (2) Distributions of Property. The distribution to any Owner of any Entity property, whether movable or immovable, real or personal, tangible or intangible,

including cash and cash equivalents ("Property") other than Available Cash;

(3) Certain Interim and Disproportionate Distributions of Available Cash. The distribution of Available Cash that is disproportionate between the Owners, or an interim distribution permitted above, which exceeds in either case, the sum of $[NUMBER];

(4) All or Substantially All of the Property. The sale, exchange, mortgage, pledge, or other transfer or encumbrance of all or substantially all of the Property of the Entity;

(5) Certain Loans to Owners or Affiliates. Loans to Owners or Affiliates that exceed the sum of $[NUMBER];

(6) Merger, Division, or Consolidation. The merger, division, or consolidation of the Entity;

(7) Calling Meetings. The call for a special meeting of Owners;

(8) Dissolution. The dissolution and liquidation of the Entity; and

(9) Other Votes. Any other event in this Agreement that expressly calls for such a vote.

(d) Express Limitation on Voting Rights. Notwithstanding any other provision in this Agreement to the contrary, no Member shall have any vote, input, or control whatsoever on any matter concerning any life insurance policy that the Entity owns that insures the Member's life.

1.2 A Company Where the Owners Work in the Business and Where One Owner Holds and Controls a Majority of the Ownership Interests

In this example, which involves an operating company where all five of the owners work in the business, one owner—of an older generation than the co-owners—owns a 60 percent majority of the interests, with each of the other four younger owners owning 10 percent apiece. This entity is an LLC that is being taxed as a partnership for income tax purposes. In entities such as partnerships and limited liability companies, it is not unusual for the buy-sell agreement to be part of the partnership agreement or the LLC operating agreement, the latter of which is where these buy-sell agreement provisions are placed. However, the language is still the same as it would be in a freestanding buy-sell agreement.

The first triggering event that they want covered is death. The majority owner is older than the younger owners, and he expects them to buy him out at his death. They've opted for a cross-purchase buy-sell agreement because they want to have the flexibility to alter the percentages of the majority owner's interests that each younger owner will purchase. This, however, can't be done with a redemption buy-sell agreement because redemption automatically increases the respective ownership interests proportionately.

They will finance the purchase of the majority owner's interest with a life insurance policy on the life of the majority owner that each pay for and own. The majority owner wants the younger owners to shoulder the burden of the life insurance premiums on his life so they "have some skin in the game." This could not be done with a redemption buy-sell agreement because the entity would have to own and be the beneficiary of the life insurance policy on the majority owner's life. This means that the owners would each bear their respective percentage ownership interests of the life insurance policy premiums—and the majority owner was not interested in financing 60 percent of his own buyout.

The majority owner has agreed to a tag along put option right in favor of the minority owners, and he also wants a drag along call option right in case a buyer for the company comes along. None of the owners have any children that want to work in the business, so there is no need for a permitted transferee clause to cover children.

The other owners have decided not to insure their own lives since they are younger and the values of their interests are not nearly as high as that of the majority owner. Therefore, the buy-sell agreement will need to permit installment payments—which all buy-sell agreements should do anyway. The only triggering event that they want to cover is the death of an owner, although they do want to give any divorcing owner the first call option right on whatever interests the ex-spouse has or subsequently obtains.

1.2.1 Death Trigger Language

The death buyout obligation. Upon the death of an Owner ("Deceased Owner"), the Deceased Owner and his Spouse and Representatives obligate and bind themselves to Transfer, and the remaining Owners shall purchase, in amount(s) proportionately to the Interests held by each of the remaining Owner(s) unless they agree in writing to a different sharing arrangement, all of the Interests owned by or for the benefit of the Deceased Owner and his Spouse upon the terms and conditions contained in this Agreement.

1.2.2 Spouse Clause

The divorce call option right could look something like this:
Spousal Election Events
(a) Death, Divorce, or Insolvency of a Spouse. Except as otherwise provided in paragraph (b) below, upon the death of an Owner's Spouse or upon the divorce or legal separation of an Owner and his Spouse or insolvency or any filing by a Spouse for relief under applicable bankruptcy laws or seizure of Interests of a Spouse by a creditor ("Spousal Election Event"), then, for a period of one hundred eighty (180) days from the occurrence of a Spousal Election Event ("Spousal Option Period"), that Owner ("Married Owner") shall have the right and option (but not the obligation) ("Spousal

Option") to acquire or receive all, but not less than all, of the Interests owned by his Spouse or his Spouse's estate. If the Married Owner timely exercises his Spousal Option during the Spousal Option Period, then the Spouse of the Married Owner and/or his Representatives shall Transfer the Spouse's Interests pursuant to the terms and conditions contained in this Agreement, it being understood that the Spouse of the Married Owner may Transfer his Interests with or without consideration to the Married Owner at any time. If the Married Owner fails to timely exercise his Spousal Option within the Spousal Option Period, then the Entity shall have one hundred eighty (180) days from the expiration of the Spousal Option Period or receipt of notice of non-exercise of the Spousal Option by the Married Owner, whichever is earlier ("Follow Spousal Option Period"), within which to exercise an option ("Follow Spousal Option") to acquire the Spouse's Interests, pursuant to the terms set forth in this Agreement. If the Entity timely exercises its Follow Spousal Option during the Follow Spousal Option Period, then the Spouse and his Representative shall Transfer the Spouse's Interests to the Entity pursuant to the terms and conditions contained in this Agreement. If the Married Owner does not timely exercise his Spousal Option, and the Entity does not timely exercise its Follow Spousal Option, then the provisions of this Agreement shall nevertheless continue to apply to the Spouse's Interests.

(b) Extension of time. Notwithstanding the provisions of Section (a) above, if a Married Owner has control over his Spouse's Interests by virtue of being a Representative, or by having the power to vote said Interests, directly or indirectly, then the Spousal Option in favor of the Married Owner shall not lapse until ninety (90) days after he loses control of his Spouse's Interests ("Extended Spousal Option Period"). The

Owner's loss of control shall be deemed a Spousal Election Event. The Follow Spousal Option in favor of the Entity shall expire within the time limits set forth in Section (a) above commencing from the expiration of the Extended Spousal Option Period or receipt of notice of non-exercise of the Spousal Option by the Married Owner, whichever is earlier.

With respect to the life insurance policies that each younger owner has on the life of the majority owner (four policies in all since there are four minority owners), the parties want to require each to continue to maintain the life insurance policies on the life of the majority owner by timely paying the life insurance premiums and to provide proof of payment of the premiums to the majority owner—who wants as much protection as can be given that the life insurance premiums will be paid on time and that the life insurance policies can't be used as collateral for loans.

1.2.3 Life Insurance Clause

This is how the buy-sell agreement part of the operating agreement reads with respect to the life insurance policies and premium obligations of each minority owner:

Generally. Each Owner (other than [MAJORITY OWNER]) shall apply for and be the owner of a life insurance policy on the life of [MAJORITY OWNER]. In order to secure performance of this Agreement, namely, the purchase of the Interests of [MAJORITY OWNER] at death, each such Owner shall be empowered to purchase, from time to time, additional insurance on the life of [MAJORITY OWNER]. Each Owner shall possess the same rights with regard to these new life insurance policies as exist with respect to previously issued life insurance policies.

Life Insurance Policies and Premiums. All life insurance policies pertaining to this Agreement shall be listed on the

Schedule "Life Insurance" that is attached to this Agreement, which schedule shall be kept current to reflect all life insurance policies on the life of [MAJORITY OWNER] that are to be used for the purchase of the Interests of [MAJORITY OWNER] at death. Each policy owner agrees to pay the first and all subsequent life insurance premiums as they become due and shall provide proof of payment to [MAJORITY OWNER] within ten (10) days after the due date of a premium. If a premium is not paid within twenty (20) days after its due date, [MAJORITY OWNER] may make the premium payment, which shall be considered a loan to the policy owner, and [MAJORITY OWNER] shall be reimbursed by the policy owner directly out of the policy owner's share of Entity profits and cash flow. Each policy owner agrees to take all necessary actions to allow disclosure of information to [MAJORITY OWNER] pertaining to the policies insuring [his/her] life.

No Encumbrances. No policy owner shall execute any loans against, impair, or in any manner encumber any of the above described life insurance policies to the detriment of this Agreement without the written consent of all other parties to this Agreement, except that each policy owner may exercise any dividend options or dividend rights provided by the life insurance policy without obtaining the consent of any of the other parties to this Agreement.

Insurance Proceeds. Except as provided in the following section, payment for Interests acquired pursuant to the death of an Owner pursuant to this Agreement shall be made in cash within ten (10) days of receipt of proceeds from all policies of life insurance on the life of a Deceased Owner and/or his Spouse to the extent that the price of the Interests do not exceed the net proceeds of any policies of life insurance owned that insured the life of the Deceased Owner and/or his Spouse that are owned by any party obligated to purchase the Interests of the Deceased

Owner and/or his Spouse pursuant to this Agreement, unreduced by loans against such policies or loans secured by those policies.

1.2.4 Tag Along and Drag Along Clauses, Tag Along Put Option Rights, Drag Along Call Option Right

The drag along call option right and tag along put option right language could look like this:

(a) Tag Along Put Option Rights. If one or more Owners, either individually or collectively own greater than fifty percent (50%) of the Interests (collectively, "Majority Owners"), offer, agree to accept a Bona Fide Offer to Transfer Interests or Transfer Interests pursuant to this Agreement over a period of twenty-four (24) months commencing from the date of the first event to a purchaser (or to purchasers who are Affiliated) or who vote to sell all or substantially all of the assets of the Entity, and if, following any such sale, Transfer or proposed Transfer, the remaining Owners ("Minority Owners") collectively own or would own less than fifty percent (50%) of the Interests and/or would not receive a proportionate share of the projected price (including amounts to be paid to individual Owners under any separate agreement or arrangement including, without limitation, consulting agreements, leases, licenses, noncompetition/ confidentiality agreements, severance packages, etc.), then the Majority Owners shall provide notice of the terms of all offers or Transfers, together with full disclosure of the identity of the purchaser(s) or prospective purchaser(s) and the total amount of consideration or other remuneration that the purchaser(s) or prospective purchaser(s) has or have paid, caused to have paid, will pay or will cause to be paid in the future to the Majority Owners, including, without limitation, for stock, options, agreements not to compete, leases, employment and consulting agreements, prepaid salary or bonuses, to the Minority Owners, and the Majority Owners shall negotiate with prospective purchasers on behalf of the Minority Owners for the same terms and conditions for the purchase of the Majority Owners' Interests ("Tag Along Rights") by the purchaser or prospective purchaser. The Tag Along Rights granted to the Minority Owners in this Section shall be in addition to the rights granted elsewhere to Owners in this Article. A Minority Owner shall have thirty (30) days to accept or reject the offer from receipt of information from the Majority Owners about the offer.

(b) Put Rights. If a Majority Owner sells or agrees to Transfer Interests or to sell all or substantially all of the assets of the Entity in contravention of the Tag Along Rights afforded to Minority Owners in Section (a) above, each Minority Owner shall have the right and option (but not the obligation) to sell to the Majority Owner ("Tag Along Put") all, but not less than all, of the Interests of all Minority Owners at the higher of the total amount per percent of Interests (or fraction thereof) paid to the Majority Owner as described in Section (a) by the purchaser or the price as determined pursuant to Article __ for cash within ten (10) days of receipt of notice of the Minority Owner's exercise of the Tag Along Put pursuant to this Section (b), and each Majority Owner shall be jointly and severally liable for the purchase of the Interests that are subject to the Tag Along Put.

(c) Drag Along Call. If a Majority Owner receives a Bona Fide Offer from an outside party to purchase all of the Majority Owners' Interests or all or substantially all of the assets of the Entity, and if the Majority Owners, after exercising the Majority Owners' fiduciary obligation to the Minority Owners to carefully review and consider said Bona Fide Offer, a copy of which the Majority Owners shall provide to the Minority Owners (who shall maintain as confidential the existence of the Bona Fide Offer, together with all of its terms), has determined that it is in the best interests of all Owners to accept the Bona Fide Offer, the Majority Owners shall have the right and option (but not the obligation) ("Drag Along Call") to call all Interests owned by the Minority Owners to be Transferred to the outside party, and all Owners who have not tendered their Interests shall be required to Transfer their Interests to the outside party at the same price and on the same terms and conditions as were offered to the Majority Owners pursuant to the Drag Along Call.

1.3 Language for an LLC That Operates a Real Estate Rental Business Where the Equal Owners Are Merely Passive Investors

In this example, which involves an LLC that operates a real estate rental business, the equal owners want the maximum flexibility to transfer interests for estate planning purposes.

1.3.1 Permitted Transferee

In this situation, the "permitted transferee" clause could look like this:

"Permitted Transferee" means the Entity, an Owner's Living Trust [OR A FAMILY MEMBER], if such transferee is or becomes a party to this Agreement and holds the Interests subject to the provisions of this Agreement by signing an Addendum in the form attached hereto as Annex "Adoption Addendum."

1.3.2 Family Member

The operating agreement could broadly define "family member" as follows:

"Family Member" means any of the following with respect to a particular Owner:

(i) Identification. [NAME(S) OF PARENTS] and their descendants [OR THOSE DESCENDANTS WHO ARE ACTIVE IN THE ENTITY], and any trust for the benefit of one of those individuals [AS LONG AS THE TRUSTEE OR A CO-TRUSTEE IS A FAMILY MEMBER].

(ii) Spousal Trust. A trust for the benefit of an Owner's Spouse, as long as the trust terms do not allow principal distribution of Interests to the Spouse during the term of the trust or on its termination, and on termination of the trust the Interests pass to a Family Member as defined in (i) above.

1.3.3 Living Trust

The operating agreement should contain a definition of "living trust" that could look like this:

"Living Trust" means a trust of which an individual Owner is a grantor and the initial trustee or co-trustee, over which the individual Owner has the full right of revocation, and that will function during the Owner's life primarily for the benefit of the Owner. However, if a subsequent amendment to such a trust would cause the trust to function during the Owner's life other than primarily for the Owner's benefit, that action is to be treated as a Transfer to someone other than a Permitted Transferee (unless the trust after such changes otherwise would qualify as a Permitted Transferee). For all purposes of this Agreement, the Interests owned by a Living Trust shall still be considered as owned by the individual grantor of the Living Trust, and all references to the death of an Owner, or any other provision that would apply to an individual and not a trust, shall be considered as applying to an individual grantor of the Living Trust. However, for purposes of making payments to an Owner (such as dividends, liquidating distributions, and payments in exchange for the Interests owned by the trust) or the Owner's estate, those payments shall be made to the

Living Trust. The trustees, successor trustees, and all present and future beneficiaries of a Living Trust shall be fully bound by the provisions of this Agreement. Any notices required to be given to an Owner whose Interests have been Transferred to a Living Trust shall be mailed to the individual grantor as trustee of the living trust, or to any successor trustee of whom the Entity has been notified in writing.

1.3.4 Exceptions to the Buy-Sell Agreement

The operating agreement could cull out exceptions to the various triggers to the buy-sell agreement language for certain transfers with a section like this:

Exceptions. Notwithstanding any provision in this Article, any Owner may Transfer, whether during lifetime or at death, his Interests (i) via a will, Living Trust, other trust (revocable or irrevocable) or an entity that is controlled by Family Members to or for the benefit of any Permitted Transferee, any entity that is controlled by Permitted Transferees and/or an Owner's Spouse that makes specific legacy or allocation of all or any part of that Owner's Interests to or for the benefit of a Permitted Transferee even if a Spouse or persons other than a Permitted Transferee also are beneficiaries of the legacy or revocable trust; provided, however, that an Owner be given control over the Interests, pursuant to the terms of this Agreement; or (ii) via lifetime Transfer to or for the benefit of a Permitted Transferee of all or any part of the Owner's Interests, said transferring Owner being permitted to take a pledge of the sold Interest as security for payment of the purchase price; it being understood that an Owner need not treat Family Members equally in any Transfer; provided, however, that an Owner be given control over the Interests, pursuant to the terms and conditions of this Agreement. A surviving Spouse may only enjoy lifetime income rights; provided, however, that no surviving Spouse shall be granted the power to sell or to vote the Interests of the Spouse's deceased spouse.

1.3.5 Transfer

The operating agreement should define "transfer" very broadly to include a sale or a gift, as follows:

"Transfer" means (i) when used as a verb, to gift, sell, exchange, assign, redeem, transfer, pledge, hypothecate, encumber, bequeath, devise or otherwise dispose of, directly or indirectly, whether voluntary or involuntary or whether arising from a divorce, separation, death, attachment, execution, bankruptcy, foreclosure, judicial order, operation of law or otherwise; (ii) when used as a noun, the nouns corresponding to such verbs; and (iii) when used as an adjective, the adjectives corresponding to such verbs. A "Transfer" also shall include a Transfer by sale or exchange of fifty percent (50%) or more of the Interests during a twelve- (12) month period.

2. Redemption Buy-Sell Agreement Examples

The following sections include some redemption buy-sell agreement clause examples.

2.1 A Company Where the Equal Owners Also Work in the Business

In the example below, the five equal owners also work in the entity's business, which is an S corporation. The owners decide to use a redemption buy-sell agreement format in order to minimize the number of life insurance policies needed, with the entity owning and being the sole beneficiary of the life insurance policies. The owners want triggering events of death (mandatory buy-and-sell), disability (entity call option right for cases of presumptive disability, but an owner put option right in all other cases of disability), and termination of employment for cause (entity call option right, which requires 80 percent owner approval, i.e., unanimity of the remaining owners). However, the owners want the rights to be different if the owner is terminated for cause versus termination for no cause (an owner put option right).

Two of the owners have children who are presently working full time for the business and who the owners will permit to become owners in the future. The owners acknowledge that any child of an owner willing to follow the prescribed guidelines to become eligible to become an owner (which requires a bachelor's degree from an accredited university, three years of outside work experience, and five years of active full-time work experience with the entity) can be a permitted transferee of shares.

2.1.1 Permitted Transferees

The permitted transferee clause could look something like this:

"Permitted Transferee" means the Entity, [A CURRENT OWNER], an Owner's Living Trust [A FAMILY MEMBER], or a Potential Owner who meets the Eligibility Requirements, if such transferee is or becomes a party to this Agreement and holds the Interests subject to the provisions of this Agreement by signing an Addendum in the form attached hereto as Annex "Adoption Addendum."

In order to be a Permitted Transferee, the transferee must be qualified to be a shareholder in an S corporation and the Transfer must not cause the total number of shareholders to exceed the number then allowed for S corporations under the Code (which is currently 100). Prior to the Transfer of any Interests to a trust, a copy of the trust instrument and all documents related hereto shall be submitted to counsel for the Entity for determination of whether the Transfer of the Interests to such trust shall cause or result in an inadvertent termination of the Entity's S corporation status.

2.1.2 Eligibility Requirements

The owner eligibility requirements could look something like this:

Eligibility Requirements. Prior to becoming an Owner, a person must meet the following requirements: (i) being a Potential Owner; (ii) obtaining a college undergraduate bachelor's degree from an institution that is accredited by any of the current recognized regional accrediting associations, namely, Middle States Association of Colleges and Schools, New England Association of Schools and Colleges, North Central Association of Colleges and Schools, Northwest Commission on Colleges and Universities, and the Western Association of Schools and Colleges, or the successors and assigns of any of the foregoing, or any other college undergraduate institution that is not accredited by any of the foregoing but which is recognized internationally or in the United States for academic excellence, as determined by the Board of Directors (with an example of this latter category being Harvard College); (iii) three (3) years of active outside full-time work experience with an employer that is neither owned by nor affiliated with an Owner and that is engaged in the same industry as the Entity or in a similar industry; and (iv) five (5) years of active full-time work experience in the Entity.

"Potential Owner" is a person who is a descendant (by blood or by adoption) of an Owner.

2.1.3 Death Trigger

The following language could be used when considering the death trigger:

Death. Upon the death of an Owner ("Deceased Owner"), except with respect to Transfers to Permitted Transferees, the

Entity shall purchase, and the Deceased Owner and his Spouse and Representatives obligate and bind themselves to Transfer, all of the Interests owned by or for the benefit of the Deceased Owner and his Spouse upon the terms and conditions contained in this Agreement.

2.1.4 Definition of Disability

The disability clause could read like this:

Disability. "Disability" means a condition resulting from sickness or injury that occurs while an Owner is employed with the Entity on an active, full-time basis, which renders the Owner unable to perform the duties of the occupation that the Owner was engaged in with the Entity when the condition commenced, and which condition is continuous and uninterrupted for a period of twelve (12) consecutive months [IDENTIFY WHATEVER SALARY CONTINUATION, IF ANY, THAT WILL BE PAID TO THE PRESUMPTIVELY DISABLED OWNER DURING THE DISABILITY PERIOD PRIOR TO THE BUYOUT]; provided, however, that, except as provided below, the following events shall constitute presumptive "Disability" for purposes of this Agreement: (i) an Owner's failure to physically report in person to work at any of the then existing public establishment(s) of the Entity to which that Owner was assigned in writing and/or had up until occurrence of the sickness or condition giving rise to the possible Disability spent more than one-half (1/2) of his work time for a consecutive period of ninety (90) business days; (ii) an Owner's failure to submit to a medical, psychiatric, or psychological examination by an authorized medical representative (which may, but need not be, a licensed physician or psychologist; it could be a nurse, social worker, or geriatric caregiver) designated by the Entity or by any Owner within ten (10) days of delivery of notice of such request to the Owner or his Spouse or Representative (collectively,

(i) and (ii) shall be referred to as Presumptive Disability); or (iii) a determination by the Social Security Administration that the Owner is eligible for SSI or other disability benefits; provided, further, however, that if the Entity has purchased and maintains a policy of disability insurance on the Owner and that policy contains a different definition of disability or waiting (elimination) period before benefits commence thereunder, then, notwithstanding any other provision herein, the definition of disability and/or the waiting (elimination) period contained in the policy and the determination of disability made by the issuing insurer shall control for purposes of this Agreement, and the Entity, on the Effective Date, owns the policies of disability insurance of the lives of the Owners as are more fully described on Annex "B" to this Agreement.

Upon a determination of Presumptive Disability, the Entity shall have the right and option (but not the obligation) to purchase any and all of the Interests owned by the Disabled Owner, his Representative and/or his Spouse ("Presumptive Disability Option"), and the Disabled Owner, his Representative and/or his Spouse shall Transfer, all of his Interests pursuant to the terms and conditions contained in this Agreement. In all other events of Disability, the Disabled Owner, his Representative and/or his Spouse ("Disabled Owner Election Event"), and for a period of one hundred and eighty (180) days from the occurrence of a Disabled Owner Election Event ("Disable Owner Option Period"), the Disabled Owner, his Spouse and/or his Representative shall have the right and option (but not the obligation) to offer ("Disabled Owner Put Option Right") to the Entity for sale, in a single transaction, as much of the Interests in the Entity owned by the Owner and/or his Spouse as the Owner, or his Representative, shall desire to Transfer ("Offered Interests"), and the Entity shall purchase, and the Offering Owner and his Representative and Spouse shall Transfer, all of the Offered Interests upon the terms and conditions contained in this Agreement.

The owners want the maximum flexibility that an S corporation offers, while adding every provision that can be added to protect the S election.

2.1.5 Termination of Employment

Termination for Cause. Upon the involuntary termination of employment for cause as defined in this Agreement of an Owner ("Terminated Owner"), and for a period of one hundred and eighty (180) days (Termination Call Option), the Entity shall have the right and option (but not the obligation) to purchase all or any part of the Interests ("Called Interests") of the Terminated Owner and his Spouse, and the Terminated Owner, his Representative and his Spouse shall sell the Called Interests pursuant to the terms and conditions contained in this Agreement. For purposes of this Agreement, the term "cause" means engagement in personal conduct of such serious nature as to render the Owner's continued association with the Entity professionally detrimental to the interests of the Entity as determined by the unanimous vote of all of the other Owners, including, by way of illustration and not exclusively, (i) any final and non-appealable federal or state conviction of an offense involving fraud or malfeasance or final and non-appealable determination of civil liability arising out of an offense involving fraud or malfeasance; (ii) final and non-appealable loss, or suspension for a period of one (1) year or more, of any professional license required for the Owner to actively participate in the business of the Entity; (iii) competing, directly or indirectly, with the Entity; or (iv) embezzlement or misappropriation of funds of the Entity in excess of $[INSERT AMOUNT].

Termination without Cause. Upon the involuntary termination of employment with the Entity other than for

Cause as voted on by the unanimous vote of all of the other Owners ("Owner Election Event") of an Owner ("Terminated Owner"), and for a period of one hundred and eighty (180) days from the occurrence of an Owner Election Event ("Owner Option Period"), the Terminated Owner, his Spouse and his Representatives, shall have the right and option (but not the obligation) to offer ("Owner Option") to the Entity for sale, in a single transaction, as much of the Interests in the Entity owned by the Terminated Owner and/or his Spouse as the Terminated Owner, his Spouse and/or his Representative, shall desire to Transfer ("Offered Interests"), and the Entity shall purchase, and the Offering Owner and his Representative and Spouse shall Transfer, all of the Offered Interests upon the terms and conditions contained in this Agreement.

2.2 Where One Owner Holds and Controls a Majority of the Ownership Interests

The following sections show clauses for a redemption buy-sell agreement where one owner holds and controls a majority of the ownership interests.

2.2.1 Right of First Refusal — Separate Classes of Interests

These owners want only the minimal protection of right of first refusal (which will include a right of first offer), which could look something like this:

Right of First Refusal. Any Owner desiring to Transfer all or any part of his Interests ("Offering Owner") or who has received a Bona Fide Offer to purchase the Owner's Interests must first offer said Interests ("Offered Interests") to the remaining Owners of the same class of Interests as the Offered Interests, and, for a period of one hundred eighty (180) days from receipt of notice of the offer, the remaining Owner(s) shall have the right and option (but not the obligation) ("First Refusal Option") to purchase all, but not less than all, of the Offered Interests at the price determined pursuant to this Agreement ("First Refusal Option Period"), or, if the price is set forth in a Bona Fide Offer that is received by the Offering Owner from a person who is not an Owner and if that price, in present value, is higher, then at that price ("Offer Price"). Each such Owner (other than the Offering Owner) shall have the right and option ("First Refusal Option") to purchase such portion of the Offered Interests at the Offer Price as the percentage of the Interests owned by that Owner in the same class of Interests as the Offered Interests at the commencement of the First Refusal Option Period shall bear to the total percentage of Interests owned by all other Owners of the same class as the Offered Interests who are eligible to and exercise the First Refusal Option in the Offered Interests at the Offer Price (or percentage thereof) on the terms described above. However, if all of the remaining Owner(s) do not exercise the First Refusal Option, then the Offered Interests over which the First Refusal Option is not exercised may be exercised in similar proportions by the said remaining Owners, and so forth, it being understood that only one (1) owner may end up with the right to purchase all of the Offered Interests if that Owner is the only Owner who exercised his First Refusal Option.

Second Refusal Option. If all of the remaining Owners of the same class of Interests as that of the Offered Interests fail to timely exercise their First Refusal Option, for a period of ninety (90) days from the expiration of the First Refusal Option Period or receipt of notice of non-exercise of the First Refusal Option by all of the Remaining Owners of the same class of Interests as the Offered Interests, whichever first occurs ("Second Refusal Option Period"), then the Offered Interests shall then be offered to the Entity ("Second Refusal Option") at the same price and on the same terms, which shall then have the right and option to acquire the Offered Interests.

Terms of Payment. The terms of payment of the Offer Price for Interests on exercise of a First Refusal Option or Second Refusal Option with respect to those Interests shall be as provided in Article [] herein; provided, however, that if the terms of payment that are set forth in a Bona Fide Offer are more favorable to the purchaser than the terms set forth in Article [IDENTIFY WHERE THESE TERMS ARE CONTAINED], then those terms shall be used. If a Bona Fide Offer does not contain all of the terms set forth in Article [IDENTIFY WHERE THESE TERMS ARE CONTAINED], e.g., no interest rate provision or an installment payout, then Article [IDENTIFY WHERE THESE TERMS ARE CONTAINED] shall supply the missing terms.

Limited Right of Disposition. If the Entity and the Owners do not exercise the First Refusal Option or the Second Refusal Options granted in this Section, then the Offering Owner shall be free to dispose of the Offered Interests as provided herein without other restriction other than that the transferee be an Eligible Owner for a period of sixty (60) days from the expiration of the Entity's Second Refusal Option or receipt of notice of non-exercise by the Entity of its Second Refusal Option. If the Offered Interests are not disposed of within that sixty- (60) day period, then the Offered Interests shall continue to be subject to all of the terms and conditions of this Agreement, and the right of first refusal process shall begin anew.

3. Hybrid Buy-Sell Agreement Examples

The following sections include example clauses from hybrid buy-sell agreements.

3.1 Two Equal Owners and a Hybrid Wait-and-See Buy-Sell Agreement

Two equal owners want to put together a wait-and-see buy-sell agreement for their C corporation, in which each shareholder would own life insurance on the life of the other shareholder. They want disability and death triggers, together with a Russian roulette deadlock provision. The death trigger would have the wait-and-see feature, but the disability trigger would be an entity purchase with an installment payout method.

3.1.1 Deadlock Provision

The Russian roulette deadlock provision might look something like this:

Owner Deadlock Put and Call Option; Voluntary arbitration. If the Owners are equally divided with respect to the management of the Entity's property, business, or affairs, or are equally divided in any question, dispute, or controversy, and this division concerns the proper subject for action by the Owners, each Owner shall have the right to make an irrevocable offer, which shall be evidenced by a written notice to the Offeree ("Put or Call Notice") specifying a value for the Owners' Interests ("Deadlock Price") and offering (i) to sell the offering Owner's ("Offeror") Interests at the Deadlock Price or (ii) to purchase the other Owner's ("Offeree") Interests at the Deadlock Price, free and clear of all liens and encumbrances. If both Owners give a Put or Call Notice to each other at or around the same time, the Put or Call Notice with the earlier postmark or delivery date, if hand delivered, shall control, and if the notices are postmarked or delivered on the same day, the Put or Call Notice providing the highest Deadlock Price shall control.

Procedure. The Offeree shall, within [NUMBER OF DAYS EXPRESSED IN WORDS] (NUMBER) days after receipt of the Put or Call Notice, give written notice to the Offeror of the

Offeree's election to sell or purchase pursuant to the terms of the Put or Call Notice. In the absence of a timely written election by the Offeree, the Offeree shall be deemed to have elected to [SELECT ONE: sell/buy] his or her Interests at the Deadlock Price. The purchaser, whether the Offeror or the Offeree, shall pay the entire Deadlock Price by certified or cashier's check or wired funds that are available at the Closing, which shall take place at a date designated by the purchaser, which date shall not be more than [NUMBER OF DAYS EXPRESSED IN WORDS THAT SHOULD BE AT LEAST TWICE AS MANY DAYS AS ABOVE] (NUMBER) days following the receipt of the Put or Call Notice by the Offeree.

Default. If the purchaser, whether the Offeror or the Offeree, breaches the terms and conditions of this Section and fails to close and/or pay the Deadlock Price as provided for in this Section ("Defaulting Purchaser"), then the non-breaching party ("Defaulted Owner") shall have the option, exercisable by written notice within [NUMBER EXPRESSED IN WORDS] (NUMBER) days after the original closing date, to purchase the Interests of the Defaulting Purchaser at a price equal to [SOME PERCENTAGE LESS THAN 100%] of the Deadlock Price by certified or cashier's check or wired funds at a closing that shall take place at a date designated by the Defaulted Owner, which date shall not be more than [NUMBER EXPRESSED IN WORDS] (NUMBER) days following the date of exercise of the option on default.

Death Prior to Closing. Notwithstanding the foregoing, if an Owner dies after the issuance of a Put or Call Notice but before the closing provided for in this Section, the procedure and provisions of this Section shall be deemed to have lapsed and the provisions of this Agreement for the purchase of an Owner's Interests on death shall apply instead.

3.1.2 Death Trigger

With respect to the death trigger, the hybrid wait-and-see buy-sell agreement could provide as follows:

Death. Upon the death of an Owner ("Deceased Owner"), all the Interests owned by such Owner at his death shall be sold by the personal representative of such Deceased Owner at the price determined as set forth in this Agreement and on the other terms as hereinafter set forth. There shall be a cascade of call options to purchase the Interests of the Deceased Owner, and the order of call options shall be as follows:

(a) First Call Option Right. For a period of thirty (30) days following written notice of the Deceased Owner's death, the Entity shall have a first call option right (but not an obligation) to purchase all or any part of the Deceased Owner's Interests, said purchase to take place within ten (10) days of exercise of the first call option right;

(b) Second Call Option Right. If the Entity does not exercise its call option right to purchase all of the Deceased Owner's Interests pursuant to its first call option right, then, for a period of thirty (30) days following the expiration of the Entity's first call option right, or receipt of written notice from the Entity that it does not intend to exercise its first call option right over all of the Deceased Owner's Interests, whichever first occurs, then the other Owners ("Remaining Owners") shall have the pro-rata call option right to purchase any such Interests of the Deceased Owner that the Entity did not purchase, said purchase to take place within ten (10) days of the exercise of the second call option right; and

(c) Entity Obligation. Within sixty (60) days of the expiration of the Remaining Owners' second call option right or receipt of written notice from the Remaining Owners that they do not desire to exercise their second call option right over all of the Deceased Owner's Interests, whichever first occurs, the Entity shall purchase the Interests of the Deceased Owner that the Remaining Owners do not purchase.

3.1.3 Disability

The disability trigger language that the owners want (i.e., an entity option) could look something like this:

Disability. "Disability" means a condition resulting from sickness or injury that occurs while an Owner is employed with the Entity on an active, full-time basis, which renders the Owner unable to perform the duties of the occupation that the Owner was engaged in with the Entity when the condition commenced, and which condition is continuous and uninterrupted for a period of twelve (12) consecutive months ([IDENTIFY WHATEVER SALARY CONTINUATION, IF ANY, THAT WILL BE PAID TO THE PRESUMPTIVELY DISABLED OWNER DURING THE DISABILITY PERIOD PRIOR TO THE BUYOUT]); provided, further, however, that if the Entity has purchased and maintains a policy of disability insurance on the Owner and that policy contains a different definition of disability or waiting (elimination) period before benefits commence thereunder, then, notwithstanding any other provision herein, the definition of disability and/or the waiting (elimination) period contained in the policy and the determination of disability made by the issuing insurer shall control for purposes of this Agreement, and the Entity, on the Effective Date, owns the policies of disability insurance of the lives of the Owners as are more fully described on Annex "B" to this Agreement.

Upon a determination of Disability, the Entity shall have the right and option (but not the obligation) to purchase any and all of the Interests owned by the Disabled Owner, his Representative and/or his Spouse ("Disability Call Option Right"), and on exercise of the Disability Call Option Right over all or any part of the Interests ("Affected Interests") of the Disabled Owner and his Spouse, the Disabled Owner, his Representative and/or his Spouse shall Transfer the Affected Interests pursuant to the terms and conditions contained in this Agreement.

RESOURCES

To download my Interest Transfer Agreement and guide,
visit www.paulhoodservices.com.

BUY-SELL AGREEMENT REVIEW CHECKLIST

1. **Type of buy-sell agreement:**
   [ ] Redemption?   [ ] Cross-purchase?   [ ] Hybrid?
2. **Parties:** Who should be a party to the buy-sell agreement?
   [ ] All of the owners or less than all of the owners?
   [ ] The entity?
   [ ] Spouses of owners?
   [ ] Prospective owners?
3. **Right of first refusal:**   [ ] Yes?   [ ] No?
   If yes, what are the terms?
        [ ] Terms contained in a third party offer?
        [ ] Does the third party offer have to be a proven "bona fide offer?"
   What proves the bona fide offer?
        [ ] A deposit of earnest money?
        [ ] Proof of financial ability to consummate the purchase?
        [ ] Does the right of first refusal provide relative to whether it is the buy-sell agreement price and terms?
        [ ] Is the rights exercise price the **higher** of the third party offer or the buy-sell agreement?

[ ] Or is it the **lower** of the third party offer or the buy-sell agreement?

[ ] Will the owner who exercises a right of first refusal be able to pay in installments, or is that owner bound by the terms of the third party offer, such that if it is a cash offer, then the rights terms are all cash at the closing?

4. **Transfers:**

   [ ] Does the buy-sell agreement prohibit **all** transfers except those made pursuant to the buy-sell agreement? If not, what are the exceptions?

   [ ] Are there any permitted transferees to whom transfers won't trigger the buy-sell agreement? If so, who are they? Family members? If so, which ones, i.e., descendants, in-laws, spouses, etc.?

5. **Triggering Events: [ ] Gift?   [ ] Death?   [ ] Divorce? [ ] Disability?**

   If so, who determines disability?

   [ ] The insurance company?

   [ ] The leadership of the entity?

   [ ] Is there any ground of presumptive disability?

   What happens if there is a presumptive disability determination?

   What is the definition of "disability?" Is it an "own occupation" or does it require absolute disability? How long must the disability last before the buy-sell agreement is triggered?

   [ ] Must disability be permanent?

   [ ] **Termination of employment for cause?**

   If so, is cause defined in the buy-sell agreement, and what is that definition?

   [ ] **Termination of employment without cause?**

   [ ] **Competition with the entity?**

   [ ] **Disclosure of confidential information to a competitor?**

   [ ] **Retirement?**

   [ ] **Voluntary termination of employment?**

[ ] **Seizure of an interest?**
[ ] **Loss of license or other qualification?**
[ ] **Deadlock among the owners?**
[ ] **Attempted transfer?**
[ ] **Other?**

6. **Responses to triggering events:**

[ ] **Gift:** Is this a permitted transfer or will it trigger a right under the buy-sell agreement? If so, what right?

[ ] **Death:**
    [ ] No action?
    [ ] Unrestricted permitted transfer?
    [ ] Restricted permitted transfer?
    [ ] Right of first refusal?
    [ ] Mandatory sale but with only a purchase option?
    [ ] Mandatory purchase and sale?
    [ ] Put option right but not a mandatory offer?
    [ ] Co-existent call option right and put option right?
    [ ] Does the buy-sell agreement require all of the interests of the deceased owner be purchased or sold?

[ ] **Disability:**
    [ ] Not Covered?
    [ ] Right of first refusal?
    [ ] Mandatory sale but with only a purchase option?
    [ ] Mandatory purchase and sale?
    [ ] Put option right but not a mandatory offer?
    [ ] Does the buy-sell agreement require all of the interests of the disabled owner be purchased or sold?

[ ] **Divorce, or death or bankruptcy of a spouse:**
    [ ] Not covered?
    [ ] No action?
    [ ] Call option right in favor of the spouse owner?
    [ ] Call option right in favor of all owners?
    [ ] Call option right in favor of the entity?

[ ] **Involuntary termination of employment for cause:**
  [ ] Not covered?
  [ ] No action?
  [ ] Call option right in favor of the other owners?
  [ ] Call option right in favor of the entity?
  [ ] Put option right in favor of the terminated employee owner?

[ ] **Involuntary Termination of employment without cause:**
  [ ] Not covered?
  [ ] No action?
  [ ] Call option right in favor of the other owners?
  [ ] Call option right in favor of the entity?
  [ ] Put option right in favor of the terminated owner?

[ ] **Competition with the entity:**
  [ ] Not covered?
  [ ] No action?
  [ ] Call option right in favor of the other owners?
  [ ] Call option right in favor of the entity?

[ ] **Disclosure of confidential information to a competitor:**
  [ ] Not covered?
  [ ] No action?
  [ ] Call option right in favor of the other owners?
  [ ] Call option right in favor of the entity?

[ ] **Retirement:**
  [ ] Not covered?
  [ ] No action?
  [ ] Call option right in favor of the other owners?
  [ ] Call option right in favor of the entity?
  [ ] Put option right in favor of the retired employee owner?

[ ] **Voluntary termination of employment:**
  [ ] Not covered?
  [ ] No action?
  [ ] Call option right in favor of the other owners?
  [ ] Call option right in favor of the entity?

[ ] Put option right?

[ ] Seizure of an interest:

    [ ] Not covered?

    [ ] No action?

    [ ] Call option right in favor of the other owners?

    [ ] Call option right in favor of the entity?

    [ ] Put option right?

[ ] Loss of license or other qualification:

    [ ] Not covered?

    [ ] No action?

    [ ] Call option right in favor of the other owners?

    [ ] Call option right in favor of the entity?

    [ ] Put option right?

[ ] Deadlock among the owners:

    [ ] Not covered?

    [ ] No action?

    [ ] Call option right in favor of the other owners?

    [ ] Call option right in favor of the entity?

    [ ] Put option right?

[ ] Attempted transfer:

    [ ] Not covered?

    [ ] No action?

    [ ] Call option right in favor of the other owners?

    [ ] Call option right in favor of the entity?

    [ ] Put option right?

[ ] Other triggering events:

    [ ] Not covered?

    [ ] No action?

    [ ] Call option right in favor of the other owners?

    [ ] Call option right in favor of the entity?

    [ ] Put option right?

7. **Valuation:**
   [ ] Is the price the same for every triggering event? If not, what are the differences?
   [ ] **Appraisal?**
      If so, who determines the value and who picks the appraiser?
      [ ] Are there any minimum qualifications for the appraiser?
      [ ] Is the appraiser given any valuation guidance?
         [ ] If so, standard of value?
         [ ] Level of value, i.e., whether valuation discounts are to be applied?
      What is the date as of which the appraisal is to be conducted, i.e., the "as of" date?
      Who pays for the appraisers?
      Is there a floor minimum value, e.g., the amount of the life insurance proceeds on the death of an owner?
   [ ] **Book value?**
      [ ] If so, are there any adjustments to book value of assets to bring them to fair market value?
      [ ] Are there any other adjustments to book value? If so, what are they?
      As of when is the book value to be determined, i.e., the "as of" date?
      Who determines book value?
      [ ] The CPA for the company?
      [ ] The leadership of the entity?
   [ ] **Formula, including capitalization of earnings methods?**
      Who made up the formula?
         [ ] Has it ever been tested or used?
      Who makes the formula calculation?
      Is there any failsafe opt-out valuation procedure in the buy-sell agreement where the formula produces an absurd result?
   [ ] **Fixed Price?**
      If so, how often is the price redetermined?

Who determines the price?

What happens if the owners are incapable of agreeing on a price?

How long will the price last, i.e, can it go stale?

[ ] Is there a failsafe alternative backup price determination plan if the price has gone stale or where the owners can't agree on a price?

[ ] **Special Deadlock Pricing:**

[ ] Does the buy-sell agreement provide for a special pricing procedure if there is deadlock between the owners on a significant event?

[ ] **Payment for interests:**

[ ] Cash only?

[ ] Installment payout?

[ ] Cash to the extent of life insurance death proceeds with the balance payable in installments?

[ ] Another combination of cash and installments?

Whose option is it on how to pay?

[ ] The seller?

[ ] The buyer?

[ ] Or does the buy-sell agreement stipulate how interests are to be paid for?

[ ] **Miscellaneous:**

[ ] **S corporation:**

[ ] Is the entity an S corporation for tax purposes?

[ ] If so, does the buy-sell agreement protect the S election against loss?

[ ] Does the buy-sell agreement stipulate a method for allocating income in a year where an owner transfers some interests?

[ ] If so, is it the pro rata method or the per diem (per day) method?

[ ] Are there any restrictions the entity from issuing different classes of ownership other than voting and non-voting?

[ ] What about not taking on debt other than "safe harbor debt.?"

Minimum Distributions:

[ ] If the entity is an S corporation or a partnership for income tax purposes, does the buy-sell agreement mandate any minimum cash distributions to the owners? If so, how much?

Corporate Redemption Limitations:

[ ] If the entity is a corporation and the buy-sell agreement is a redemption agreement, does the buy-sell agreement provide what happens if the corporation can't redeem stock for any reason, e.g., to do so would violate the minimum capital requirements or would violate a loan covenant?

Alternate Dispute Resolution:

[ ] Does the buy-sell agreement allow for either mediation or arbitration, or both, for disputes about the buy-sell agreement, or is the buy-sell agreement silent?

Termination:

[ ] Does the buy-sell agreement provide for when it terminates? If so, when?

Tag along (co-sale) or drag along call rights:

[ ] Does the buy-sell agreement provide for either "tag along" or "drag along" provisions, or for both?

Amendment:

What is the procedure for amendment of the buy-sell agreement?

What is the required vote?

[ ] Unanimity?

[ ] A mere majority?

[ ] A super majority?

[ ] **Governing Law:**

> [ ] Does the buy-sell agreement provide for which jurisdiction's laws govern?
>
> If so, what jurisdiction?

[ ] **Legend:**

> [ ] Does the buy-sell agreement contain language about its existence that must be placed on all outstanding certificates of ownership?

[ ] **Purposes of Buy-Sell Agreement:**

> [ ] Does the buy-sell agreement list out the purposes for the buy-sell agreement? If so, what purposes are listed?

Buy-Sell Agreement Life Insurance Notice and Consent Provision

It is anticipated that the Entity or Owners may from time to time obtain life insurance policies on the lives of the Owners. If those policies fall within the definition of "employer-owned life insurance policies" as defined in Code section § 101(j), it is intended that the policies qualify for an exclusion from those rules (and thus making the proceeds income tax–free) and that this Agreement comply with the notice and consent requirements necessary to obtain that exclusion. Therefore, each Owner is hereby given written notice that the Entity or Owners intend to insure his or her life by purchasing life insurance policy(ies) in the maximum face amount of $[ENTER AMOUNT], and that the Entity or Owners will be the owner and beneficiary of that policy and of any proceeds payable on such Owner's death. Each Owner (by signing this Agreement) hereby gives advance written consent to being insured under such policy(ies) and to the continuation of the policy(ies) after such Owner ceases to have an Interest in the Entity or otherwise terminates employment (as defined in Code section 101(j)(4)(B)) with the Entity (and no inference is intended that a Member is an "employee" for any purposes other than the possible application of Code section 101(j)). The Owners also agree to enter into a specific notice and consent containing these terms with regard to each policy obtained before the issuance of that policy.

Buy-Sell Agreement Necessary Documents Checklist

[ ] Articles of Incorporation that are on file with the state secretary of state, together with all amendments

[ ] LLC Articles of Organization that are on file with the state secretary of state, together with all amendments

[ ] Articles of Partnership/Limited Partnership, together with all amendments

[ ] Corporate By-Laws presently in effect

[ ] LLC Operating Agreement

[ ] Buy-Sell Agreement(s) presently in place, together with all amendments and waivers

[ ] Franchisee Agreements, together with all amendments

[ ] Distributor agreements, together with all amendments

[ ] Entity Loan Agreement(s) presently in place

[ ] Insurance Bonding Agreements presently in place

[ ] All ownership options, warrants and similar agreements that could give someone the right to acquire an interest in the entity

[ ] ESOP documents

AUTHOR BIO

L. Paul Hood, Jr. is a frequent speaker and commentator on estate, charitable, and tax planning issues. His articles have been published in many journals, including *CCH Journal of Practical Estate Planning*, *Trusts & Estates*, *Probate Practice Reporter*, *Estate Planning*, *Digest of Federal Tax Articles*, *Louisiana Bar Journal*, and *Tax Ideas*. In addition to serving on the Louisiana Board of Tax Appeals, he was a sponsored speaker for distinguished law schools such as Duke, Georgetown, Notre Dame, NYU, LSU, Tulane, and Loyola New Orleans. He is also the author of seven other books on estate planning, charitable planning, and business valuation.

Along the way, Paul has been a father, godfather, husband, lawyer, trustee, director, president, partner, trust protector, director of planned giving, expert witness, agent, professor, judge, juror, respondent, and defendant. He uses his expertise and experience in these myriad roles to guide others.

Paul is an author speaker, and consultant on tax, estate, and charitable planning. He is also a Vice President with Thompson & Associates, a charitable estate planning firm. paul@paulhoodservices.com.

OTHER BOOKS BY L. PAUL HOOD, JR.

The Tools & Techniques of Estate Planning, 19th edition

The Tools & Techniques of Charitable Planning

www.ingramcontent.com/pod-product-compliance
Lightning Source LLC
Chambersburg PA
CBHW071548210326
41597CB00019B/3160